Seeing Voices

OXFORD STUDIES IN MUSIC THEORY

Series Editor
Steven Rings

Seeing Voices

Analyzing Sign Language Music

ANABEL MALER

OXFORD
UNIVERSITY PRESS

Oxford University Press is a department of the University of Oxford. It furthers
the University's objective of excellence in research, scholarship, and education
by publishing worldwide. Oxford is a registered trade mark of Oxford University
Press in the UK and certain other countries.

Published in the United States of America by Oxford University Press
198 Madison Avenue, New York, NY 10016, United States of America.

Library of Congress Cataloging-in-Publication Data
Names: Maler, Anabel, author.
Title: Seeing voices : analyzing sign language music / Anabel Maler.
Description: New York : Oxford University Press, 2024. |
Series: Oxford studies in music theory |
Includes bibliographical references and index.
Identifiers: LCCN 2024030412 (print) | LCCN 2024030413 (ebook) |
ISBN 9780197601983 (paperback) | ISBN 9780197601976 (hardback) |
ISBN 9780197602010 | ISBN 9780197602027 | ISBN 9780197602003 (epub)
Subjects: LCSH: Music for hard of hearing people. |
Deaf musicians. | Sign language.
Classification: LCC ML3838 .M25 2024 (print) | LCC ML3838 (ebook) |
DDC 780.87/2—dc23/eng/20240815
LC record available at https://lccn.loc.gov/2024030412
LC ebook record available at https://lccn.loc.gov/2024030413

DOI: 10.1093/oso/9780197601976.001.0001

Paperback printed by Marquis Book Printing, Canada
Hardback printed by Bridgeport National Bindery, Inc., United States of America

This book is dedicated to my husband, Robert Komaniecki, our two daughters, Harriet and Maeve, and above all, to the members of the Deaf, hard-of-hearing, and DeafBlind communities who so generously shared their musical knowledge with me.

Contents

Note on the Cover Art

Title of the artwork: *The Symphony* (2023)

Artist: Pamela E. Witcher

Medium: Digital art, acrylic on paper

Artist Biography: Pamela E. Witcher—Multidisciplinary artist, interpreter, translator, cultural mediator and museum curatorship, Pamela finds it necessary to overlap old and new discoveries that have the power to change views and ideas. When the Deaf communities create information through art and documentation, our existence becomes concrete, known, and valued. Pamela's works have been featured at Partition/Ensemble Conference, Dyers Art Center, Edinburgh International Book Festival, Écomusée du fier monde, Quebec on the Move!, À Bâbord, and Signed Music: A Symphonious Odyssey. Pamela's signed music performances were portrayed at Phenomena Festival; VIBE Symposium: Challenging Ableism and Audism through the Arts; and Celebration of Sign Language: Revisiting Language, Literacy, and Performing Arts Symposium.

Acknowledgments

This book has been more than a decade in the making. I first became curious about sign language music in 2011, when a signed music video sparked my interest in the early days of YouTube, and have been thinking, researching, reading, and writing about the subject in one way or another ever since. Along the way, my thinking has been shaped by conversations with far too many people to thank individually; nevertheless, I am grateful for each of these encounters and exchanges.

The inquiries that would someday lead to this book were first developed at McGill University, in the form of a term paper for a course taught by Nicole Biamonte. I am grateful to Nicole for encouraging my interest in the topic, as well as to faculty members at McGill who have continued to guide and encourage me over the years.

Although my dissertation focused on an unrelated topic, my time studying at the University of Chicago was truly formative for my conceptualization of sign language music. Many of the projects that would later coalesce into this book began at the University of Chicago, including a study on the perception of sign language music generously funded by the Center for Gesture, Sign, and Language, as well as my first ethnographic and historical work on sign language music and Deaf music-making. Larry Zbikowski, in particular, has supported my work in this area since our very first meeting—before I even matriculated at UChicago—and his guidance has continued to be invaluable at every stage of this project. I was also challenged and encouraged throughout my time in Chicago by numerous other faculty members, including Martha Feldman, Seth Brodsky, Kaley Mason, Berthold Hoeckner, Philip Bohlman, Thomas Christensen, Bob Kendrick, Janet Schmalfeldt, and especially Jennifer Iverson and Steve Rings. Jennifer Iverson has been an endlessly supportive presence throughout the writing of this book, and her kind yet critical comments have shaped the project in new and exciting ways. Jennifer also encouraged me to submit the book for consideration to Oxford's Studies in Music Theory series, edited by Steve Rings. Steve has been a wonderfully enthusiastic editor and mentor throughout the writing process. My editor at Oxford, Norm Hirschy, has been patient, generous, and supportive of the project since our first contact, and I am forever grateful for his guidance.

Conversations with my friends and colleagues at the University of Chicago shaped much of my early work on this project. My colleagues at the University of Iowa have also helped and supported me in many ways; in particular, Katie Buehner has helped locate resources and provided guidance on copyright issues. Outside of these institutions, my colleagues have provided valuable insights and assistance, including Jessica Holmes, Jeannette Di Bernardo Jones, Joseph Straus, and Phil Ewell. I am thankful to my students at the University of Iowa, especially in my graduate seminars on disability and voice, whose insightful commentary inspired and challenged me.

I am grateful to the University of Iowa for generously supporting the writing of this book through a research leave in Fall 2022, an Old Gold Fellowship, and an Arts and Humanities Initiative grant that allowed me to conduct the interviews in Chapter 2; and to the National Endowment for the Humanities, whose generous funding through a Summer Stipend supported my research throughout the summer of 2021. The completion of the book was made possible through a generous subvention grant from the Society for Music Theory.

Conducting this research was made possible by the generosity of my Deaf, hard-of-hearing, and DeafBlind collaborators and colleagues; in particular, Jason Listman, Teresa Blankmeyer Burke, Raven Sutton, Paris Glass, Matt Maxey, Harmony Baniaga, Rosa Lee Timm, Marko "Signmark" Vuoriheimo, Warren "Wawa" Snipe, and my ASL teachers, Susan Weinfurtner and Rafie Legene. I owe my gratitude to Anne Liversidge, who helped with the ASL-English glossing in examples throughout this book, and especially to Pamela Witcher, who not only spoke with me at length about her artistic process but also created the incredible cover art for this book.

My family has shaped this book in many important ways. My parents, Leonard Maler and Sabine Boetel, were the first supporters of all my endeavors both musical and academic. During the course of writing this book, I gave birth to my two daughters, Harriet and Maeve, and watching them grow and become enamored with music is a constant source of inspiration. Most of all, I must thank my husband, Robert Komaniecki, my partner in life, music, and scholarship, who has supported me both personally and intellectually through the writing of this book. During our many conversations on long walks and over shared meals, Robert contributed critical insights to the book's content, and his endless support and love have made their mark on every page. Writing this book would not have been possible without him.

Some of the material that follows has previously appeared in other publications and is used here by kind permission of the publishers. This material includes portions of my article "Music and Deafness in the Nineteenth-Century U.S. Imagination," originally published by the *Journal of the Society for American Music* 16, no. 2 (2022), and an article coauthored with Robert Komaniecki, "Rhythmic Techniques in Deaf Hip Hop," originally published in *Music Theory Online* 27, no. 2 (2021).

About the Companion Website

www.oup.com/us/SeeingVoices

This book features a companion website that provides material that cannot be made available in a book, namely a collection of over 100 videos illustrating the book's materials. The reader is encouraged to consult this resource in conjunction with the chapters. Examples available online are indicated in the text with Oxford's symbol ⊙.

Introduction

Music Beyond Hearing

Imagine the following: it is 9 P.M. on a hot weekend in Washington, DC, at the end of June. The popular artists Ashanti and Ja Rule have taken the stage at a music festival. You feel the thump of the bass vibrate through your chest, your feet, your jaw—sweat drips through your hair and down your forehead, stinging your eyes. Purple and blue lights flash onstage as smoke drifts out from behind the performers. You see the passion and joy on the performers' faces as they move to the music. You can smell the smoke in the air, mixed with the scent of sweat, old beer, and the dirt kicked up by dancing feet. Your mouth is somewhat dry from exertion in the heat, but you taste sweat, the last beer you drank, perhaps a lingering hint of the hamburger you purchased from the concession stand. You feel the excitement, electric and tangible, from the concertgoers around you. You also feel the heat rise from your skin, sunburned from a day in the DC heat, the chalky layer of sunscreen you applied this morning a distant memory now. The straps of your mini backpack are digging into a particularly sunburnt spot on your neck. The person next to you is dancing, his arm lifted high in the air, his mouth moving alongside familiar lyrics. His excitement is contagious: you lift your arm as well, fingers stirring the hot, sticky air, as your body sways to the rhythm of the pounding bass.

The careful reader may have noticed that none of the musical experiences I just described involves sound or hearing. I have instead foregrounded the senses of sight, touch, taste, and smell. Although scholarship on music tends to focus on the sounds we hear, humans make use of multiple senses when experiencing music, whether at an outdoor festival, an indoor concert, or even at home, through headphones, while doing the dishes or mopping the floor.

We tend to think of music in terms of what Edgard Varèse called "organized sound." Varèse's pithy phrasing has persisted for a reason—it captures what we feel is at the heart of all musical experience, across history and

Seeing Voices. Anabel Maler, Oxford University Press. © Oxford University Press 2024.
DOI: 10.1093/oso/9780197601976.003.0001

culture: the very human act of intentionally organizing sounds into patterns, and perceiving them primarily through the sense of hearing. While music-making has taken many different forms over the course of human history—from mothers singing to their infants, to the first known instruments, to Renaissance polyphony, to Balinese gamelan—we understand fundamentally that music involves sounds, transmitted from one body to another's ears.

Consider our concertgoer again. Perhaps she looks up at the stage once again and notices, to one side, a woman dressed in a black jumpsuit and a long yellow button-down shirt (see Example I.1). Her hair is swept into a tidy bun. Her body bounces to the rhythm; her hands sweep in front of her, carving out the shape of a song. Her face is animated, adding new emotional dimensions to the sounding music. Her name is Raven Sutton, and she is performing the music in American Sign Language as a Deaf Interpreter. Both the Deaf and hearing audiences take in her movements and find their experience of the concert visually enriched.

Example I.1 A still image of Raven Sutton interpreting for Ashanti and Ja Rule, June 19, 2022.

Music performed in a signed language poses considerable challenges to the established definition of music as organized sound. It raises important questions about the kind of analytical resources that are afforded by the work's musical parameters, which are created by the moving, signing bodies of the performers. In other words, for Western music theory, which is so practiced at analyzing musical sound, sign language music poses a fundamental definitional problem. Performances like Raven Sutton's are defined culturally as music, but they do not necessarily make sound their only—or even primary—mode of transmission.

Indeed, other sign language songs may not involve sound at all. For example, the song "Boat, Drink, Fun, Enjoy" uses only sign language with no auditory component. The song was first performed by George Kannapell and captured on film by Charles Krauel in 1939 (Supalla and Dannis 1994). This piece is an example of what Ben Bahan calls "percussion signing," an original rhythmic song created in sign language by Deaf people (Bahan 2006; Cripps et al. 2017; Padden and Humphries 1988). While our music-theoretical toolbox has many resources for making sense of sounding music, it has very few resources for making sense of "Boat, Drink, Fun, Enjoy," or performances like Raven Sutton's. Given this information, one might decide to either exclude sign language music from the purview of music scholarship, or change the definition of music. If music is not sound, however, then what *is* it?

Performances like Raven Sutton's and songs like "Boat, Drink, Fun, Enjoy" involve language, which is typical of many songs, and measured, rhythmic, directed motion through space. In order to conceptualize these pieces of sign language music *as* music, we need a definition of music that includes movement, with or without accompanying sounds.

I.1 Music as Movement

The notion that musical concepts are rooted in bodily states and motions is not unprecedented. In the monograph *Conceptualizing Music*, Lawrence Zbikowski (2002) reveals how George Lakoff and Mark Johnson's theory of conceptual metaphors and cross-domain mappings allows us to correlate the musical domain with other domains like that of gesture or space. For example, Zbikowski identifies the conceptual metaphor at work in describing pitches as "high" and "low" in Western music theory as PITCH RELATIONSHIPS

ARE RELATIONSHIPS IN VERTICAL SPACE, a metaphor that maps spatial orientation onto pitches.[1] By mapping pitch onto the concept of verticality in Western culture, we are thus able to conceptualize musical pitch in terms of ascending and descending intervals.

In this conceptualization, music and movement are still fundamentally separate: there is music, and there is movement in physical space—the two may combine and interact in a conceptual blend, but they are made of fundamentally different stuff. For example, a sound-based phenomenon, like a series of pitches, may blend with the physical concept of movement upward in space. On its own, then, Zbikowski's theory of conceptual metaphors does not adequately explain how sign language music is music. Sign language music does not involve a blend between musical ideas and movements in physical space; instead, the movements themselves *are* music.

We must go a step further in order to include sign language music within our existing concept of music. Consider the conceptual metaphors that Zbikowski discusses for pitch: vertical space, waterfalls, size, and age. While each conceptual metaphor reflects different cultural values and understandings of music, they all involve *movement*: movement through space, the movement of water, the movement of vibrations, or movement through time. It seems, then, that we might find common cultural ground by defining music primarily in terms of movement rather than sound.

The ancient Greeks recognized the basis of music in motion as well, albeit in an abstract sense. Plato presented his mathematical model for the "harmony of the spheres" in the *Republic*, the *Laws*, and the *Timaeus*, and the anonymous *Division of the Canon* (4th–3rd century BCE) "defines the physical basis of sound as a series of motions" (Mathiesen 2002, 115). Boethius, in transmitting Platonic thought, famously divided the knowledge of music into *musica mundana* (the "music of the universe"), *musica humana* (the music of the human body and soul), and *musica instrumentalis* (the sound of instruments). *Musica mundana*, in addressing the harmony of the universe, concerns the motion of planets and the rhythm of the seasons, the sound of which, of course, cannot reach human ears (Boethius 1989). Audible music, in this tradition, acts as the tangible expression of the principles of *musica*

---

[1] As Zbikowski points out, not all cultures make use of the same conceptual metaphors: for example, the Kaluli of Papua New Guinea "describe melodic intervals with the same terms they use to characterize features of waterfalls," in Bali and Java pitches are "small" and "large," which "reflects the norms of acoustic production" in that "small things typically vibrate more rapidly than large things," and the Suyá of the Amazon understand pitches as "young" and "old," reflecting how the "pitch of the voice becomes deeper with age" (Zbikowski 2002, 67–68).

mundana. In their study of signed music and its role in the Deaf community, Jody Cripps and his colleagues note that ancient Greek attitudes about music and movement are of "special interest for Deaf people and signed music" (Cripps et al. Forthcoming).

The topics of music, language, speech, gesture, and deafness came under particular scrutiny in France in the eighteenth century, when French Enlightenment thinkers began to ponder questions about the origins of language and music, the relationship between the senses and thought, and the relationship between language and society (see Fulka 2020; Downing 1995; Mirzoeff 1995). Philosophers and critics Jean-Jacques Rousseau and Denis Diderot were particularly interested in the relationship between deafness and music. Josef Fulka describes how each author approached the problem. In his treatise *Émile, or On Education*, Rousseau proposes training deaf students to perceive sounds through the sense of touch (Rousseau 2010, 279). Diderot, by contrast, "confronts the deaf person with a fashionable invention, a machine that transforms sounds into colors," in order to supplement the deaf person's sensory experience of music. This supplementation, Fulka notes, involves a process of translation from "that which cannot be grasped by the ear into what can be by the eye" (Fulka 2020, 95). Diderot goes on to argue that the deaf subject, confronted by this invention, perceives music as a kind of language (Fulka 2020, 95).

More recently, there has been a great deal of interest in the biological origins of music, the relationships between music and speech, and understanding which aspects of music perception are domain-specific or domain-general. Research has shown that some aspects of speech and language are processed by the brain in similar ways using overlapping neural circuitry, and even that processing some musical events may involve using Broca's and Wernicke's areas, which had previously been thought to process speech exclusively (Patel et al. 2008). Furthermore, multiple studies have found that, from infancy, humans respond to the musical aspects of their mothers' speech, also known as "motherese." Anne Fernald has described how, in comparison to speech with other adults, both mothers and fathers speak to infants more slowly, with higher pitch, greater pitch variability, shorter vocalizations, and longer pauses (Fernald 1992, 398). In other words, these exaggerated pitch contours resemble musical melodies. These exaggerated melodies induce higher states of infant "attention, arousal, emotion, and language comprehension" (Fernald 1992, 403). The prosodic contour of motherese promotes not only attention but speech discrimination (Liu,

Kuhl, and Tsao 2003) and the parsing of speech into units (Kemler Nelson et al. 1989; Jusczyk et al. 1992).

The attributes of motherese extend to infant-direct singing, or "songese," as well: when singing with infants, parents used a slower tempo, longer interphrase pauses, and higher pitch (Trainor 1996; Trainor et al. 1997). The musical information conveyed during this infant-directed singing is not only auditory in nature—a study conducted by Elena Longhi on the temporal structure of mother-infant singing revealed that the synchronous behaviors used by mothers and infants, such as head movements, nodding, and body bouncing, were important for establishing temporally coherent segmentation of the flow of the song (Longhi 2009). From a very young age, then, infants rely just as much on bodily movements to understand and parse musical information as they do on sound alone.

A study by Nobuo Masataka revealed that motherese is also used by deaf mothers with their deaf infants who communicate using a signed language, and that deaf infants respond to signed motherese in the same way as hearing infants do with aurally perceived motherese (Masataka 1996). An additional study showed that hearing infants who had not previously been exposed to sign language also respond to signed motherese, as they do with aural motherese. Unfortunately, no studies on songese in signed languages have been undertaken at the present time. Given, however, that motherese and songese share many traits, and that physical movement is already a crucial component of aural songese, we might predict that a mother singing to her baby in sign language would prompt similar heightened attention, arousal, emotion, and understanding of musical segmentation in an infant. While the effects of signed songese in particular have not yet been studied, a case study on the effects of ASL rhyme and rhythm on Deaf children's classroom engagement showed some promising effects of ASL rhyming and rhythm in helping with accuracy in recitation (Holcomb and Wolbers 2020).

Chakraborty and Jarvis even speculate that brain pathways for vocal learning might originate from motor pathways in birds and mammals, arguing that "changes in the regulation of some genes that may allow greater vocal–motor–auditory integration in vocal learning systems could have influenced changes in the surrounding motor areas to allow greater auditory–motor entrainment and synchronizing of body movements to the rhythm of music for dance in parrots" (Chakraborty and Jarvis 2015, 4). The findings of Phillips-Silver and Trainor further show a strong connection between body movement and auditory rhythm processing for humans beginning in infancy, revealing that "the experience of body movement plays an important role in musical rhythm perception" (Phillips-Silver and Trainor 2005, 1430).

Recent scholarship on music cognition supports the notion that music perception is both embodied (Leman 2007) and multimodal (Godøy, Haga, and Jensenius 2005). Rolf Inge Godøy's research in particular supports the notion that music always involves the cooperation of multiple senses, rather than relying purely or exclusively on the sense of hearing (Godøy 2003, 317). Godøy argues for a motor-mimetic understanding of music cognition, in which we "mentally imitate sound-producing actions" when we listen to music (Godøy 2003, 318). He further suggests that our experience of music is "enhanced by concurrent experiences of gestures," arguing that musical works are "rich, multidimensional gestural scripts" (Godøy 2010, 122).

Given the historical and biological evidence that music and movement are closely linked, I submit that music can be defined more broadly as *organized movement*. The physical and cognitive phenomenon that we call "sound" is merely one type of musical movement, one that depends upon pressure waves that move through the air meeting with the inner workings of an ear, which a brain, through complex processing, perceives as sound. But before there was sound, there was always movement: the particular case of aurally perceived music happens to involve the movement of pressure waves through the air. Perceiving, cognizing, and creating music, then, are processes that are not limited to the sense of hearing. In a "typical," sonic musical instantiation, one might see the vibration of strings, and one's ears might feel the pressure waves that the brain will interpret as musical sound. But our understanding of music as movement must go beyond this typical situation to include touching a vibrating surface, seeing another's hands, body, and face in motion, feeling another's body move, and moving *with* another body, either in physical space or in our minds.

Is dance music, then? In short, sometimes. A more thorough response is that dance is music if a particular culture defines it as such. The particular types of movement that are understood and interpreted as music must be agreed upon by a group of humans. In that sense, all music is organized movement, but not all forms of organized movement are understood by all human cultures as musical. There are many cultures in which dance and music are viewed as one and the same: for example, the South Asian classical dance traditions in which music and dance are both contained in the word "sangeet" (Nimjee 2018, 2019; Clayton, Dueck, and Leante 2013;

Rahaim 2012); the South African competitive music and dance practice ngoma (Meintjes 2017); the Haitian rara (McAlister 2002); and the drum dancing of the Inuit, the dance songs of the Dene, and the social dances of the Choctaw (Browner 2002, 2009).

How we perceive and cognize music *as* music, then, depends both on the affordances of a particular type of movement and on the perceiver's relationship with her environment. By "affordance," I refer to Donald Norman's notion of the potential uses or actions latent in materials (Norman 2013). Affordances are relational, in that they are equally determined by the properties inherent in the object itself and the abilities and inclinations of an interacting subject. When interacting with a particular type of movement, a perceiver may make use of her senses of hearing, sight, touch, smell, or taste, as well as her learned understanding from within a particular human culture, to determine the affordances of that movement. At the same time, Terra Edwards's research on re-channeling language and infrastructure among DeafBlind people reveals that re-channeling a language (i.e., transforming channels of communication from sight to touch) begins "not with the affordances of particular channels of transmission, but with the complementarity of the language user qua organism and its environment" (T. Edwards 2018, 286). In other words, re-channeling emerges first from residence within the world, and then from representations of it. When we think about channels of musical transmission, we might also think in this DeafBlind, protactile manner: we might imagine "what it would mean to be in the world together and what that world might have to offer," rather than thinking simply about how to transmit a linguistic or musical sign from one party to another (T. Edwards 2018, 276). Michele Friedner's work on deafness and cochlear implant infrastructures in India supports the notion that our environments and infrastructures both produce and constrain our sensory experiences and possibilities (Friedner 2022).

The re-definition (or re-channeling) of music as organized movement means that sign language music, rather than being peripheral or extraneous to histories and theories of music, is in fact central and crucial to our understanding of all musical expression and understanding. Sign language music can teach us a great deal about how, when, and why movement becomes musical within a particular sensory environment. And as the concertgoer at the opening of this volume demonstrated, sign language music urges us to think of all music as a multisensory experience that goes beyond the sense of hearing (a notion supported by the work of Godøy, Leman, Zbikowski, and others). While some music rewards a more hearing-centric style of perception, other music may reward more visual, tactile, or multisensory ways of knowing. How we categorize and understand this music ultimately depends upon its affordances and on our own sensory relationships with our environment.

I.2 Sign Language Music and Deaf Culture

The preceding definition of music as organized movement does not quite go far enough. "Organized movement," after all, could include anything from walking, to trees swaying in the breeze, to a cat pouncing on a toy. We must also consider how music is defined and understood within a particular cultural context: thus, music is *culturally defined, intentionally organized movement.* Studying sign language music requires an approach that is closely tied to Deaf culture. As an outsider to Deaf culture, my intent is not to speak for Deaf communities in regard to their musical practices. Instead, the book has three central aims. My first—and perhaps most important—aim is to center the experiences and knowledge of Deaf persons, who have historically been excluded from music education and research (a topic that I explore in great detail in Chapter 1 of this volume). I do so by making space for the Deaf musicians whose work I study to speak for themselves throughout the book, through interviews transcribed in English and available in English and/or ASL on the book's companion website. The second aim is to bring the long and rich history of sign language music to the attention of music scholarship, to engage with it seriously and thoughtfully as a musical art, and to grapple with the methodological quandaries that it raises for the discipline of music theory. My third and final goal is to challenge the notion that music is transmitted from hearing knowers of music to Deaf non-knowers. The assumption that Deaf persons do not have an interest in music, and that music is purely or primarily a sonic discipline, is very much alive and well today.

This book centers and takes seriously Deaf ways of knowing about music. As recent scholarship demonstrates, Deaf persons have a great deal of knowledge about sound. Mara Mills's work has revealed that Deaf persons were historically treated as prodigious hearers in the realm of communication technology, and their experiences shaped the development of communication technologies (Mills 2011b, 2014, 2011a, 2015). Jessica Holmes urges us to understand Deaf listeners as "expert listeners" whose listening practices lead us to a "pluralistic understanding of what listening expertise entails" (Holmes 2017).

As Holmes reveals, listening and music-making practices within the Deaf and hard-of-hearing communities are as rich and diverse as those within the hearing community. This book focuses on one particular form of musical experience: music created in a signed language. Specifically, this book aims to highlight the history, context, and analysis of music created in American Sign Language. Sign language music has been the subject of some recent interest in the fields of music theory and analysis (Maler 2013, 2015; Maler and Komaniecki 2021), music and disability studies, musicology (Holmes 2016; J. D. Jones 2015), ethnomusicology (Best 2015/2016, 2018), performance studies (Cripps and Lyonblum 2017; Cripps et al. 2017), sound studies, music cognition and perception (Mangelsdorf, Listman, and Maler 2021), and Deaf studies (Listman, Loeffler, and Timm 2018; Loeffler 2014). All these scholars have pushed back against the audist notion that deafness precludes musical understanding and experience, and have highlighted the wide variety of musical practices among Deaf and hard-of-hearing individuals.[2]

Sign language music involves signs and/or classifiers. It involves movement of the face, hands, head, and body. Like sign language poetry, it involves different types of movement—such as holds, specific movement paths, movement emphasis, and different movement durations—in order to create a musical experience for the viewer. These movements are fundamental to creating rhythm in signed poetry as well. Rachel Sutton-Spence observes that "rhythm in sign language poetry can be described in terms of the changes that occur within signs or in the transition between signs ('movements') and periods of no change ('holds')" (Sutton-Spence 2005, 45). Clayton Valli (1993) establishes four fundamental movement types that can create poetic rhythm: the first is hold emphasis, which can involve long pauses, subtle pauses, or strong stops; the second is movement emphasis, which can involve long, short, alternating, or repeated movements; the third is movement size, which can involve an enlarged movement path, shortened movement, reduced movement path, and accelerating movement; and fourth, movement duration, which can be regular, slow, or fast. These four movement types form the foundation of all expressive, musical motion in

---

[2] Some examples of this scholarship include Maler (2013, 2015); Holmes (2017); J. D. Jones (2015); Cripps and Lyonblum (2017); Cripps et al. (2017); Listman, Loeffler, and Timm (2018); Loeffler (2014); Straus (2011); Best (2015/2016, 2018); Friedner and Helmreich (2012); amd Mills (2011b).

sign language music, and, accordingly, act as fundamental building blocks for sign language music analysis.

I.3 Chapter Summaries

This book is organized into two parts. Part I contextualizes our present-day understanding of Deaf musicality by situating it within the history of Deaf musical education in America and recent trends in sign language music. Part II engages in close music-analytical readings of sign language music through the lens of several parameters: vocal technique, rhythm and meter, melody, meaning, and form.

Chapter 1, "Music and Deafness in America, 1820–1965," traces the history of Deaf musical culture in America. Music has played a role in Deaf culture and artistic practice since at least the mid-nineteenth century in America, and yet in music scholarship, scholars, composers, and performers of music are typically presumed to possess normal hearing. That the dominant hearing community has only very recently recognized the musical practices of the Deaf community today—in spite of abundant examples of Deaf musicians and music enthusiasts—suggests that our model of knowledge for music has been constructed to exclude Deaf persons as producers of musical knowledge. When music is posited as something that is totally foreign to Deaf existence, it obscures Deaf musical experiences and understanding from our collective knowledge about how music works. In order to understand how this framing of Deaf music-making came about, I argue, we must understand the history of how music has been used in Deaf education since the early nineteenth century in the United States.

In Chapter 2, "Deaf Culture's Musical Presents," I explore the many and varied signed musical practices that exist today, and their social contexts across Deaf and hearing cultures. I showcase these different practices and perspectives through interviews I conducted with ten Deaf signing musicians over a period of ten months. By centering Deaf voices, I reveal the richness, complexity, and diversity of modern sign language music practices within Deaf communities. The contributions of my interlocutors suggest that the historical exclusion of Deaf knowledge from musical discourse, which I explored in Chapter 1, has ongoing implications for signing musicians in the present day.

Chapter 3, "The Signing Signing Voice," conceptualizes sign language vocality, or what I call the "signing voice." Voice studies has grappled with the idea that the singing voice is material and embodied. However, recent efforts to formalize the voice run the risk of limiting it to a phonocentric concept. One issue with existing research into sign language music is that the concept of a signing voice remains untheorized, making it difficult to analyze melody and counterpoint in this music. In this chapter, I use Brian Kane's tripartite model of the voice as sound, meaning, and site to define the signing singing voice as involving motion rather than sound. By developing a theory that celebrates the signing voice as a singing voice, I aim to complicate our understanding of "voice" as limited to air vibrating through the vocal folds. I also examine how our dominant phonocentric ideologies of voice have caused damage to the Deaf and signing communities and to our understanding of Deaf vocality.

Chapter 4, "Rhythm and Meter," explores the concepts of entrainment, pulse, rhythm, meter, and phrase rhythm, and how they emerge in the visual-kinesthetic art form of sign language music. I focus primarily on the rhythmic techniques used in signed rap, or "dip hop," a musical movement that originated in the early 1990s. Specifically, I ask how the paradigms of vocal hip hop, signed songs, and signed poetry interact and intersect in signed rap songs. In doing so, I identify some of the primary rhythmic and metric techniques used by dip-hop artists. I suggest that the unique format of signed rap—which involves simultaneous rapping in two natural languages in different modalities—engenders unique rhythmic strategies and paradigms, involving four movement types that are found in sign language poetry: hold emphasis, movement emphasis, movement size, and movement duration. Finally, I show how analyzing the rhythmic techniques of dip-hop artists sheds light on the message and meaning behind their rapping.

Chapter 5, "Melodic Techniques," builds upon the framework of the signing voice established in Chapter 3 in order to discuss how sign musicians use directionality of movement, location of signs, holds, movement size, and movement duration in order to establish kinetic lines that are equivalent to melodic lines in aural music. I make use of Gino Stefani's everyday definition of melody as "what everybody sings or whistles" (Stefani 1987, 23) in defining the elements of signing melodic behavior as well as signing vocal behavior. I define these elements of signed melody using several different interpretations of "The Star-Spangled Banner," which has been frequently covered by signing musicians over the past century. Having established the nature of melodic lines in sign language music, I then thoroughly explore the melodic lines in one ASL cover song: Rosa Lee Timm's interpretation of Carrie Underwood's song "Blown Away."

Chapter 6 uses the analytical framework established in Chapters 3–5 in order to build a theory of affect, meaning, and form in signed music. I survey existing theories of song, form, and affect in order to understand how pieces of purely signed music, with no auditory component, are capable of expressing musical meaning. I explore the formal structure of sign language music through an analysis of Russell Harvard's cover of Paula Abdul's "Straight Up." I then discuss how two signing musicians create musical meaning in their original signed music (Rosa Lee Timm, "River Song," and Jesse Jones III, "One World, Two Hands").

I.4 The Resilience of Music

In her book *The Resilience of Language*, Susan Goldin-Meadow reflects upon her research on language development among Deaf children who were not exposed to language, and her resulting search for universal or "resilient" language properties in humans (Goldin-Meadow 2003). By "resilient" properties, Goldin-Meadow refers to those properties of language that appear in a child's communication regardless of whether that child is exposed to a language model that they are able to perceive.

Faced with music's persistent place in Deaf culture in spite of extraordinary obstacles, we might similarly understand there to be resilient properties of music: properties that appear whether or not a person is exposed to music in early childhood. In writing this book, I interviewed several Deaf musicians and performers (excerpts from which are featured in Chapter 2), including my former ASL teacher, Susan Weinfurtner. I asked Susan whether she was exposed to music growing up, and she responded that she was not. Her only exposure to music came through seeing her family and friends enjoy music in the car and feeling the rhythm of the bass, as well as seeing singing in church and on TV. Only in adulthood did Susan begin to enjoy music. She described how she finds sign language music calming and relaxing, and she enjoys following song lyrics and feeling an emotional connection to the music through translating it into sign language. Now, she posts her sign language music covers on her Facebook page and is learning to play the piano and guitar. Susan's story resonates with those of several other Deaf musicians

I interviewed as well: despite not having access to music in the traditional sense in early childhood, they sought out musical experiences later in childhood or adulthood. Interview by interview, it became clear to me that music, like language, demonstrates extraordinary resilience.

In the chapters that follow, I explore the resilience of music by studying how sign language music has evolved within Deaf and hearing cultures, how it pushes us to ask questions about the nature of musicality more broadly, and how voice, rhythm, melody, and emotion act as resilient properties of music by shaping music across visual, kinesthetic, and aural modalities.

PART I
CONTEXTS

1

Music and Deafness in America, 1820–1965

1.1 Introduction

On a cold December morning in 2021, I logged on to Zoom to meet with my colleague Teresa Blankmeyer Burke. We chatted for over an hour about her varied experiences of music as a Deaf woman: she is fond of opera, has played the piano since childhood, and enjoys watching Deaf signing musicians perform.[1] But of all these experiences, one quick, off-the-cuff anecdote from Burke's early childhood has stayed with me in particular:

> Oh, here's the irony: so I had speech therapy as a child, and almost always they pulled us out when it was music and arts time. So I never really got that instruction in the classroom because . . . I was learning how to pronounce my t's, or my ch's, or what have you.

Burke related this story in a cheerful tone, laughing about the irony of this music-obsessed child being taken out of music class to learn to pronounce her t's. The story bothered me, though, because it seemed indicative of a broader tendency to routinely exclude Deaf children from the musical experiences that hearing children receive effortlessly and constantly over the course of their lifetimes. Moreover, Burke's experience of being excluded from music class was directly tied to a pedagogical method that emerged in the nineteenth century called "oralism," which aims to teach Deaf children to communicate through speech and lip-reading rather than a sign language.

---

[1] Carol Padden and Tom Humphries established the convention of referring to audiological deafness with a lowercase "d," while membership within Deaf culture is identified through the uppercase "D" (Padden and Humphries 1988). More recently, however, there has been a shift toward more inclusive language. Following the guidance of the Deafhood Foundation, I use "Deaf" as an inclusive term that encompasses a variety of experiences. When referring to historical figures and events, however, I exclusively use the lowercase-d "deaf," since these concepts were not available until the latter part of the twentieth century.

Seeing Voices. Anabel Maler, Oxford University Press. © Oxford University Press 2024.
DOI: 10.1093/oso/9780197601976.003.0002

Oralist methods caused immense harm to the Deaf community (see, e.g., Edwards 2012; Baynton 1996). Some of those harms directly pertain to music. I doubt that it was mere coincidence that Burke's speech therapy conflicted with music class: rather, I would venture that her exclusion was at least partly the result of a persistent stereotype that Deaf persons are uninterested in music.

Historical accounts reveal that this stereotype is based in fiction rather than fact. In 1820, for example, several American periodicals reprinted a letter described by the *National Recorder* as an "interesting account of the fondness for music of an artist born deaf," excerpted below:

Some years back, probably five or six, a young gentleman of the name of Arrowsmith . . . came down into this country, and resided some months in Warrington. . . . He was quite deaf, so as to be entirely dumb. . . . It will scarcely be credited, that a person thus circumstanced should be fond of music, but this was the fact in the case of Mr. Arrowsmith. He was at a gentleman's glee club . . . and as the glees were sung, he would place himself near some articles of wooden furniture . . . and would fix the extreme ends of his finger nails, which he kept rather long, upon the edge of the wood or some projecting part of it and there remain, until the piece under performance was finished, all the while expressing, by the most significant gestures, the pleasure he experienced from his perception of the musical sounds. He was not so much pleased with a solo, as with a pretty full clash of harmony; and if the music was not very good, or, I should rather say, if it was not correctly executed, he would show no sensation of pleasure. But the most extraordinary circumstance in this case is, that he was most evidently delighted with those passages in which the composer displayed his science in modulating his different keys. When such passages happened to be executed with precision, he could scarcely repress the emotions of pleasure he received within any bounds; for the delight he evinced seemed to border on ecstasy. (Anonymous October 21, 1820)

The letter, written by an Englishman named G. Chippendale and originally printed in the *Bath and Cheltenham Gazette* in 1818, describes how Mr. Arrowsmith enjoyed musical experiences by placing his fingernails upon objects in order to experience vibrations. Not only that, but according to Chippendale's interpretation of events (and unfortunately we do not have access to Mr. Arrowsmith's own thoughts on the matter), Arrowsmith demonstrated a sensitive and discerning understanding of the music that he was experiencing, preferring full harmonies over solos, correct execution over performances with mistakes, and modulations over single-key pieces.

If printed today, Chippendale's anecdote might seem nearly as novel as it did in 1820. Why, nearly 200 years later, might the idea of Deaf musical experiences remain foreign or surprising, in spite of accounts like Chippendale's? In the introduction to this volume, I suggested that the basis of music is in movement rather than in sound, and that as a result, sign language music—which emerges from Deaf and hard-of-hearing experiences of music—is central to our understanding of human musicality. If, indeed, sign language music speaks to the very core of musical experience, then we might also wonder why music scholars have not been writing about it since the first occasion on which a piece of sign language music, a rendition of "The Star-Spangled Banner," was recorded on film in 1901.

A sampling of media headlines from the last decade on the topic of music and deafness suggests that Deaf people have only recently discovered music. For example, the following three articles were written about one man, Austin Chapman, who received new hearing aids: "What It's Like for a Deaf Person to Hear Music for the First Time," "We Spoke to a Man Who's Been Deaf His Whole Life about Hearing Music for the First Time," and "Deaf Filmmaker Truly Hears Music for the First Time" (Rosen August 29, 2012; Wilkinson January 9, 2014; Brunell October 2, 2012). All three articles frame Chapman's experience of music as novel, unprecedented, and achieved only through his new hearing aids. None of the interviewers asked about Chapman's musical experiences before he had his new hearing aids, or mentioned sign language music at all. An article about a woman named Jo Milne who received a cochlear implant, entitled "Formerly Deaf Woman Hears Music for the First Time in 40 Tears—Watch," similarly frames music as something that can only be accessed through the medium of sound, transmitted through the technological innovation of the cochlear implant (Haigh 2014).[2]

Even sign language music is often framed in terms of hearing interpreters who bring music to the Deaf community through their interpretations.[3] Sign language interpreters like Amber Galloway Gallego, Holly Maniatty, and

---

[2] Cochlear implantation remains a controversial subject in Deaf culture, having been likened to a form of cultural genocide. For more on this controversy, on the framing of deaf identity in terms of a cultural and linguistic minority group, and on audism (discrimination against those who cannot hear), see Dunn (2008); Gertz (2008); Hyde and Power (2005); Lane, Hoffmeister, and Bahan (1996); Lane and Bahan (1998); Lane (2008).

[3] E.g., see Caswell (2017).

Linsday Rothschild-Cross have each gone "viral" for their live interpretations at concerts, where they provide a valuable and essential service for deaf concertgoers. Reports on sign language music interpreting often tell only part of the story of sign language music and how it has developed within Deaf culture over the past century or more.

Members of the Deaf community have been singing, playing, signing, composing, and otherwise engaging with music for at least two centuries. Today, Deaf musicians and artists like Sean Forbes, Warren "Wawa" Snipe, Marko "Signmark" Vuoriheimo, Rosa Lee Timm, Jason Listman, Christine Sun Kim, Janis Cripps, Pamela Witcher, and many others are producing original signed hip hop, sign language interpretations of pop songs, and original signed music and sound art. The contradiction between the evidence of these historical and ongoing musical traditions and the idea that deafness is "the deepest imaginable antithesis to music" begs further analysis (Abbate 1991, 130).

In this chapter, I argue that Deaf musical knowledge became excluded from music-theoretical systems of thought as the result of a battle between two competing philosophies of deaf education in the nineteenth century: the manualist school and the oralist school. Ideas about morality, authenticity, and technology also colored American views of Deaf musicality, shaping the reception of Deaf music-making throughout the twentieth century until today. Ultimately, this chapter tells the story of how Deaf music-making came to be forgotten and rediscovered, again and again, in the American consciousness. In the sections that follow, I trace the history of Deaf musical practices in the nineteenth and early twentieth centuries to reveal how institutional knowledge about music came to exclude deafness as a critical concept.

1.2 Music and Manualism

In order to understand how Deaf musical knowledge came to be excluded from modern musical discourse, we must understand how music was framed by the two dominant strains of Deaf education in the nineteenth and twentieth centuries: manualism and oralism. By understanding how educators and thinkers explicitly framed Deaf persons as either knowers or non-knowers of music, we can trace how the exclusion of Deaf knowledge came to be established as normal and unmarked in musical discourse.

In 1817, Thomas Hopkins Gallaudet, with the help of Laurent Clerc (a deaf teacher at the Royal Institution for the Deaf in Paris), founded the first school for deaf students in the United States. The school, which was named the American Asylum for the Education of the Deaf and Dumb, largely employed manual methods of instruction, using sign language rather than teaching the speech and lip-reading of the oralist schools in England (Winefield 1987, 6). Over thirty more schools for the deaf were opened by both deaf and hearing teachers following the establishment of the American Asylum.

R. A. R. Edwards has suggested that there was some debate about manualism and oralism already in the early nineteenth century (Edwards 2012, 13). An 1807 article that compared a presentation of an orally trained deaf girl with the presentations of Abbé Sicard, the French pioneer in the instruction of the deaf using sign language, reveals that some found the use of speech among the deaf unnatural or even uncanny: "There was something in her voice extremely distressing, without being absolutely discordant; a plaintive monotonous sound, rather tending to excite melancholy than pleasure" (Anonymous 1807).

Ideas about sign language and speech were thus already bound up with ideas about naturalness, artificiality, and the automatic in America even before the founding of America's first deaf school in 1817. As Douglas Baynton has observed, the manualist method was the product of the Evangelical Protestant reform movement during the Second Great Awakening, which emphasized moral regeneration and salvation (Baynton 1992, 220). Baynton argues that manualists in the early nineteenth century saw "the language of signs" as natural, in comparison to the artifice of spoken languages. Benjamin D. Pettingill, a teacher at the Pennsylvania Institution, wrote that "all artificial languages are destitute of any life or meaning in themselves. They are based upon a natural language, and derive their significance from it. This natural language consists chiefly of expressions of the countenance, gestures, and involuntary muscular movements; the varied intonations of the voice; the actions which accompany words spoken or written, and pictures, whether made in the air or on paper, or otherwise" (Pettingill 1873). Sign language, the "natural language of the deaf," was thus framed in opposition to the "automatic," which was caught up, as Baynton writes, "in the nineteenth-century debate over materialism and the question of whether human life was inspired by more than mere mechanical impulse" (Baynton 1996, 124). And since Evangelical Protestants saw God as the author of nature, for manualists, sign language was nature's—and therefore God's—remedy for deafness.[4]

Early nineteenth-century religious instructors of the deaf therefore took an active interest in the moral education of their students. For Edward Miner Gallaudet, son of T. H. Gallaudet and leader of the late nineteenth-century manualist movement, religious and moral advancement was in fact the primary goal of deaf education. In 1875 he wrote that the manualists' compassion for the deaf was "not more called forth by the consideration that their ears are closed to all the sweet harmonies of sound, and their tongues useless ... than by the reflection that their minds are dwarfed, their sensibilities undeveloped, their social natures warped and soured, their moral perceptions nebulous, and their religious feelings unawakened."[5] In this passage, Gallaudet insists that deaf-mutism goes beyond the "merely physical" and toward a "deplorable" moral condition when the deaf individual does not receive an education: what Gallaudet calls "mental deaf-mutism" (Gallaudet 231–232).

Music, of course, has long been employed in religious education. But the idea that music could also be used in the moral education of the *deaf* was one that intrigued early nineteenth-century writers. Mr. Arrowsmith, the subject of Chippendale's 1820 letter, provides one example of how music was tied to morality in the early nineteenth-century understanding of deaf education. Arrowsmith's brother, who reprinted the same letter in his own book on instructing the deaf, framed Arrowsmith's musical experience as a means of aiding religious education. He instructed parents to allow their deaf children to sit close to the organ in church, so that they could experience the same enjoyment of music as his brother (Arrowsmith 1819, 74).

In 1847, the American Asylum began publishing the *American Annals of the Deaf and Dumb*, which allowed educators to discuss matters pertaining to the instruction of the deaf in a public forum. The topic of music arose frequently in the first volumes of the *Annals*. This new interest in music among educators of the deaf came about at the same time as educational reformers were pushing for music education to be included in public schools more broadly (Mark and Gary 2007, 119). The views of proponents of music education in the early nineteenth century are directly linked to the Protestant reform movement's emphasis on moral regeneration. The manualist educators

---

[4] For more on the connection between nature and sign language, see Baynton (1996, 108–131).
[5] Quoted in Winefield (1987, 97).

who contributed to the *Annals* were deeply concerned with the moral condition of the deaf, which they saw exemplified in the deaf person's seeming inability to experience music. Henry Camp, for example, argues that "it is the *moral* condition of this class of persons, which, more than all besides, should enlist our sympathy in their behalf" (Camp 1848, 213). The unfortunate moral state in which uneducated deaf people found themselves was, according to Camp, caused by the deaf being cut off from two "chief sources of enjoyment": the ability to hear "the pleasant voices of friends, the songs of birds, [and] the melody of musical instruments, [which] afford exquisite pleasure to the ear of man," and the ability to "utter articulate sounds" (Camp 1848, 214).

William E. Tyler echoed this sentiment in 1856, writing that "before education," the "deaf-mute" has "no knowledge of God or a future state. The treasures of history and science are closed to him. The music of nature, of art and of song can never thrill his soul or attune his heart to praise" (Tyler 1856, 202). In other words, manualists saw the deaf as cut off from an important source of moral and intellectual betterment due to their inability to perceive music. This lack could be remedied by finding ways to instruct the deaf in musical matters. Tyler goes on to write that if the "deaf-mute" "is so fortunate as to meet with a skillful teacher who can bear the torch before him, he must still stumble for some time in the gloom, before he can reach the perfect light of day," reflecting the attitude that manualist educators acted as the moral saviors of their deaf pupils (Tyler 1856, 202). William Wolcott Turner, principal of the American Asylum for the Deaf, and David Ely Bartlett, who taught at the New York School for the Deaf and the American Asylum, further argued for the inclusion of music in deaf education in 1848:

> If the question be raised, "Cui bono?"—what possible benefit can result from teaching music to the deaf or from exercising them in musical performances when learned?—it may be answered: What benefit is ever derived from teaching music? It is a source of intellectual gratification. It is a means of intellectual cultivation. (Turner and Bartlett 1848, 5–6)

Bartlett suggests that the deaf derive pleasure from the "rhythmical character of the movement, which can be perceived by the sense of sight alone, and yet more perfectly by sight and feeling together." He also notes that another source of musical pleasure for the deaf is "the pleasurable effect of vibrations gently exciting the nerves. This kind of sensation, although far inferior to that of perfect tune acting upon the perfect ear, is nevertheless in a degree a pleasurable one" (Turner and Bartlett 1848, 5–6). The language used by Bartlett in justifying including music in deaf education resonates with the justifications used for including music in public school curricula in Boston ten years prior. These justifications were intellectual, moral, and physical: music was positioned as "an intellectual art" that produces only "good, virtuous, and kindly feelings," and that helps exercise the organs, thus warding off disease (Mark and Gary 2007, 160–161).

Manualists thus acknowledged, at least in part, that there was value in including music in deaf education, that it had the same moral, intellectual, and physical benefits for deaf children as for hearing children, and that deaf students could indeed experience music in some pleasurable way through vision and touch. Deaf musical practices were, in other words, accepted as ways of knowing about music, and through these established ways of musical knowing, deaf pupils could be taught morals and religious principles.

In the next volume of the *Annals*, though, another manualist instructor expressed skepticism about deaf musical expression. J. A. Ayres describes a piano performance by a girl who was deafened in infancy, in which he asserts that she exhibited "expression, accuracy and skill" in the performance:

> No one hearing it would have dreamed for a moment that the performer was destitute of the sense of sound, or unable to drink in with a full soul the harmony which she was, in a measure, unconsciously creating. It is true this was, to a great extent, only a display of mechanical skill; yet as an effort, under great disadvantages, to take one step further in the world of acquisition, it was an exhibition full of both wonder and interest. (Ayres 1848, 26–27)

This passage reveals an underlying current of anxiety about the status of deaf persons with respect to musical knowledge. The notion that deaf people could have musical knowledge that would allow them to perform musically and indeed *authentically* on a musical instrument was a potential source of anxiety even for manualists who encouraged deaf musical knowledge production for its potential to lead to moral and intellectual betterment.

Whence did this anxiety originate? As I have noted, manualists were particularly interested in preserving the natural, or godly, in deaf education, as opposed to the artificial or mechanical. Manualists were thus concerned about any display that encouraged the "unnatural" in a populace they saw as "innocent" and "less corrupted than hearing people" (Baynton 1996, 130). Using speech and, it seems, performing music were seen by manualists as unnatural, going against the mode of expression that God had deemed appropriate for the deaf. Attitudes toward mechanical music-making and musical automata had also undergone a shift at the beginning of the nineteenth century. We can understand fears and anxieties about mechanical music-making in the context of a shift away from the android forms of musical automata of the eighteenth century. While Enlightenment thinkers on music like D'Alembert and Diderot embraced automata and musical machines, Carolyn Abbate notes that by 1800, animated musical objects had become terrible, the stuff of nightmares (Abbate 1999, 476). Thus, the performance of a young deaf girl on the piano became a locus for broader cultural anxieties about the unnaturalness of speech and music for the deaf, the authenticity of mechanical reproductions of music, fears about machines and technology, and anxieties about the mechanical man who "robs us of a prize, our soul" (Abbate 1999, 476).

Deaf music-making was thus inextricably bound up with ideas about authenticity and the mechanical even in the early part of the nineteenth century. But at the same time, manualists expressed the notion that the moral state of the deaf can and should be improved through music. Most important, manualist thinkers tentatively agreed music could be experienced by means other than hearing sounds.

1.3 The Oralist Method, Music, and Technology

Already by the 1840s, manualism had several prominent and powerful opponents: most significantly, Horace Mann, Samuel Gridley Howe, and, in the latter part of the nineteenth century, Alexander Graham Bell. These educators instead supported the oral method, which proposed eliminating sign language in classrooms and replacing it with the exclusive use of lip-reading and speech. As R. A. R. Edwards argues, the attacks on manualism by Mann and Howe were crucial to oralism's ultimate victory over manualism and dominance in the field of deaf education by the end of the nineteenth century (Edwards 2012). The first oralist schools founded in America were the Clarke Institution, founded by Harriet Rogers in 1867, and the Horace Mann School for Deaf-Mutes, opened by Sarah Fuller in 1869 (Winzer 2006, 114). By 1880, eleven more oral schools had opened. Mann, Howe, and their followers believed that deafness had a "horrifying impact on the character of the afflicted child" and that deaf children should be "fashioned accurately into the likeness of the hearing majority" (Edwards 2012, 185). Throughout the latter half of the nineteenth century, more and more educators and parents came to believe that an oralist education offered the only solution for this assimilationist goal. As Margret Winzer points out, hearing, female teachers led the oral reform, ultimately elevating oralism "to the dominant ideology by the opening decades of the twentieth century" (2006, 112).

In 1880, the Second International Congress on the Education of the Deaf, commonly known as the Milan Congress, dealt a heavy blow to manualism by resolving to ban the use of sign language in educating the deaf in favor of the oral method. Baynton argues that oralism was the result of an altered reform atmosphere after the Civil War, in which the emphasis shifted from the individual reform of the Second Great Awakening to the creation of natural unity (Baynton 1996, 16). In keeping with that goal, the primary objective of oralism was the assimilation of the deaf into the hearing world, and its champions believed that an oral education would lead to greater assimilation. While oralist schools did not completely discourage the deaf student's acquisition of language skills or their pursuit of other academic achievements, these were given substantially less emphasis than the teaching of speech and lip-reading. As Richard Winefield has noted, "oralists advocated integration as the primary desired outcome. While not eschewing language skills and other academic attainments, they saw these more as a means to an end, that end being assimilation" (Winefield 1987, 80).

Under the oralist regime, deaf education had what Simi Linton calls a "taming function." Its aim was to contain, to control, "to civilize creatures seen as not quite human" (Linton 1998, 56). The leader of the oralist movement in the late nineteenth century was inventor and eugenics advocate Alexander Graham Bell, who "thought it best for the race that all people be able to hear and, short of that, that all people at least be able to understand speech and communicate orally" (Winefield 1987, 96). For oralists like Bell, the word "natural" had a different meaning, one that aligned more closely with the nineteenth-century ideas of the "normal" or "average."[6] In 1884, Bell captured this new understanding of the "natural" in his reply to a question about whether teachers should vocalize while teaching deaf students:

---

[6] For a detailed analysis of the concept of normalcy and how it was constructed during the nineteenth century, see Davis (1995, 23–49).

I think we should aim to be as natural as we can. I think we should get accustomed to treat our deaf children as if they could hear, and if we get into the habit of articulating to deaf children without voice in this way we make a distinction between them and hearing persons. We should try ourselves to forget that they are deaf. We should teach them to forget that they are deaf. We should speak to them naturally and with the same voice that we speak to other people, and avoid unnatural movements of the mouth or anything that would mark them out as different from others. ("Convention of Articulation Teachers of the Deaf—1884: Official Report" 1884, 11)

The advancement of normality as the goal of oral instruction was tied up with ideas about eugenics and the ideal human, ideas promoted by Bell. In November 1883, Bell famously delivered the paper "Memoir upon the Formation of a Deaf Variety of the Human Race" to a meeting of the National Academy of Sciences at Yale University. In the lecture, he carefully documented the marriages and familial relations of the deaf in America, revealing intense anxiety about the intermarriage of deaf individuals, which he imagined would lead to the establishment of a deaf variety of the human race, weakening American society and requiring a remedy: the assimilation of deaf people into a "normal" educational environment.[7]

For oralists—who saw the deaf as requiring assimilation into the hearing world lest they form a race of their own—music could not have the same educational and cultural function as it did for manualist instructors. Manualists acknowledged that deaf people experienced music in a variety of ways—including through touch and sight—and accepted the experiences of deaf knowers as valid. This view of deaf musicality was not compatible with the version of deafness constructed by the oralist movement. Oralists wanted deaf people to experience music in only one way: through hearing. For oralists, "only the *normal* behaved *naturally*" (Baynton 1996, 139) (emphasis original), and since those with "normal" hearing understood sound to be fundamental to musical participation, the only natural way for the deaf to experience music would be through the sense of hearing; other ways of experiencing music were both abnormal and unnatural. If a deaf person could be made to hear music in the same way as a hearing person, then that would be a truly remarkable sign of their assimilation into what oralists saw as "normal," hearing culture. For this to happen, deaf persons could not be

---

[7] For a detailed exploration of Bell's eugenic views, see Greenwald and Van Cleve (2014).

framed as having any musical knowledge outside of this "normal" experience of music, through the mechanism of the ear. The ongoing musical experiences of deaf individuals therefore needed to be obscured from our collective understanding of musical knowledge.

A representative example of the oralist attitude towards music can be found in Arthur Hartmann's 1881 oralist publication *Deafmutism and the Education of Deaf-Mutes by Lipreading and Articulation*. Hartmann describes a "totally deaf girl in the Royal Deaf and Dumb Institution" who had "received at home pianoforte lessons for several years and had acquired such skill that she learned to play pieces not only from music but also by heart" (Hartmann 1881, 88). Hartmann goes on to describe this type of instruction as "useless" for the deaf child. Since, Hartmann opines, "every care has to be taken with the intellectual education of a deaf-mute, . . . it seems injudicious and disadvantageous to employ the time and attention of a deaf-mute child with such a purely mechanical and useless occupation" (Hartmann 1881). Hartmann does, however, acknowledge that "a not inconsiderable amount of deaf-mutes are able to hear music, and . . . these are passionately fond of it" (Hartmann 1881). In these quotations, Hartmann largely dismisses the deaf experience of music as useless. He speaks of music as an exclusively "heard" experience, rather than a phenomenon that can be experienced through sight or touch. Although he acknowledges that some deaf people are "passionately fond" of music, he does not recognize that the primary means by which these deaf people experienced music may have been visual, tactile, or kinesthetic.

Hartmann's portrayal of deaf music-making as "mechanical" for the deaf child resonates with J. A. Ayres's account of the deaf pianist's "display of mechanical skill" in 1848, and with the report on a deaf girl's display of speech in 1807. For Ayres and the anonymous reporter, the mechanical or artificial displays of speech and music were understood as going against the natural, God-given use of gestures for deaf expression and communication. But in 1881, only two years before Francis Galton coined the term "eugenics" and Alexander Graham Bell cautioned against the formation of a deaf race, the idea of the mechanical takes on more ominous resonances. It calls to mind the idea of disability as spectacle, as other, as a threat to the normal bodily state, and even as monstrous. It also creates a link between deafness and the concept of the human as machine—which, like the metaphor of the human as animal, is designed to dehumanize. As Scott Selisker observes, "the automaton, mannequin, or robot, and its attendant dilemma, became central to a wide range of representations of subhumanity in the twentieth century" (Selisker 2011, 572). Colleen Lye has explored how instigators of the "Yellow Peril" in the early twentieth century likened Asian Americans to machines: "the brute is typically a kind of 'wild man,' desire incarnate loosed from social control, denoting the figure of primitivism within modernity. The coolie signifies a different kind of monstrous presence, not the ambivalent pleasure of the body's libidinal release, but, on the contrary, the prospect of its mechanical abstraction" (Lye 2004, 56).[8] All these resonances are at play in the characterization of deaf music-making as mechanical by oralist thinkers, whose notions of normalcy and assimilation were grounded in eugenic modes of thought—what Rosemarie Garland-Thomson calls eugenic logic (Garland-Thomson 2012).

The characterization of music as existing beyond the reach of the deaf—who could only hope to mechanically reproduce it—would become dominant among oralists by the turn of the century as they established the primacy of speech and lip-reading, and encouraged the use of technology to facilitate what they saw as a more normal, "heard" experience of music. In 1897, the publication of an article by Harvey Lincoln entitled "Music for the Deaf and Dumb" goes one step further, arguing that the deaf can only experience music—and thus become more like the typically hearing majority—through technological interventions. In this passage, Lincoln describes a new technology that would enable the deaf to hear music:

> There is music for the deaf! Professor McKendrick, of Glasgow, is its discoverer. He is to the ear-drum what Koch is to the lungs. . . . The restorer of the normal condition! With the aid of Professor McKendrick's invention deaf persons can attend the opera and occupy their boxes in any part of the house, however remote. They can dress as others dress, converse as others converse, do as others do, with nothing conspicuous about them. . . . This applies to all deaf people and especially to the deaf and dumb who will, for the first time, enjoy musical rhythm and hear the notes of human warblers. (Lincoln 1897, 66)[9]

---

[8] Scott Selisker explores the racial aspects of the mechanical metaphor further through the example of the Haitian zombie, introduced to US culture by travel writer William Seabrook. Selisker characterizes the threat of the zombie, as portrayed by Seabrook, in terms of exoticized technology. Angus McLaren further discusses how fears about mechanized men were colored by eugenics in early twentieth-century British literature (Selisker 2016; McLaren 2012).

[9] While the article describes a technology developed by a Glaswegian, it is important to recall that ideas about music, technology, and deafness circulated in a transatlantic framework.

John McKendrick's invention used a combination of a phonograph, telegraph, and electric battery to allow the user to "hear as well as though he were in possession of normal aural organs." Lincoln even ventures that the apparatus allows the deaf person to "hear an opera better than a person with good ears." A large phonograph is placed as near to the stage as possible, and connected via electric wires to seats where deaf people are located. Then the deaf person places his hands in a saline solution, into which the wires are passed. The result, claims Lincoln, is sound. He even describes the deaf person's total focus on the music while using the device as an advantage, since he will not hear the interruptions of people speaking to him. Ultimately, he concludes that even though the device is highly expensive, "it is a great invention . . . and will relieve a large class of men and women who suffer a slow martyrdom of sound."

Lincoln characterizes the deaf population as having been wholly bereft of musical experiences before the invention of a specific technology. Normal hearing, provided by modern technology, is positioned as an essential element of musical enjoyment. Other musical activities that had previously been mentioned by manualist writers, such as feeling vibrations or seeing rhythmic patterns, are completely absent from the author's conception of music. An important element of Lincoln's account is the notion of assimilation; he advertises McKendrick's invention as a means for deaf people to pass as hearing, with "nothing conspicuous about them." The idea that deaf people could pass perfectly as hearing was common among oralists. In 1884, Alexander Graham Bell encouraged other oralist educators to teach their students "to forget that they are deaf" and to avoid anything "that would mark them out as different from others" (Baynton 1996, 136).

Concurrently with McKendrick, Miller Reese Hutchison was engaged in the invention of the first electrical hearing aid, the Akoulathon. He soon refined the hearing aid into the first model of the Acousticon, a portable, battery-powered hearing aid. A flurry of articles emerged in 1903 in *The National Magazine*, *World Today*, and *Scientific American* advertising Hutchison's Acousticon, using music as a prime example of the invention's powers. In *The National Magazine*, Bennett Chapple describes the visit of the Metropolitan Opera's Suzanne Adams to the home of the Akouphone Manufacturing Company. A photo accompanying the article, reproduced as Example 1.1, shows Adams "singing to the hearts and souls of those who have never before heard music—music, the language of hearts," through a related instrument called the Akoulalion (Chapple 1903). The photo is

Example 1.1 Suzanne Adams singing to Orris Benson, a DeafBlind child, through the Akoulalion. Printed in *The National Magazine*

captioned: "The engraving shows Mme. Susanne (sic) Adams, the famous grand opera soprano, singing to the blind, deaf and dumb boy Orris Benson, through the Akoulalion. Thus was the magic of great music conveyed to the eager soul of this thrice unfortunate boy, past the barricaded avenues of his natural senses" (Chapple 1903).[10] Chapple positions technology as part of a musical cure, in which the child's deafblindness is a barrier to musical under-standing, to be overcome by the power of the Akoulalion.

Suzanne Adams was not the only opera singer called upon to demon-strate the abilities of devices like the Acousticon. In 1903, A. L. Griffith tells of six pupils of the New York Institute who tested the hearing aid by going to the opera, where they were "particularly impressed and delighted with the voice of Mme. Sembrich." Three deaf-blind children also "heard Sousa's

---

[10] For a discussion of Helen Keller's encounters with famous opera singers of the early twentieth century, see Accinno (2019).

marches played on a piano and then heard a phonograph repeat the sounds" (Griffith 1903). These public tests or experiments were common in the early days of the Acousticon and were often conducted on children and young adults from deaf schools, with music used as the ultimate tool in assessing the new technology's effectiveness on these musical non-knowers. The claims of miraculous musical recoveries made possible by Hutchison's technology rely on the foundation of hermeneutic injustice. An article appearing in *Scientific American* entitled "New Instruments for Enabling the Deaf to Hear" describes how the Acousticon allowed a young woman who had lost her sight and hearing at age six to "listen rapturously to the sounds of musical instruments and the human voice, conveyed to her for the first time since her affliction, by the new instruments." The author also points out that there exist modifications of the Acousticon, one of which he calls the "opera outfit." This version is contained within a small box for greater portability and ease of disguise, so that the previously mentioned girl "was able to enjoy the music at the opera in New York City, as if she had never been stricken." Once again, the central function of the device is to restore "normal" hearing for the purpose of positioning deaf persons as musical non-knowers, who can only gain an epistemic foothold as knowers through becoming assimilated into the paradigm of "normal" hearing.

New technologies like the Acousticon, which were advertised across America and which quickly found a place in deaf classrooms nationwide, were meant to improve the condition of the deaf through assimilation.[11] The ultimate proof of that assimilation was the ability of the deaf technology user to hear music normally. The desire for the deaf to integrate into hearing culture so seamlessly that they could pass as hearing, and the use of music as proof of that integration, contrasts sharply with manualists' fears about the use of music as a tool for "passing." At the same time, oralists still feared what they saw as the mechanical aspects of deaf music-making and questioned the morality of instructing the deaf in musical matters.

Although music was no longer used for the moral and religious education of the deaf, the participation of the deaf in musical activities was certainly viewed as morally problematic by oralist educators. Hartmann, for example, viewed music performed by deaf children as "purely mechanical

---

[11] The Acousticon occupied a special place in the ad sections of America's newspapers throughout the twentieth century. These advertisements often contained outrageous claims about the device's ability to cure deafness. They also addressed more mundane concerns, such as portability and ease of concealment by wearing the device as a watch or hidden in a woman's hairstyle.

and useless" (Hartmann 1881, 88). In fact, music was used specifically as a means of dehumanizing the deaf and heightening their comparison to emotionless machines: in a 1903 article from *The Association Review* on the proceedings of the Department of Special Education of the National Education Association, Edward E. Allen characterizes the deaf as "less emotional, less sympathetic, less altruistic than the blind or the normal," because "music and the voice, by which the feelings are best expressed, do not appear in the world of the deaf" (Allen 1903, 345). It is important to note that Allen was an educator and administrator at schools for the blind, where music and the voice were highly valued in blind pedagogy. This led educators of the blind, like Allen and Samuel Gridley Howe, to ally themselves with oralism (Winzer 2006, 114; Edwards 2012).

Three years later, in 1906, a report by the Italian G. Ferreri on the state of American institutions for the deaf includes similar language that associates deaf music-making with automata and machines. Ferreri is highly critical in his assessment of a display at the Chicago school, where children were "not only exhibited to give proof of their ability in speech (and in this there was no harm done) but also in choral singing and dancing." In the following passage, he attributes this musical event to the deaf person's ability to mechanically execute rhythmic movements, without actually understanding or experiencing music:

> The facility of the execution is owing principally to the mathematical element of the rythm [*sic*]. . . . The deaf-mute is capable of following and of executing himself a succession of rythmic [*sic*] movements, whether with the voice, arms, or legs. . . . Now when these movements are accompanied by sound, the illusion is an easy one, and it seems to the public that the deaf-mute moves himself, dances, and sings from musical impulse. (Ferreri 1906, 402–403)

For Ferreri, the most harmful demonstration the children made was not of speaking, but of singing and dancing. To "pretend" to experience music in any way as a deaf person was the most pernicious kind of deception, one that could trick the audience into thinking that the deaf could participate in musical culture without any technological mediation.

Proponents of manualism and oralism, although they disagreed about how music should be used in educating the deaf, shared the fear that the music produced by deaf people was mechanical, and thus in some way deceitful and immoral. The oralists' fears were, however, exacerbated by the influence of the eugenics movement on oralist thought. In an example of eugenic logic, oralists specifically associated deaf music-making with metaphors of the mechanical and automatic, capitalizing on eugenicists' anxieties about humans as machines, in order to eliminate culturally Deaf modes of musical thought in favor of technologically "normalized" music-making. The idea, promoted by Alexander Graham Bell, that the deaf could and would form a race separate from mainstream America was not acceptable to late nineteenth- and twentieth-century supporters of eugenics. The concept of a deaf race presented an epistemic threat to musical knowledge as well, in that it would take deaf persons outside of the realm of hearing musical knowledge structures and into a culture that Bell feared would have its own language, literature, and artistic practices (Bell 1883, 44). The elimination of specifically deaf ways of knowing and thinking about music was, therefore, one of the unspoken aims of the American oralist program.

1.4 Music and Deaf Education after 1900

Although the Milan Congress of 1880 dealt a severe blow to America's deaf citizens, sign language certainly did not disappear from their lives or even their educations. The National Association of the Deaf, founded in the same year the Milan Congress took place, fought against oralist pedagogy and defended sign language against its attackers. At certain schools for the deaf, particularly those that still employed deaf teachers, deaf culture thrived in spite of the Milan decision. Deaf journals like *The Silent Worker* and *The Deaf-Mutes Journal*, launched in the 1870s and 1880s, quickly became popular sources of news and gossip for deaf Americans, providing a sense of community that spanned the nation. In these journals, as in almost nowhere else, we can observe traces of the musical culture in deaf spaces (Buchanan 1993). However, these musical cultures were shaped as well by oralist pedagogical techniques involving rhythm and pitch as aids for speech production, as Abby Lloyd documents. Lloyd recounts how the use of rhythm and pitch exercises at the piano, as well as the formation of deaf and hard-of-hearing bands, is directly tied to oralist thought and technique (Lloyd 2017). At the same time, though, deaf persons did derive pleasure and satisfaction from these musical experiences, per their accounts.

Articles published in *The Silent Worker* reveal an abundance of musical events at American and Canadian schools for the deaf. These events included the singing and signing of hymns, solo performances on musical instruments such as the piano or percussion, and performances by deaf bands. Music acted as a source of entertainment, an amusing pastime, an educational or therapeutic tool in the context of oral schools, and a source of income for the deaf people described in these articles. In 1905, for example, Herbert Roberts described a tradition, begun by Professor Samuel T. Greene at the Ontario School for the Deaf and Dumb in Belleville, of "training the deaf scholars in the art of signing hymns." Since Greene began this practice, Roberts writes, "almost every female graduate of that school is an expert in the art of hymn reciting, and the more they practice the more grace and charm is observed as they sweetly warble off their melodies in the quietest and most fascinating way imaginable" (Roberts 1905, 137). Outside of this particular school for the deaf, there are several documented instances of hymns being signed by both deaf and hearing individuals.[12]

One of these instances involved the signing of the hymn "Nearer, My God, to Thee" by a young girl named Marion Ballin. This was the daughter of Albert Ballin, artist, actor, advocate for sign language education, and author of *The Deaf Mute Howls*. Ballin recounts the story of how his daughter came to sign the hymn:

> By the time my oldest child reached her eighth year, I had taught her to sing in signs the hymn "Nearer, My God to Thee," using the sign method that I had worked out. I made her blend one gesture into another until every verse resembled what we might call "visible music." It was not dissimilar to the rhythm of Greek dancing. (Ballin 1998, 65)

In this passage, Ballin tells how he taught his daughter his own system of sign language singing, which she then performed for church audiences. Despite developing the system for singing in signs, however, Ballin had his hearing daughter perform in his stead—perhaps because she was young and thus more entertaining, or perhaps because hearing audiences would be more accepting of a hearing child's musical performance in signs.

The earliest examples of signed songs captured on film originate from the early twentieth century as well, the oldest known recording

---

[12] See, e.g., "An Impressive Incident" 1898; "Bible Class Gives a Funny Show" 1905.

being a performance by a deaf woman of "The Star-Spangled Banner" in 1902. Charles Krauel, as filmed in Ted Supalla's documentary "Charles Krauel: A Profile of a Deaf Filmmaker," identifies ASL performers as "singers" who create music with sign language (Supalla and Dannis 1994). Some of the music identified by Krauel are signed interpretations of songs like "The Star-Spangled Banner" or "Yankee Doodle," but he notes that others were entirely conceptualized in sign language, such as "Voices of Animals." Supalla's documentary shows several examples of these popular sign language songs from Krauel's films of the early twentieth century. Cripps et al. observe that this signed musical practice continued in theatrical performance in America through the National Theatre of the Deaf, which "produced My Third Eye for both the stage and television during the 1970s. Both translated songs (i.e., Three Blind Mice) and singing in an ensemble format are found in this production" (Cripps et al. 2017, 3).

Several oralist schools for the deaf developed musical curricula in the early twentieth century, including the New Jersey and New York Schools for the Deaf. Lloyd lists four such band programs: (1) the Illinois School for the Deaf; (2) the New York Institution for the Deaf; (3) the Tennessee State Deaf School; and (4) the Minnesota School for the Deaf. As Lloyd observes, "the bands were formed as extensions of rhythm programs already in place at the schools for the deaf and/or as extensions of military marching programs at schools that embraced military traditions" (Lloyd 2017, 31).

In 1914, *The Literary Digest* reported that the principal of the New York Institution, a military school for the deaf, saw the boys banging on walls and other solid objects and decided to introduce them to the drum, and later the fife, bugle, and other instruments, so that by 1913 a "forty to fifty member band, entirely made up of students, was achieved." Another article adds that the band was "invited to participate in high-grade concerts given by hearing musicians in New York City" (Porter 1917). The New York band is pictured in Example 1.2. Multiple sources reported that the band was also invited to participate in concerts given by hearing musicians. The audience for this deaf music, in other words, was not limited to members of the deaf community.

In 1917, an article entitled "Rhythm Work in the New Jersey School for the Deaf" described the practice of using musical rhythm in schools for the deaf, specifically in the case of a drum band ("Rhythm Work in the New Jersey School for Deaf" 1917). The author depicts how, when their "'orchestra' of

Example 1.2   The Deaf Band at the New York Institution for the Instruction of the Deaf. Printed in *The Silent Worker*

drums starts up at one of the Saturday evening parties, . . . [the] youngsters gather round and fairly gorge themselves like gluttons with the vibrations." The students feel the drums, the author writes, "in every bone and muscle and fiber of their beings" ("Rhythm Work in the New Jersey School for Deaf" 1917, 105).

The band at the New York Institution for the Deaf also inspired the formation of other deaf bands, like the Illinois School for the Deaf Band (Sheldon 1997). In her discussion of the history and formation of the Illinois School for the Deaf Band, Deborah Sheldon quotes the words of the school's students on the benefits of musical participation:

Many people ask this question: "What is the use of having such a band at a state school for the deaf?" The answer [*sic*] to this question are given below:

1. It develops the cultural side of life.

2. It teaches team work (or co-operation) by ensemble playing.

3. It develops the dormant remnant of hearing that is found in a certain percentage of children in every school for the deaf.

4. It makes the band boys more alert in their other studies and removes that feeling of hopelessness which arises at every seemingly different problem.

5. No one can call the study of music a waste of time. Each band boy spends at least five hours a week at it.

6. It puts not only the band boys, but the entire school more in touch with the outside world, in that it appeals to the public in a way which the regular school work does not. (Sheldon 1997, 591)

It is evident from the preceding quotation that the deaf students who were a part of the band or who witnessed them performing found pleasure in this musical experience and framed it in terms of their culture, their community, their personal development, and their relationship with the hearing world. Given that they spent a large part of their lives participating in this musical activity, it is clear that these students had a great deal of musical knowledge and expertise, of which they felt proud.

The practice of using the piano in deaf education continued as well, mostly in the form of rhythm training, as Lloyd documents (Lloyd 2017). At the New Jersey School, as at many other schools for the deaf, the piano was used therapeutically to help the children with their speech.[13] Example 1.3

Example 1.3 "A Class in Rhythm at the Piano," printed in *The Silent Worker.*

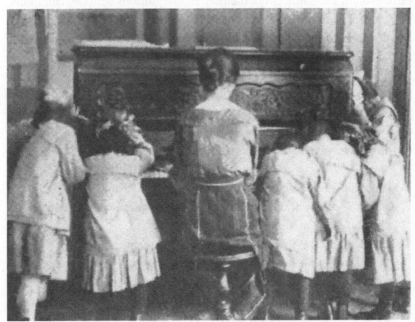

[13] As Michael Accinno (2019) documents, Helen Keller undertook similar instruction in rhythm and piano in her education at the Perkins Institute for the Blind.

shows a picture of deaf students around the piano at the New Jersey School, where they "used the piano as a means of aiding the children to change the pitch of their voices," but also for rhythm work ("Rhythm Work in the New Jersey School for Deaf" 1917, 106). Lena Herschleifer, a pupil at the New York School for the Deaf, writes the following testimony about her own experiences of music:

> We, the deaf, are often asked if we hear the tones of the piano or the voices of people. We don't hear sound vibrations, we only feel the thrill of the music—but hearing persons appear not to understand our sense of feeling.
>
> Sometimes we happen to feel some great sound which makes us start, and people think we hear it.
>
> We can feel the vibrations pass from our feet to our head when the piano is played or a person is singing or if we hold a paper or sit at a distance. (Herschleifer 1917)

Herschleifer's words reveal her awareness of the epistemic gap between deaf and hearing knowers in the musical realm. Her explanation of how she experiences vibrations, and how hearing persons do not understand her experience of music, reveals that deaf persons were thinking about their own musical experiences in different terms than were hearing persons of the same time. Although oralist educators promoted music as a therapeutic tool for improving speech production for deaf students, it is possible that this understanding of music and rhythm work presents a contributory injustice: while oralist educators only attended to the possible effect of rhythm work on speech, deaf students may have been conceptualizing their musical experiences in other ways.

For some deaf students, the piano could also be a tool for musical artistry. A 1918 article in *The Silent Worker* described Leah Wenger's talents at the piano: "Although the beauty of the notes produced on the piano by her nimble fingers falls on unreceptive ears, Miss Wenger appreciates the various works of the great composers through her sense of rhythm and imagination. . . . 'Piano playing,' she declared, 'is nothing more than dancing with the fingers and feeling the time and rhythm" ("Deaf Girl Is Expert Pianist" 1918). For Wenger, music is fundamentally *movement*: she sees rhythm and meter as the foundations of her musical experience and practice.

The Silent Worker ceased publication in 1929, when superintendent Alvin Pope dismissed its editor, George Porter, an influential figure in the

American deaf community. A staunch supporter of oralism, Pope censored the debate over oralist and manualist methods by systematically dismissing deaf teachers, like Porter, who spoke out against oralism. With Pope's take-over of *The Silent Worker*, the newspaper's coverage of music education for the deaf became overwhelmingly focused on speech development at the expense of fostering musical enjoyment and understanding. By the late 1930s and 1940s, the epistemic exclusion of deaf knowers from the realm of musical knowledge, at least in the mainstream hearing narrative, seemed complete. In the *Music Educators Journal*, for example, Karl Wecker writes:

> Children classed as totally deaf do not possess even the rudiments of music. They have had no experience with speech rhythms, thus they lack even that natural relationship of music and language which every normal child entering an elementary school has unconsciously absorbed. They have never heard musical sounds and are unequipped mentally to orientate pitches, timbre and other qualities of sound.
>
> Faced with these facts, Frederick Lewis, supervisor of the Federal Music Project at Lansing, Michigan, recently initiated experiments in cooperation with the Lansing public schools, to determine whether the completely deaf child could be brought to an appreciation of music, and, through appreciation, to a self expression in music somewhat approximating that of the normal child. (Wecker 1939, 45)

By positioning musical knowing as exclusively belonging to the "normally" hearing child, Wecker and Lewis reveal a fully oralist approach to music instruction for deaf students and deny the possibility that deaf children could experience music in ways other than through sound alone. They further call for the assimilation of the deaf child into "normal" modes of appreciating and understanding music.

Throughout the twentieth century, other hearing educators of the deaf continued the oralist program of assimilation using music. In 1965, for example, Lois Birkenshaw writes that the goal of teaching music is, ultimately, assimilation: "in teaching music to deaf children one must always remember that music is only a means to an end, never the end in itself. The end is the satisfactory adjustment of the child in a hearing society and this adjustment is accomplished, for the most part, through the development of clear, understandable speech" (Birkenshaw 1965). The tenacious thread of deaf musicality, stretching all the way back to the first days of Gallaudet's American

Asylum, was by the mid-twentieth century irrevocably tangled in a web of oralism, assimilationism, speech therapy, eugenics, cure propaganda, hearing aids, and, later in the century, cochlear implants.

1.5 Conclusion

The story of music and deafness is one of rediscovery. Time after time, writers have discovered "music for the deaf," shaping and reshaping their definition of that music according to their belief in manualist or oralist ideals. I have argued that the result of the oralist school's redefinition of music as belonging exclusively to the domain of sound and "normal" hearing—or hearing "normalized" through technology—has led to the lasting exclusion of deaf ways of thinking and knowing about music.

Fortunately, Deaf musical practices have persisted in many forms, although some may not have survived to be transmitted to the present day. As Holmes observes, the present-day testimony of members of the Deaf community, hearing aid wearers and cochlear implant recipients, and musicians with hearing loss "amounts to a diverse record of musical experiences that fall squarely within the full spectrum of listening" (Holmes 2017, 173). We now have the opportunity to deepen our knowledge of the kinds of musical understanding and expression that come from Deaf knowers, and in doing so, come to a more expansive understanding of the possibilities for musical knowledge. In order to accomplish this, we must reconsider the very definition of what it means to possess musical knowledge. My goal, in the chapters that follow, is to do exactly that: to rethink what we know about music through the lens of Deaf musical practices.

The history of music and deaf education underscores two essential and interrelated features of music and its role in societies: first, that music forms tight social bonds, and second, that musicality is resilient. Oralists advocated strongly for music use in the classroom for several reasons, not least of which was music's perceived power to create social cohesion. If deaf children could form social bonds through music with their hearing peers, then the eugenicist fear of a deaf race might not become reality. Of course, deaf students also formed social bonds through music by performing sign language hymns and playing in deaf bands, and these shared musical practices would contribute to a sense of shared cultural identity that eventually emerged publicly as the Deaf President Now and Deaf Pride movements of the late twentieth century.

But given the weaponization of music by oralist educators, why did music persist in American deaf communities throughout the twentieth century? With every reason to shun music (and some deaf people *did* shun it, after all), why did deaf social groups engage in percussion signing together, and why do deaf artists continue to create music in sign language? The answer lies in what I am calling the resilience of music. The history of music in Deaf education reveals that musicality is resilient across modalities: when one form of music-making has been discouraged in a Deaf community, another form takes its place. In the next chapter, I explore how these different types of music-making have evolved and changed in more recent history.

2

Deaf Culture's Musical Presents

2.1 Introduction

A video begins with the gentle sound of a folksy guitar, which fades in as two blurry figures gradually appear on the screen. We soon recognize them as a couple dancing, before a cross-fade reveals a young woman swaying to the music at center stage. She soon begins signing rhythmically and smoothly in American Sign Language as she dances, swaying back and forth to the beat. An American flag hangs in the background: the setting is a high school dance, the music playing is the song "Get Together" by the one-hit wonder the Youngbloods, and the tape is titled "A Night at the High School Hop," filmed at Gallaudet University, a Deaf liberal arts university, on February 11, 1975.

Early twentieth-century recordings of sign language music are rare. Only a handful are extant: two percussion songs captured on tape by pioneering Deaf filmmaker Charles Krauel, a film of an anonymous woman signing "The Star-Spangled Banner" in 1901 (see Chapter 5), and a few scattered instances at meetings of the National Association of the Deaf. But in the 1970s, recordings like "A Night at the High School Hop" begin to appear in the Gallaudet University video archives: in addition to the High School Hop tape, they include a 1976 tape entitled *Poetry and Songs in Sign*, as well as an undated tape featuring songs by the group "The Joyful Sign," an ensemble who performed religious music in the 1970s (Rensberger 1979). In 1981, a trio of Deaf musicians and actors named Rita Corey, Bob Hiltermann, and Ed Chevy formed the Musign Theater Company. In 1983, the *New York Times* described their combination of music, dance, and signing as "witty" and "dramatic" (Dunning 1983).

As Katelyn Best has documented, the 1990s saw the beginnings of a new genre, Deaf hip hop or "dip hop," championed by Warren "Wawa" Snipe (Best 2015/2016, 71). By 2005, artists like Darius "Prinz-D the First Deaf Rapper" McCall, Sean Forbes, Warren "Wawa" Snipe, and Marko "Signmark" Vuoriheimo were beginning to release their music (Best 2015/2016, 73).

Seeing Voices. Anabel Maler, Oxford University Press. © Oxford University Press 2024.
DOI: 10.1093/oso/9780197601976.003.0003

Beginning in the mid-2000s, the advent of video-sharing platforms such as YouTube and Vimeo allowed people to easily upload video content to the internet, including recordings of sign language music. Additionally, social media websites and apps like Facebook, Twitter, Instagram, and later TikTok made it possible to widely share sign language music to a large online audience. As I'll discuss later in this chapter, this has led both to innovation in sign language music and to some serious issues involving the appropriation of sign language music and Deaf culture by members of the hearing community.

Today, sign language music takes many forms, and its practitioners come from a variety of backgrounds. Types of sign language music that exist today include traditional percussion songs, translated songs that involve interpreting a preexisting song in sign language, original songs created in sign language, and signed music that involves no signed words (Bahan 2006; Cripps and Lyonblum 2017; Cripps et al. 2017; Maler 2013, 2015). The category of translated signed songs includes live music interpretation services or performances by signed song artists, videos featuring the performance of an original signed song or of a preexisting song translated into ASL (Maler 2015), and what Jody Cripps et al. call "signed music video performances," which involve "highly abstract meanings and encourage artistic interpretation" (Cripps et al. 2017, 7).

To capture some of the richness and diversity of today's signed music practices, I conducted virtual interviews with ten Deaf signing musicians over a period of ten months in 2021 and 2022. This chapter centers their experiences and knowledge in showcasing the innovations and issues in sign language music today. I have organized the interviews by topic: I introduced each topic briefly before letting the artists speak for themselves.

The Deaf musicians featured in this book are Raven Sutton, Paris Glass, Rosa Lee Timm, Harmony Baniaga, Teresa Blankmeyer Burke, Susan Weinfurtner, Matt Maxey, Marko "Signmark" Vuoriheimo, Warren "Wawa" Snipe, and Pamela Witcher.

2.2 Ten Signing Musicians: An Introduction

I selected ten musicians who varied in their backgrounds, relationships to Deaf and hearing cultures, amateur or professional status, and musical genre(s). Raven Sutton, Paris Glass, Harmony Baniaga, Rosa Lee Timm,

Susan Weinfurtner, and Matt Maxey all produce ASL covers of auditory music. Rosa Lee Timm and Pamela Witcher produce original signed music, and Marko "Signmark" Vuoriheimo and Warren "Wawa" Snipe produce original hip hop in both English and sign language (dip hop). Weinfurtner uploads her covers to Facebook for her friends, family, and some of her ASL students to enjoy, while Maxey, Snipe, Vuoriheimo, and Timm have been or are currently professional musicians. Teresa Blankmeyer Burke does not produce any signed music; rather, as a Deaf philosopher and lover of signed music and music in general, she provides a valuable audience perspective. I provide brief biographies for each of my interlocutors below.

Harmony Baniaga (HB) is a Deaf Filipino woman who was born in Seattle, Washington. She attended a Deaf and hard-of-hearing program from kindergarten to fifth grade, when she transferred to a mainstream classroom. She is currently attending Gallaudet University, where she studies ASL with a minor in dance. She describes watching shows like MTV as a child and being fascinated with the music videos, turning the volume up to feel the vibrations.

Teresa Blankmeyer Burke (TBB) grew up in Southern California, where she attended a mainstream school. Her mother noticed that she was hard of hearing at the age of three, although she notes that medical professionals initially did not believe that Burke was hard of hearing. Burke was raised in a musical family and took piano lessons for fourteen years, beginning at the age of seven. She majored in music in college.

Paris Glass (PG) grew up in Houston, Texas. They grew up hearing and became deaf later in life. They went to college for ASL interpreting and worked as an interpreter until they lost their hearing. They now work at a private school for neurodivergent children. Glass creates ASL covers of a variety of musical genres, including punk and musical theatre. Glass grew up hearing, in a family of "musical theater buffs." They played the violin for eleven years before losing their hearing and shifting toward creating sign language music.

Matt Maxey (MM) was born in Decatur, Georgia, and grew up in Texas, Mississippi, and Atlanta. He identifies as a hard-of-hearing but culturally Deaf man. He grew up in a musical family, where his mother sang and his grandparents were heavily involved in their church choir. His interest in hip hop was sparked by his father, who introduced him to groups like A Tribe Called Quest, Nas, Jay-Z, and Outkast. Maxey is the founder of DEAFinitely Dope, a company that provides sign language interpretation for live music events. He currently resides in Atlanta, where he teaches, presents, performs, and interprets. His goal is to "break barriers and bridge gaps through sign language and music."

Warren "Wawa" Snipe (WS) was born and raised in Philadelphia. Growing up, he was the only Deaf individual in his family, although he later discovered that several of his extended family members were Deaf as well. He attended college at Gallaudet University, where he learned ASL, discovered Deaf culture, and started creating music. He grew up in a musical family and was particularly interested in rap music, with its strong bass and drums. Snipe would feel the vibrations from a speaker while simultaneously reading the rap's lyrics and his sister's lips as she spoke them out loud, which would help him memorize the song. He began by writing poetry, which he converted into his own signed raps. He was also involved in dance at Gallaudet University, where he was a founding member of the all-male dance company the Wild Zappers. He has released three albums of his music: *Deaf, So What?!* (2016), *Wamilton* (2021), and *Unapologetically* _____ (2021).

Rosa Lee Timm (RLT) was born in California to a Deaf Seventh-day Adventist family. Her older brother is also Deaf and her younger brother is hearing. She grew up in Oregon, where her mother home-schooled her and her siblings. Her family then moved to Nebraska for her father's work, where she initially attended a mainstream school, followed by a Deaf school. She now lives in Maryland. When Timm was five, she began using hearing aids, which led to her love of music. She took guitar lessons and quickly began signing along to music on VH1 as an eight-year-old child.

Raven Sutton (RS) is from Birmingham, Alabama. She attended the Alabama School for the Deaf and Gallaudet University, where she studied social work. She currently lives in Maryland and works as a survivor resource specialist, working with the Deaf community who have experienced domestic violence in the DC area. Sutton mainly creates covers of rap and hip hop. She grew up as the only Deaf person in a musical family, and she has danced throughout her life.

Marko "Signmark" Vuoriheimo (MV) was born in Helsinki, Finland, where he currently resides. He grew up in a Deaf, signing family and attended a deaf school growing up. He became interested in music at the age of seven or eight, when his hearing grandparents would play the piano and sing Christmas carols in another room, apart from the rest of his Deaf family. Vuoriheimo was curious and began to sign along with the carols for the rest of his family. He later began to write his own raps in sign language, eventually releasing four hip-hop albums: *Signmark* (2006), *Breaking the Rules* (2010), *Silent Shout* (2014), and *Dream Awake* (2018).

Susan Weinfurtner (SW) was born in Cocoa Beach, Florida. She was born hearing but became deaf at the age of two. She grew up oral, without access to sign language, and graduated high school as the only Deaf student in her class. She then attended college at the Rochester Institute of Technology, which is where she encountered Deaf culture for the first time and began to learn sign language. She is now an ASL teacher and lives near Atlanta. Growing up, Weinfurtner did not enjoy music. She saw her family and friends listening to music in the car, attended some concerts, and saw singers on TV, but did not appreciate music until very recently, when she saw Deaf artists like Sean Forbes creating sign language music. She currently posts some of her own ASL covers of music on her Facebook page.

Pamela Witcher (PW) was born in Montréal, Québec, to a Deaf family. She attended the Mackay School for the Deaf. She attended a mainstream high school, followed by the cégep Dawson College. She then attended McGill University, where she received a Bachelor's of Social Work, and Montmorency College, where she received a degree in Applied Museum Studies. She currently resides in Elmer, Québec. Growing up, she wanted to become a singer. She became involved in translating music into sign language for a band, after which she joined a Deaf drum group. In 2009, she decided to no longer use hearing aids and to explore her relationship with music by disassociating it with sound.

2.3 Topics in Sign Language Music

Motivations

Due to the different backgrounds and musical histories of each of my interlocutors, each musician took a unique path toward discovering music in sign language. In an effort to understand what motivates signing musicians to take up and hone their craft, I asked each of my interviewees to explain what drove their interest in sign language music.

Raven Sutton emphasizes accessibility as a motivating factor in her decision to create and distribute ASL covers of music (▶ Video Example 2.1). She also points out the importance of having Black Deaf people signing Black music for cultural and accessibility reasons.

RS: I guess I would have to say that with music I want it to be accessible for us. . . . I got kind of tired of hearing people not recognizing the Deaf creativity and what we have in deafness and how we can express ourselves through sign. . . .

I like different Black artists, I like Black Deaf people signing because some of the words that are used in the music are not culturally acceptable for white people to be signing or saying. And also I feel that for Black artists, what they say in their music is like a Black person's experience. We know how to translate this music. Whereas a white interpreter or a white person would translate that music and it will not be 100% accessible because maybe they are not choosing an accurate translation or they do not know how to express what the artist is saying and the attitude and how it will come through. And the movements that go with it and how you get that vibe, that song. With hip hop it's not the kind of music where you just stand there and sign it. Hip hop is all about movement and rhythm and dance. So I use that in my ASL translations because I want Deaf people to watch my video and feel it and want to move with me, just like a hearing person would if they were listening to it. Deaf people are very visual and they can get that sense of what is happening and sometimes with white people when they are signing music, it is just not 100% accessible. Because there are things culturally that just do not match up. Maybe they use the wrong sign for some specific thing. And of course, when they are saying are signing the N-word, that also, just can tailspin into a lot of problems. That is why as a Black Deaf woman I prefer signing hip hop and translating that more accurately.

Harmony Baniaga describes how she began signing along to songs on the TV in Signed Exact English (SEE), an invented system for representing English grammar and vocabulary using a mixture of ASL signs and unique English signs (Miller 2010) (▶ Video Example 2.2).

HB: I think I was eleven or twelve. At that time, she [my mom] was like working out. And I saw like the captions on the TV, there was a woman who was singing, while the other woman was working out. And my mom would like follow that workout video. And I saw the captions, you know, it was like a really slow song. And so I just kind of like started signing the captions, kind of playing around with it. At that time I was using SEE signs which is like more English, not really ASL. At the time I hadn't had any exposure to that, or like the Deaf community or Deaf culture or anything just yet. So, when I got into like middle and high school that was when I did continue signing music, because I kind of got into it that way. And then I did a talent show in high school. You know you sit on the stage and I was signing with a dance that they were doing. And people kept asking me to do that because they were really interested by it. They like to see it. And when I got into Gallaudet people said that they had seen my videos and they wanted me to get into the show business. And so we would go to like restaurants and bars where they would have stages for events. Every last Friday of the month, people would come in and they would do poetry or music or really anything, sort of artistic, and I would go in and do music there.

Marko "Signmark" Vuoriheimo explains how he began by translating songs into sign language, but a violent encounter at a nightclub, in which he was attacked for signing a song, led him to start writing his own raps (⯈ Video Example 2.3).

MV: I started with translating only, I was just translating the lyrics. There are thousands and thousands of Deaf people who are translating music and I started to get bored, and I think this is so boring. It's better if I write my own songs and that's how I started to create my own music and write it. So how I started this was a little bit interesting. I think I was twenty-one or twenty-two, or something like that, and started to think that I'd like to translate the music. But when or how, I have no idea. But then one night I was in a nightclub dancing, and I knew the song they were just playing, it was Coco Jambo. I knew that, and I went to the dance floor. I started sign it, to translate it, and very quickly a pint of beer was thrown on my neck, on my back. Three men attacked me and started to fight me and hit me, and it was a really bad fight, and I was thrown out of the nightclub. The doorman said, "the guys were just losing their temper because you're using your hands, you're like a monkey or something," and they thought I was signing something about them, mocking them and that's why they attacked me and I was the one thrown out. At that point I said fuck it, enough is enough. And I decided that well, I was not allowed to go back into the nightclub, and I said, Okay. I went to the nearby petrol station, got a cup of coffee and piece of paper, and I started to write. I didn't know how I would perform it. In a way it was like a diary for me at that point. Then I start to look into who are the true artists who are producing music in the world, who are making music from the start to the end. The whole project, the whole process by themselves, and I didn't find any Deaf musicians like that. They were just well, some dancing groups or translators, but that was not something that I was interested in. I just wanted to be the person who does everything from the start to the end, and also who knows how this connects to the rap music and the rhythm and rhyming the lyrics. So you have to know about these issues. And I didn't find anyone.

Matt Maxey describes how his musical career emerged from a culture clash between his hearing upbringing and Deaf cultural norms at Gallaudet University, against which he initially rebelled (▶ Video Example 2.4).

MM: Honestly, it was just more of, my mind worked way too fast. So when I first went to Gallaudet University, I had to take ASL 101, pretty much the introduction. And I didn't really quite conform to the ASL culture, it was more me rebelling against it, but still curious enough to learn about sign language. And with music it felt more fast-paced and more of a challenge and more intriguing for me to try to use everything that I learned sign language–related, and applying it, applying it to music. And I started off with people like Bone Thugs-N-Harmony, Twista, Eminem, like I started at the top. And you know it was challenging, it was more my speed of helping me to understand how ASL works, how the sign language vocabulary could become memorized, how all of this can be applied in conversation, and the more I applied it to music, the easier conversation became and it just continued from there.

Honestly [at Gallaudet] it was so many cultural rules that I didn't understand. So for example, I remember my first summer there I went there early, for a new signers' program, and when I went there the first thing they told me was get off the phone, talking to my mom. So I'm thinking wait, what? Why are you telling me to not talk to my mom on the phone? Again, I didn't know, some may consider it audist, but I came from a hearing background, so I was learning as I went. So with that being said, it kind of made me rebel even more, because you want me to be like you; I don't want to be like you, I want to keep my identity, my upbringing, my background, my cultural heritage, wherever you want to label it as, I want to keep that. But at the same time. I'm trying to understand what it means to be Deaf, hard of hearing in a Deaf world instead of a hearing world.

Pamela Witcher reflects on how she wanted to find Deaf representations of sound, which led to her piece of signed music called "Experimental Clip" (▸ Video Example 2.5).

PW: Yeah, so . . . around the year of 2006, I began to question myself. Internet went virtual, it became expansive, and we became more visible to each other. There came video editing, filming, and documenting. So, that made me think . . . what if one day, I decide to remove audible sounds? It's finished. What if there have never been any hearing people on earth, none at all? What if there are only deaf people? What would become of music? The visual sounds, yeah the visual sounds—this is how we sign the "visual sounds" and this is how we sign the "audible sounds"—yeah, the audible sounds in ASL and the visual sounds in ASL. How can we take ownership of that word "sounds"? Yes, the sounds. . . . And hum . . . so I decided to make a first clip called "Experimental Clip." Maybe you have already seen it? Yeah, that's my first, yeah, the first but it wasn't a live performance, it was an edited video. So, when I played with music through signing and through editing. So, that process is different from a live process. Yeah, so, that was my first diffusion and people began to look at it, became interested, they began to look at it with curiosity and all that. Then, a friend of mine, he's a hearing musician and he was fascinated by the music video. He added the audible sounds, yeah, ok . . . the audible sounds added to that video that became a second version. Yeah, so, now there are two versions, the original one without the audible sounds and the second version with the audible sounds. Both have the visual sounds but they have different impact on the audience.

Expression and Emotion

One commonality among my interlocutors was their motivation to express emotions and stories through sign language music. Although I did not specifically ask about expression and emotion in each interview, the topic inevitably arose when each signing musician described their passion for music, and specifically for creating music in a signed language.

Rosa Lee Timm points out the importance of experiencing music through one's native language, and of understanding the emotional content of a song when creating a translation (▸ Video Example 2.6).

RLT: Really ASL is my first language. So for me to understand the music and to really appreciate the words, I needed to be able to sign it and get the linguistics of it, so I would sign it so I could understand the music better. Because I would put it into my first language. I could hear some and I started to catch inflections of the sound of the voice going up and down, I would catch the beat, when it would pause. So I had kind of like purpose, I knew when to emphasize what it was, what the emotions were, what was the point of what they were trying to represent, the perspective of language, what were they saying, what did it mean. It was just feeling it and experiencing it was different. The one frustration was with my family being deaf, they didn't understand music. They were just like yep yep yep, it's just this that and the other. They didn't really understand what it was about, the deeper levels that go with music, it's not just a beat. What the artist was wanting, what they want to you to feel, to experience, to get out of this music. And so with my natural language, we'd do that through my CODA [Child of Deaf Adults] brother. He is in the same boat where his heart is deaf, his family is deaf, but he is only one who can hear. So when he hears music he can understand it and sign it to me, to help me follow along with the lyrics or what is being said, where the rests are. And I'd ask something like, why are you making that face at that moment? And he'd say oh because the voice goes up high or hitting a high note or doing something different, and you know that's when I learned about the emotion when the voice goes up or something like that. So there are different music emotions and ways to express it and how it can impact you by using that voice up and down. So he explained a lot of that to me and that really painted a picture for me. And it told me that accent, whether they are southern or country or heavy metal, or whether the voice is monotone, or a young voice, a deep voice. He could give me those colors that I could paint with, and it was just so fascinating, that world, and trying to sort of take that all in and take that artistic piece out of it and put it in ASL, and Deaf people can experience it on that same level, not just watch and listen but experience it. That is what I think is one of [the] biggest gaps in our community.

Raven Sutton emphasizes using the body to tell a story, revealing how emotion, movement, ASL, and music are integrated across the senses to create a unified experience (▶ Video Example 2.7).

RS: Expression with the body and movement is a big part of ASL. So music, you see a story, it's what the singer is saying. It is like oh no, they just broke up and they are single and having a party. Or whatever. And hearing people can hear that in the words, in the lyrics. They can hear that. They hear that in the instruments. Maybe there is a drum or guitar or piano or violin. But they can hear that and how it kind of crescendos and there is a lot of big roles of that. You are feeling what the artist wants you to feel—and I feel that through ASL and when I bring that to life and I show what I am feeling, my emotions and the movement, it's like dancing in a way. And I am interpreting with my body, with my expressions, whether I am sad, or when I'm excited I look like this with a smile on my face. Or if I am excited or bouncing around. So whatever they are saying is what I'm showing. It is like acting. We are providing that and we are bringing it to life. People are making those connections and they are seeing the visual art, and I know that hearing people depend on their ears. They can listen to something but they are also visual, and if you like plays and movies, if you like to see dancing, ASL is a big part of that. When you are hearing, and sighted and hearing together, it can be the most amazing imagery with motions. You can see it. That is one of the things I love about making my videos, is that I get lost in the character. That is why I do so much studying ahead of time because I want to understand what the artist is telling me and what is the feeling that they want me to get from their music. I think about situations where I have had that same feeling in my own life. And how did that mood make me feel and when I put all that together and I am signing it accurately and I see my emotions and I see my anger and I see my happiness, I can see what the artist is trying to say. I think that is 100% music and Deaf culture married together. Just like dancing. It is universal. You don't need to know—you don't have to have captions for communication. It is like you can feel it and you can see ASL in the translation and with the emotions are. What they are trying to say and convey and what you are hearing and feeling, what does it feel like. You're signing it and you are seeing it. It's like different senses. You use all of those senses integrated.

Paris Glass describes the cathartic effect of this kind of musical expression for the signer (▶ Video Example 2.8), and Susan Weinfurtner recounts how she uses sign language music to uplift herself and others during dark times (▶ Video Example 2.9).

PG: Signing something as emotionally charged as a song with all the expression that comes with ASL, there is nothing more cathartic in the world. It feels so good to just let loose and go for it, especially if you are having just a really bad day. To just express yourself to the point of exhaustion. And because I already had a platform I was like well, I can share that. I did not expect anything of it. At the time I had a couple thousand followers, on accident. So I was like oh well you know, I will just post it because it is something that I like. And then other people liked it also. That is really validating, especially when it is a song that I have a personal deep connection with. And some of the ones that I post are just because it is fun or a funny song like the Bo Burnham stuff, but a couple that I posted have been things that I have a very deep connection with and so those videos are, as cliché as it's gonna sound, a glimpse into my soul. I take everything I feel and connect with in that music and putting it into the world physically.

SW: In the past when I'm sad about relationships, my best friend, or if my friend or anyone is going through tough times, I always look for uplifting music to sign to make them feel happy, you know? Like it'll be alright. That's very important. And when I decide to make music I must turn off my mind, my thoughts about other things, distractions, I need to close that up and focus on the music, relax, and flow, then my signing will be clear. Because if you are distracted you will mess up. Your mind and the music have to flow.

Finally, Teresa Blankmeyer Burke provides an audience perspective on the emotional impact of both signed and non-signed music (▶ Video Example 2.10).

TBB: So I engage with signed music in two different ways. Maybe more but definitely—sometimes I engage with my hearing aids on and my little assistive device and I'm trying to pull in the auditory content, knowing that my experience of processing that may be very different from someone with typical—species-typical—hearing, but it's still an aesthetic process and experience for me. Sometimes with signed music video translations of songs, I just watch. And I watch and I intentionally turn off the sound, take these [hearing aids] off, and watch. And there are very few people who can really keep my attention, and they tend to be people who are native signers, because otherwise it's like this doesn't have, for me, because I did grow up hard of hearing in an environment where I was exposed to a lot of music the emotive response I have to the sounds of music is a part of my musical appreciation experience. I don't have to have that, but if I don't have an emotive response to a signed music translation it's like, um . . . [shrugs]. So maybe the part that's important to me is having, being able to have an emotional response.

Translation

Many of the musicians I interviewed produce ASL translations, or covers, of existing music. Jason Listman, Summer Loeffler, and Rosa Lee Timm have pointed out that there is a range of translation types in translated signed songs "from literal, word-for-word translations, to translations where modifications were made for ASL, to more loose, creative translations" (Listman, Loeffler, and Timm 2018, 1). The musicians I interviewed pointed out some of the unique challenges of creating these translations in their music.

Raven Sutton emphasizes the importance of cultural awareness when translating between English and ASL, pointing out that there are idioms that make little sense in Deaf culture (⊙ Video Example 2.11).

RS: Sometimes the singer uses a lot of meanings that just go over my head. English is not my first language. ASL is my primary language. So with English sometimes I have to have a friend who is hearing kind of let me know, like "please tell me what is she saying. I have no idea." And sometimes they don't know either. Okay. So now what? So with Deaf people and ASL there could be several meanings for a sign. What are they exactly saying? We don't understand. Exact English isn't ASL. When you interpret the meaning behind the actual English, then it is understandable for Deaf people. Typically, Deaf people would not necessarily know a lot of hearing idioms. Or what those actually mean. It is kind of like "in one ear and out the other." We would not use that in ASL. But we have this sign, "it went right past me." Meaning, I did not understand what you meant or I was not paying attention to what you said. "In one ear and out the other" does not make sense to Deaf culture. But when you do the translation, Deaf people understand. They know exactly what you are talking about. When there are multiple meanings to English, it is hard to know exactly what they are saying. So the translation can be more cumbersome. I have to ask people what that means and what they are saying. Trying to make sure that I am understanding. That can be a struggle.

Paris Glass points out that some metaphors do not translate well into a visual medium (▶ Video Example 2.12).

PG: The biggest challenge is metaphors. Metaphors. (Laughing) There are some that it just clicks and I am like okay I can turn it like that and do this that or the other, right. And then there are some—what does that mean? Like, I want to grab the hearing singer and ask what does this mean. Because everything else has something there that I can relate to, I can feel. And then there's this one line that is complete and utter nonsense. Because you can do that with music. You can make complete and utter nonsense every once in a while. But when you are trying to bring it into a visual medium, what are you going to do? So a lot of music that I connect with has that issue. There are so many metaphors that have so many layers that it just doesn't work and it's very frustrating.

The immediate lyric that comes to mind is a Pierce the Veil song, "I Don't Care If You're Contagious." I was listening to it earlier. "I would rather spend my life vacations in bed with you like drunken summer kites." What does that mean? I love that song! What is a drunken summer kite?

Harmony Baniaga offers two solutions in her own work: thinking about the lyric metaphorically, or resorting to a word-for-word translation. She also points out the difficulty of matching the speed of English prosody with that of signed prosody, which sometimes necessitates editing or summarizing the meaning of the English lyrics (▶ Video Example 2.13).

HB: I did experience some challenges while I'm translating and editing the videos as well. And I'm sure you've listened to Billie Eilish before, you know who she is? Yeah, I love her music. She's an amazing singer, artist. She's wonderful, but whenever I hear her song I'll listen and I'll like it but when I look at the lyrics I'm just like what the hell does that mean? And so I have to go to Google and try to figure it out. Some of them, there's no explanation, but some of it.. . . . Do you know Genius, the website Genius? It will show the meaning of the song lyrics and so I'll take a look at those and some of it will show very clearly and some of them it won't. So there has been a few, I'll ask my hearing friends like do you know what this means? Some of them will say, Oh, I'm not sure. Some of them can explain it a little bit more but still I have trouble understanding her music sometimes, so I'll try to think of like what that lyric means as a metaphor. Or, if I still can't figure it out, just try to follow in the exact English word order, or I'll just do what I feel it means, trying to make the lyrics match with the song. Like the overall concept of the meaning of the song to kind of show the message, instead of what exactly that specific line meant in the song. It's not just Billie's music of course, there's other singers too that I have that experience with. And then, speed, the speed of a song, like the tempo. Like, I do like to challenge myself with quicker songs, or sometimes like a hip-hop song. But what they're saying can be so quick. So I'll sign either before they start talking or after they start talking trying to fit it in. And sometimes I try to think of what can be the perfect sign for that lyric for that line in the song, or you know if it's too fast, I have a time limit, I have to summarize it or edit it down.

Marko Vuoriheimo discusses translation in his original rap music. In this case, the English and ASL lyrics are both created by Vuoriheimo himself. Vuoriheimo points out some of the unique challenges of translating and English rap into ASL, especially when rhyme is involved (⊙ Video Example 2.14).

MV: So for example if you're thinking of the sign BORED and the sign SERIOUS: so that means that I just change the location of the sign. Just one part of that. And that's rhyming in sign language in a way. But in spoken language they are two different words: boring and serious. So I was thinking that I need to do almost like triple the amount of work than the hearing artists because first I have to write the lyrics, then I have to translate it in ASL, then I need to see if there's rhyming in the spoken language version and the signing version. If the rhyming matches. If there is no rhyme, then I have to go back and change the wording in the spoken language. And that took a lot of time. That was so time-consuming. But now today, in rap music, the rhyming is not the most important thing in rap music anymore. So that was a huge relief for me. It's a little bit easier now than it was about 2010, because at that time the rhyming was the most important thing in rap music. So now there's more flexibility and more flow in that sense today.

Lastly, Pamela Witcher teases out distinctions between translating and interpreting aural music, and shares concerns about the relationship between these ASL covers and hearing identity and culture (▶ Video Example 2.15).

> PW: My focus is totally on signed music. Yup, that's it. Hum. . . . because hum . . . it's a very narrow path and that field of practice is living oppression. So, I am trying to build some room, the space for this! Yes, the space. Yeah, hum . . . so, what's left outside of that space is unbelievably vast. It's so big out there, all related to audible music. Yeah, the audible. . . . There is interpretation, there is translation . . . all that over there. Yeah, so that's really the hearing culture over there . . . all set. . . . That is the hearing way of thinking, the hearing way of expressing, the hearing identity based on audible sounds . . . yeah . . . there. . . . So, now . . . some deaf people interpret, they translate. Yeah, some deaf do that kind of stuff. Hum . . . that scope is quite broad with various stuff in that. One of them is adapted kind of translation which falls in line close to American Sign Language. Let's look at it as trying hard to read, to perceive, to analyze the metaphoric meanings, all those little details and transform that information into a sign language, into full ASL. I have already seen those kinds of works, but there aren't many of them but it does work well in its own way . . . it does. But if it's direct works between text and sign, without any analysis, without really thinking about what it really means in ASL? The direct interpretation, I am not talking about translation or adaptation versions but the interpretation, during the process, the meanings are missing out along the way. Hum . . . really, it's almost as if the hearing music is right there, in our face, the facade of their spoken language and culture there. So, when Deaf people watch the audible music, we do not have our own direct interpretation. Yeah, we are not able to have our own direct interpretation. What really happens is that my perception, what I receive from the performance is based on the interpreter's interpretation, yeah.

Copyright and Accessibility

In our conversation, Raven Sutton described a unique challenge of creating and distributing sign language covers online: signing musicians often encounter copyright challenges when they post their covers on websites like YouTube or Twitter (▶ Video Example 2.16). In a sign language cover, the audio from the original song is usually unchanged, although the signed performance is of course original. Sutton points out the importance of .sign language music covers in providing necessary accessibility for a Deaf audience.

RS: Also on Twitter a few weeks ago they suspended my account because of copyrights. That was another struggle and frustration because I do not sign it for profit or money, I do it for me. I do it for my own accessibility. So right now I am trying to figure out how can I contact them and be in touch with whomever I need to, to get through with this copyright violation. I did get my account back from Twitter. However, I am not allowed to post any more videos on Twitter. Because then they will suspend me again. And that's been a struggle because I do not post for profit. I post for accessibility, that's it! Being blocked, that's another reason that a lot of people don't sign music, because of the copyright violations that can happen. So that can be quite a struggle to figure out how we can work through this.

And what is strange is that it makes your video more popular when you send it out. Maybe people want to buy your music. By me doing this obviously other people are getting interested. So these artists, it is their music, but we are helping people and we are doing a lot for the artist. And people may choose to buy their dance or their curriculum—thinking like, I like it more because I know what it is about. With ASL, it just brings more people to be interested in their music so they have more access to their music. So I think it is really strange how we are doing so much with this copyright violation when actually we are helping them to earn more money. We are not earning the money. They are the one that's making more money out of this, so it is just bizarre.

Teresa Blankmeyer Burke also emphasizes that these covers should be protected by the Americans with Disabilities Act (ADA) of 1990 (▶ Video Example 2.17).

TBB: So often, so there, there are these issues about musical copyright and YouTube and what you can put on there, what you can't, whether a signed interpretation of a song counts as an original contribution and therefore bypasses that copyright and how strict—some companies are more strict than others and so on and so forth. And I have wondered, I don't think I've seen this anywhere, but is it has occurred to me, when I'm thinking about like all my Deaf lawyer advocates that I know, is whether anyone has ever challenged these copyright violation, pulled down by YouTube, or what have you, as a matter of accessibility using the ADA.

On the Nature of Music

Sign language music offers an opportunity to think about the multisensory nature of musical experience. My interlocutors each offered their unique perspective on the nature of this multisensory experience, and how experiencing music can involve all five of our senses.

Rosa Lee Timm describes how music can be a purely visual experience, with all of the rhythm, tone, and texture of auditory music (▶ Video Example 2.18).

> **RLT**: My first exposure to music, I thought, was at church, church music. But really if I go back further, I think about being in the car and a rainstorm, the windshield wipers, and the rhythm of the windshield wipers, seeing the trees passing by, the lights twinkling through—driving on the road and having the lines that are passing by you or the cars that are passing by you. So watching all of these different visual things happening at one time, that is like music. It is like instruments, it is called texture. Because there are all those elements. So texture is one of [the] elements of music. There is the tempo, texture, tone, rhythm, all of these things are the elements of music. So that's what I could capture in the car, just visually, it's music. So it is there. It is like a phone wire, like you watch the wires and they kind of go up and down, you pass by them and they go up and down up and down and that is like the tone going up and down, so all of that is similar to music but visual of course. Growing up I loved sitting at the window watching everything pass by, the lights, the different rhythms of things, the colors. But that is not sound.

Harmony Baniaga lists just a few of the ways in which music can be experienced through sight and touch (▶ Video Example 2.19).

> **HB**: When I got here to Gallaudet I met a lot of Deaf people who love listening to music. And, you know, some can hear a little bit, some are profoundly Deaf and can't hear at all, but I have met some people who are profoundly Deaf and they only like to feel the vibrations of the song

but still they do appreciate and enjoy watching music happen in whatever way that's happening. I think music is just the same thing visually
too. It's making a visual way for people to enjoy music, just the same as
how hearing people enjoy it too. I know people who are Deaf, they use the
word Deaf to mean they can't hear music, they can't appreciate music, but
they don't look at the whole body, the whole picture. They can still feel the
vibrations, they can feel the beat. If you're on [a] wood floor you can feel it
even more. And so when you're looking at the whole thing, even you can
hold a speaker and feel the vibrations in your hands. Or like if you're in a
big group and there's loud music going on, you could feel it in your body.
I've seen that they have vests that you can put on that you can connect
to music through Bluetooth and it'll vibrate and shake with the beat. So,
there's a lot of different ways.

Marko Vuoriheimo relates his experience of teaching a hearing music producer a thing or two about listening to music through his body (⯈ Video
Example 2.20).

MV: With the first producer, we had fun together doing it, because he had
done years and years producing music, and he's been working in that field,
and he started to tell us that you know how to make the bass, etc. He tried
to explain, "yeah I know how to do this, this is very good" and I said "no no
no, it's not enough bass, it's not enough. We need more." And he just started
to wonder like, "what? There's quite a lot of bass." And he was thinking that
I'm just a Deaf person and I don't understand what the hearing people
think. So I said, "Okay. Go to the nightclub, and they have audio equipment
there, etc. Play my music there." And he did, and I said, "Can you feel it?"
And he said, "Yeah, yeah, yeah, I can, what's the difference?" And I asked to
change the song to Tupac's music. I said, "Okay, do you see the difference?"
And at that point he was just like "Oh, yeah. Now I can feel the rhythm.
I can feel the bass, the vibrations in my body." And I said "Okay, in my song,
there's only this much bass." Through this kind of experience he realized
that he had never been used to listening to music with his body. That was
this kind of an enlightening moment for him.

Finally, Pamela Witcher discusses how creating signed music can offer
people self-reparation, healing, or a form of resistance against oppression
and audism (⯈ Video Example 2.21).

PW: So this is from a Deaf perspective. It feels like auto-reparation. Healing process is really necessary to be able to find courage to share our story. But the fact that we have experienced a lot of oppression and lived criticisms. . . . "No, you are wrong. You can't. No, you can't do music," to name a few on a long list. Deaf people's insides are filled with that kind of negativity. On the outside, they may seem fine, standing tall on resistance. Often their worth is structured based on the capacity of doing translation works. Listen, that's fine but what's really going on deep inside of you, what is it? Let's imagine if we put other people's work, their creative works aside and we have nothing to do with it. What if it comes from you? Yes, from you. . . . You! So, what will happen? So, you see . . . really . . . that's where the sensitive spot hits. That challenge, I have noticed. This is where you have to be personal . . . vulnerable . . . and become exposed. Yeah, that can be challenging. . . . So, that process really needs time and we need a safe space. We need a safe space but where is it? Where can we find the location for it? Hum. . . . Where can we get together to discuss the signed music, yeah. . . . Often, it happens that hearing people are around which isn't a good idea. Hearing people around us, researching us, analyzing us, observing us. How would that give Deaf musicians the space to freely share out? That can be challenging.

Hearing People and Sign Language Music

The relationship between hearing people and sign language music has been complicated and somewhat controversial. As I have observed, creating ASL translations of aural songs remains a popular pastime for hearing people interested in ASL, including ASL students (Maler 2015). Members of the Deaf community have cautioned against hearing people posting and sharing these videos online, as they often contain inaccurate signs. Paris Glass has humorously demonstrated this phenomenon by posting music videos by hearing people with captions that accurately capture inaccurate or confusing signs (see GlassMenagerie 2021 for an example).

The quotations below reveal how hearing engagement with sign language music can be regarded as both necessary (in the case of ASL interpreters at concerts) and problematic (in the case of amateurs or students posting videos online). My interlocutors point out inequities in audience engagement and exposure: covers by hearing people tend to get more online engagement than those by members of the Deaf community, leading to greater fame and more opportunities for the hearing. Others emphasize the importance of ethics in professional music interpretation, urging professional ASL interpreters not to let their egos interfere with the goal of accessibility. Several people emphasized the importance of employing members of the Deaf community to interpret music at concerts, and specifically encouraged the use of Certified Deaf Interpreters (CDIs). CDIs are Deaf or hard-of-hearing interpreters with native or near-native fluency in ASL, who work in conjunction with hearing interpreters to provide the most culturally and linguistically accessible interpreting for the Deaf community.

Raven Sutton points out how the hearing community is biased toward watching hearing interpreters, rather than Deaf artists. She calls for more exposure for Deaf artists and proposes working in teams to provide access (▶ Video Example 2.22).

RS: It would be exposure of—hearing people tend to not want to see—how do I say it? ASL signed from Deaf people, they like to watch the interpreters. They feel more connected to hearing people and the Deaf creative artists and people who are posting things, people do not really pay attention to that exposure. The hearing person tends to sometimes maybe if they are teaching ASL, they're doing it wrong or their interpretation is not accurate. And they tend to vlog all the time. Sometimes it can be very disappointing because they think that they are providing accessibility. But in reality they are not. And they are not teaching it appropriately or they are not translating the music appropriately and some people tend to sign with exact English and so it is not really in ASL. That can be confusing. There are many ways that you can sign one word. You could pick, for example, if I say "freak," that can mean crazy, it can mean something dirty, it can mean weird. There are several meanings. When people say freak and one person will say it is crazy and someone will have another interpretation. So what freak are they intending on using? Which freak are they talking about? Following exact signed English just is not very successful. So it is either they do not know or care or understand that part of interpreting music. So that can be very frustrating.

Historically, and I am not going to say way back in the past, but over the past few years there are Deaf people who signed music. However, they do not get as much exposure when, let's say concerts or festivals, we'll ask for an interpreter to sign the music because that is the only type of accessibility that we have. But now as more Deaf people are being artists and being creative and are posting, I feel like we should be getting more exposure about that, with interpreting the music instead of how the hearing interpreter signs it. So I feel like when we need an interpreter, an interpreter should be there. However, when it comes to music, that is where we can have a Deaf person signing music. And that is accessibility. It is the artist hiring Deaf creative people to be doing this music instead of always relying on an interpreter.

We ask that people provide access, captioning their videos and having ASL interpreters at the ready when requested. And if Deaf people can do these things, then let them do it first. Get them out there first. And we are fine working in a team. Just don't leave us behind and take the easy route to pick the interpreters because that is easier for you. . . . Like, for example, today one interpreter, this white woman, she just put up her vlog, she just went viral. What was it? Some festival in Chicago recently over the weekend. She was signing WAP and it went viral. Everyone was talking about this interpreter and there were comments saying, "Deaf people don't listen to music, why is there an interpreter?" And ugh, now we have to start all over again with explaining. So it is kind of ironic because my first viral video was WAP. But still, no one has been in touch with me about signing music at that festival, or I would have been happy to look around or ask people. But it is just really easy for people to pick a hearing interpreter to sign something like that and think, "wow they are so amazing," but they are ignoring us who have been doing a lot of this work all along.

Paris Glass emphasizes the frustration Deaf people experience when they see beginner hearing signers appropriating ASL on social media, and encourages hearing people not to sign music on these public platforms. She also points out that concert interpreting can lead to fame for some interpreters, which may lead to inflated egos and unprofessional conduct (▶ Video Example 2.23).

PG: So, we will always need interpreters. Obviously. The issue is that a lot of—it's such a sticky situation and it sucks sometimes. So when Deaf people say on social media hey, don't post videos of you signing. It's not cool. The root of that is more that it is not your language, it's not your culture. And because ASL has been out of the public eye for so long until so recently, we want the people modeling our language to be native users. So when we scroll past and see an ASL 1 student trying to sign something, people with no knowledge of ASL will think that's just as good as a Deaf person signing that song even if it is completely inaccurate and makes no sense at all. So there's that frustration there. There's also so many Deaf artists who want to interpret music, who want to be the ones at the concerts because they connect with that specific artist who's playing that concert. So they know their songs already, they don't need to prepare for it. They have it on call. So there are those people and there is also a lot of Deaf people who hold trauma with hearing people not respecting them over their identity or our language. And so there are Deaf people who are like, hearing people on social media do not sign. I don't care if you are an interpreter, I don't care if you're a CODA [Child of Deaf Adults]. If you are hearing, if you have hearing, do not sign on social media. It's not yours. And for a little bit I was like that and then I kind of took a step back. And thought ok the world is not black and white. There is intention behind things. There is a lot of gray area. My personal belief at this point is that it depends on the person, the skill level, and the intention. If it's an ASL 1 student who's showing off something that they just learned, they can do that with their friends and family. But let's not try to go viral for it.

I happen to know personally two concert interpreters who are very famous because they are good at what they do. But their egos, man! And that is something very common with interpreters who go viral and interpreters who are brought on to Jimmy Kimmel, which is a thing that happened. . . . Their egos are the size of the sun because they know they are talented and they know that what they are doing is beautiful and artistic. And so the professional side of it, out the window. Completely out the window. And so there is like this diva syndrome. And makes me very wary of concert interpreters. Because I've seen what it's done to some of their egos. But at the same time it is necessary. There are not enough Deaf people who would just get up on stage and do that. A lot of us just want to chill at the concert. And sometimes we do fine without the interpreter for the actual songs but we want to know what they are saying in between. It's so widely varied that we do need the hearing person to be up there. So again, it's another really sticky thing. I feel like a lot of interpreters throw out the professional side of it once their skills get to a certain point because they feel like they are irreplaceable. And that becomes an issue.

Rosa Lee Timm notes that while there is a time and place for hearing people signing music, their translations are often too focused on sound and lack grammatical accuracy. This leads to inaccessible and ineffective ASL covers (▶ Video Example 2.24).

RLT: There is a time and place for it. I do see value in ASL students practicing signing music, but for profit, for fame, for attention, for opportunity, to move up in the ranks, to get a job, to get recognized, using sign music for that? No. I do not agree with that. I don't feel like they are doing it right. It sucks, their ASL translation. Their priority is sound, you can see it in their signing, they are dropping the ASL grammar and dropping the environment of it because they are so busy listening for the wrong reasons. It is not accessible and not about ASL even, it is about "Hey this is cool, look what I can do, I am signing these words, look at me, pay attention to me." I say no. But I'm not saying that hearing people should not sign music period, but there is time and place for it.

Harmony Baniaga explains how she came to understand why it is culturally inappropriate for hearing people to post their signed songs online. She also notes the differences between signing in SEE (Signed Exact English) and ASL (▶ Video Example 2.25).

HB: So okay, personally, myself, I did not have that much exposure to ASL, I knew English and I signed in an English way most of growing up. So, in high school, I had taken ASL for three years. And there was either a teacher or student who showed me a video of a hearing person signing a song and I thought oh you know that's cool, you know, that's fine. It's creative, I guess, I could kind of understand what they were saying, you know, I didn't understand every second, but at least they were signing something creatively and I showed it to some of my Deaf friends and they were pissed off. And I didn't understand that you know they were more ASL than me. I didn't really understand. They said this isn't clear, I don't understand what she's saying. And I was just kind of like, oh. At that time I was still kind of lost, but trying to understand the ASL like perspective, their culture, from their perspective. And then when I got to Gallaudet. That is when I kind of started to understand exactly why hearing people signing is wrong. And it's not culturally appropriate for them to be signing music on the internet in that way. From what I've noticed too, seeing, like for example, if you see two different signers signing the same song but they'll sign it differently, one's in ASL and one is in SEE (Signed Exact

English). You can compare the two of them, and the ASL one is going to be more clear. It's going to be showing the meaning and the content more effectively, while a SEE signing hearing person is going to be following the English order and not really including the facial expressions, not showing classifiers, which is another parameter of sign language, so it's harder to understand that one. From what I understand, some hearing people will post signing videos of music because they feel inspired, they are attracted to sign language, they want to be able to do what Deaf people are doing, but they don't actually understand and they're reading the English lyrics and are just signing it in that exact word order. So I started to understand why exactly it's not appropriate. And of course now we happen to be stuck in the middle of Covid, there was a lot more recognition for sign language and a lot of hearing people are starting to become more popular more viral for their signed songs compared to Deaf artists and Deaf signers who are not getting the recognition they should have. So that can be frustrating as a Deaf person.

Teresa Blankmeyer Burke points out some of the ethical issues with hearing people profiting from creating and distributing sign language music (▶ Video Example 2.26).

TBB: Sometimes the issue of the attention on the hearing person who's signing comes from that individual wanting to like monetize their YouTube channel. And sometimes it comes from something going viral because somebody at a concert recorded an interpreter, was doing their job. And that becomes challenging and problematic for (a) the interpreter; (b) for the Deaf person who requested that interpreter. Because pretty often interpreters are provided upon a Deaf person's request. It is very rare, and Sweet Honey in the Rock would be one group that I can think of that's always had that access but that's pretty rare. So if a Deaf person makes a request for access and then an interpreter becomes famous or profits from that, there's some, some layers of ethical issues and obligations and connections to—one of my areas of research in ethics is Sign Language Interpreting ethics and how an interpreter navigates that sort of sudden viral fame as an interpreter of music is . . . there are several cases where I go, mm, don't do it like that! And yet I think we're human, right? If we get attention for something we do well, we want to be acknowledged for that.

Warren "Wawa" Snipe emphasizes the discrepancies in how hearing and Deaf artists are treated, with hearing signers receiving far more attention in the form of "likes" on social media. He also expresses his dream for each major recording artist to have a team of interpreters, including Deaf performers, ready to interpret every live concert (▶ Video Example 2.27).

WS: In the beginning, I thought it was really cool. I mean I've seen a lot of interpreters with interpreted music and I was like wow, you know, it's really good and stuff, and I loved it, and I know many people have the heart for the Deaf community who really want to put out that access which I love it. Then I started seeing some people who typically, take ASL 1 or 2 or 3. Okay, and they're signing the song. Just to get this [attention], the likes, the people to say, Look at me! I know ASL. And then they proceed to start teaching sign and I'm like whoa whoa whoa whoa, and it's a wrong sign. So I saw that often, and then we see some Deaf people, and it happened to me many times too. If it's one popular song, if a Deaf person signs it, beautiful job, boom, maybe 100, 200 likes, or maybe 1,000 likes but then you have someone taking ASL 1 or 2 or 3 signing that song? Millions or hundreds of thousands, and it's like mind-blowing. I'm like, do you realize this is our language, this is what we do naturally. This is what we love. This is our communication access, our skills. We're just showing it, you're doing it for fun, you're doing it for the likes. We're doing it for the access, we're doing it for the community. I became frustrated.

But then also sorry, interpreters, there are still some interpreters who did it for the same reason. "Yeah, look at me. I did this, I could do this." And then with several interpreters before was saying, "I'm an interpreter so I have every right to do it myself, I don't *need* the Deaf community for this." Oh oh oh ok. All I'm asking, is give credit where it's due. That's all. You want to do it because you're an interpreter providing access? Great. I'm all for it, no problem. But be nice. Give the credit where it's due. And now all that's been changing. There's still some struggle, because this is still an uncharted water right now, it's untouched, still trying to figure out how to adapt, clarify the course of ethics, the rules, and stuff like that. So this is a great opportunity of how we can present this the right and the best way and the most effective way.

Now, here's the biggest dream that me and several others, several other performers, Deaf performers, interpreters, you know, for music, concert interpreters—we wish, we wish, and we're hoping this would be the goal. We want to make this the goal. Each major artist [would] have a team, an interpreting team. So any concert they go to, any concert they have is always accessible. Doesn't have to pick, it's only for this day. What if the person can't make it that day? They wanna do it this day. The placement of where you have interpreters are at, because that'd be amazing because there's about almost, I believe 80 to 800 maybe concerts a year. We have enough interpreters and DIs (Deaf Interpreters) to provide that. So if every star has their own interpreting team, beautiful. So when the performance comes up, Monday, Tuesday, Wednesday through Friday, Deaf people can pick which day themselves. They don't have to be zoned to one. Access. So it all comes down to what does total inclusion mean to you? We need that today. It's the twenty-first century, it's time.

Music and Deaf Culture

The notion of "sign language music" encompasses a wide variety of musical practices, each of which exists in a particular relationship to both Deaf and hearing cultures. Sometimes these relationships are fraught, and many are in a state of flux. Several authors have noted that feelings on music are mixed within the Deaf community; as these authors note, however, music continues to play an important and often-overlooked role in Deaf culture, through translated songs, rap, songs purely in ASL, and instrumental music (Best 2015/2016; Maler 2013; Cripps et al. 2017; Listman, Loeffler, and Timm 2018). When asked whether music is "common in the deaf community," deaf rapper Sean Forbes enthusiastically replied, "Yeah! There are a lot of deaf people who love playing music in their cars while driving. Mostly they play music that's dominated by drums and bass, like rap music and techno, because they can feel the pulse" (Mackin 2011, 11). Several of my interlocutors noted that while not all members of the Deaf community enjoy music, many of them do.

Some of the musicians I interviewed, like Rosa Lee Timm, felt that music has a natural place in Deaf culture (▶ Video Example 2.28).

RLT: Yes I would say that, yes I think music has always had a place in Deaf culture. You have to look at each culture in the world, everybody has music, all of them. Including Deaf culture. It is just that the definition is not universal: the definition is problem. Yes, it does exist. It has always been here, it has been a part of Deaf culture, it has always been rooted in our history, it's just a matter of how you label it, and having a better understanding of it, better research, more studies, that's all. That is what I tell people, is that music is already part of our culture. We just didn't realize it, we didn't know it. And we probably denied it. Maybe there was some trauma with growing up in the hearing world and not under-standing, not having access, and maybe just kind of pushing it off as a trigger. But that doesn't mean music does not fit with us. I think we've always had it. . . . Always. It is just our relationship with it has changed throughout time. Which doesn't mean it is not always there, it's rooted in our culture, whether we like it or not.

Raven Sutton points out that there are still stereotypes about deafness and music that lead hearing people to question her Deaf identity (▶ Video Example 2.29).

RS: So I realized that many musicians and artists, their art is not accessible to the Deaf community. People who can hear think that it is because we are Deaf and we can't enjoy music. And a lot of us do go to concerts. We like to go to celebrations and we like to dance. We like music. We like all of those things. So people who can hear assume that if you can't hear you don't ap-preciate music. But actually that is very false. I can definitely attest to that. I realized that if it is not accessible to us I want to show Deaf people that yes, actually, it can be, whether we can hear it or not, we can feel it. Music can be accessible to the Deaf community. And my friends would ask me to sign music for them and I have done that. However, I started posting more on YouTube and social media and Twitter and Facebook and Instagram. As I was posting my videos more people were asking me, how do Deaf people do that and how can you do this? How can you sign music? How can Deaf people be dancing? And a lot of people think that I am not really a Deaf person. Saying, "I have seen you dance and I see your music. There's no way." That was kind of a challenge to continue to educate people who are hearing that there is more accessibility in the music in our Deaf world and communities.

By contrast, Susan Weinfurtner felt more uneasiness about the relation-ship between music and Deaf culture (▶ Video Example 2.30).

SW: Hmm. . . . Deaf culture? In the Deaf community, maybe. But Deaf culture, that's complex. I haven't thought about that. No. . . . Deaf culture is more about history, family traditions, schools for the Deaf, Deaf Olympics, Deaf culture, Deaf President Now, many other things. But does music fit with Deaf culture? No, I can't agree to that. I'm sorry. It's separate.

Paris Glass emphasizes that the relationships between Deaf people and music are personal and unique to each individual, and that they vary based on one's background and personality (▶ Video Example 2.31).

PG: It depends on each individual person. There are Deaf people who view music as a hearing people thing and [think] other Deaf people who listen to music or try to engage with music are just trying to be hearing. There are Deaf people [for whom] music is their lives. They live for it, they love dancing and they love to express themselves that way. There are Deaf people who just don't care, who are completely neutral on the topic. It does not interest them. There are Deaf musicians. There's a ton of Deaf musicians that people don't even think about. People who play guitar, people who play trumpet. I can name three people off the top of my head who are Deaf and play music. So it's just like hearing community and their relationship with music. It is so personal. And it depends on your history, your background, who you are, your personality. Hearing loss level, that can also really impact how—not how but what kind of music you enjoy the most. So somebody with profound hearing loss is going to enjoy something with a lot more bass, most likely, obviously it's varied. But something that they'll feel more in their chest. Whereas I can still stick to—mainly what I was listening to before I lost my hearing. I don't really listen to much new stuff now because I just don't understand it. But the stuff that I listened to before I lost my hearing is pretty much what I still listen to, just with a hearing aid now.

Warren "Wawa" Snipe similarly points out that there is a wide range of experiences of deafness, and notes that music is for everyone, regardless of gender, race, or disability (▶ Video Example 2.32).

WS: There's a myth, many people said that Deaf people do not like music. That is not true. Yes, there's some people in the Deaf community who don't like music because they can't hear. Can't hear it, but they can feel it. But a large, large majority just love music, a variety of genres. And so, it's freedom. Music is freedom. Music is a form of expression. Just be your-self without even being judged. That kind of thing. You can come up with your own, whatever your heart feels. Do you wanna follow your heart-beat? Making beats with your heart? That's music, it's you, it's your baby, show it to the people. So yeah, that's the biggest myth. People would say, oh, Deaf people [are] not supposed to like music, because they can't hear, or Deaf people are not supposed to know music, because they can't speak. Not true. Boom, hello. There's many. Some people chose not to speak. Some people can, some people do, some people can't, it's the same with people who have vision. Some people have low vision, some are blind, some can see okay. There's a wide range of disabilities, there's a wide range of Deafness.

Music sees or feels no gender, color, disability, anything, it's for everyone.

As I mentioned at the opening of Chapter 1, Teresa Blankmeyer Burke's anecdote about speech therapy reveals how Deaf children are often excluded from musical experiences from early childhood. In this video, she recounts how she was pulled out of music and arts classes in elementary school to work on her pronunciation in speech therapy (▶ Video Example 2.33).

TBB: Oh, here's the irony: so I had speech therapy as a child, and almost always they pulled us out when it was music and arts time. So I never re-ally got that instruction in the classroom because—well I shouldn't say never, but often, my classmates in grade school were learning music and doing that kind of thing and I was learning how to pronounce my t's, or my ch's, or what have you. So it's a really good thing that I did have the private music instruction with the piano because that helped me, at least get that exposure.

Innovations in Sign Language Music

The world of sign language music has expanded enormously since the mid-2000s, when artists like Sean Forbes, Wawa, and Signmark were beginning their careers. Improvements in technology and the advent of social media resulted in new tools for video production and dissemination that made it easy to create sign language music videos.

Raven Sutton partially attributes the rapid changes in sign language music to the Covid pandemic, which has increased exposure for Deaf artists and creators (▶ Video Example 2.34).

RS: I feel like with the pandemic, people are forced to watch social media more. They are reading and they are seeing these things that I think people are paying more attention to Deaf people. I think that more and more Deaf creativity is coming out now and this is our chance, like TikTok and Twitter and Instagram, we are seeing so many creative people that are coming out of the woodwork. I feel like it's nothing new about what we do and it has been what we have been doing. But I think the exposure is new. The awareness and getting people to look at us: here we are! And we can do all of these amazing things.

As Paris Glass observes, the wider dissemination of sign language music videos has resulted in greater acceptance of Deaf people signing music publicly (▶ Video Example 2.35).

PG: The biggest shift that I've seen has been the acceptance of Deaf people signing music. For such a long time it felt like you only ever saw hearing people signing music because there wasn't—as gross as it sounds, a lot of hearing people were like, well you're Deaf, you can't enjoy music, so why would you sign it? Let a hearing person sign it for you then you can enjoy the music. And that's shifted. Which I am very thankful for because not only do I obviously enjoy signing music but watching my friends do it is just so cool. And being able to see that on a public platform, see that getting the attention not just from me but from other people, that feels good. That is the biggest shift that I have really seen, at least in my circle.

Rosa Lee Timm notes that improvements in video editing technology have also led to innovations in Deaf musical expression (▶ Video Example 2.36).

RLT: Using those textures, remember I was talking about like sitting in the car, the visual textures, and now, being able to document that in film. We're having more artists adding different visual layers, signing music, it's been really nice. Like music, the musical experience so that Deaf people can see it, they have visual additions to make it have more texture. Technology has really opened the door to a lot of different ways people can express their music. That's really exciting for me.

Communities of Sign Language Music

Where is sign language music today being created and disseminated? In the past, sign language music primarily involved live performance, but today there is also a great deal of sign language music being disseminated through social media websites and mobile apps, such as YouTube, Vimeo, Twitter, Facebook, Instagram, and, most recently, TikTok.

Raven Sutton discusses the different social media websites that are popular venues for posting sign language music (▶ Video Example 2.37).

RS: I think mostly on the internet. On YouTube, other social outlets like TikTok. That has become very popular lately especially during the pandemic. A lot of people will use TikTok for short videos that you can post. They are pretty easy and they go viral. You can videotape them pretty easily. Also Instagram and Twitter. I think there are a whole lot of different outlets on the internet and social media. But as far as festivals and in-person signing, usually it tends to be an interpreter. I think that is really mostly where it is at.

As Paris Glass and Rosa Lee Timm point out, however, live performances at parties and ASL karaoke are still important places for signing musicians within the Deaf and signing community (▶ Video Example 2.38, Video Example 2.39).

PG: In terms of before COVID, ASL karaoke—go to karaoke with Deaf people the next time that you get a chance. It is incredible. It is so much fun. I had a friend who went in blind to a song. We picked "Bohemian Rhapsody" for him. He signed it on the spot. It was incredible! And that's such an abstract song. Nobody understood what was going on. So that's a really fun thing. In terms of where I see it most, it's definitely social media because, I mean, that's where most things are happening right now. I would say definitely Twitter, TikTok, and Instagram are the biggest ones that I see quality signed music from, from Deaf people.

Part of it is because it is much easier to film a shorter video [on TikTok]. Part of it is because it's much easier to interpret a shorter clip. Part of it is because I can take my favorite clip of the song that I sign best because it's what means the most to me and I can put just that out there into the world and not the third verse that like kind of I get it but I don't really love it. And there's less pressure to finish the entire song than it would be on YouTube because why are you just gonna post a 40-second clip on YouTube? There's a whole song, why aren't you doing the whole song? So there is that. We have more flexibility on how long we want to post. And with apps like TikTok specifically you can edit in app and you can't really do that on YouTube. With TikTok I can add fun filters, I can add an effect that makes three of me in the background. You know, stuff like that. So there is this ease of being able to just do it on your phone compared to having to set up a camera, film it, edit it, caption it, post it on your computer. If you have this thing that is in your hands, even if we want to record the whole song, even if that is not the barrier, even if it's, either way you are recording the whole song. The option of editing it on your phone and not having to get software, not having to sit at your laptop, is just a lot easier and that is a huge part of the appeal.

RLT: Well, every skilled signer always signs music at parties. For example, you tend to have people signing music at interpreted concerts, you see the interpreter being up there signing music. Social media. TikTok. That is where I see them. And like at parties. Those are the most popular times that I see signed music.

The Elements of Sign Language Music

Sign language music is a multisensory art form that can make use of visual/tactile language, non-linguistic gestures, sounds, tactile elements like vibrations, and additional visual effects such as costuming and video editing effects. I asked my interlocutors about the elements of sign language music that they felt were the most important to their own musical expression.

In her response, Rosa Lee Timm emphasized the importance of storytelling. By this, she means setting the scene for the viewer: while a hearing person might immediately get a sense of a song's genre, style, and affective content when listening to the beginning of a track, a Deaf person might not receive that information if the translation is not carefully thought out (▶ Video Example 2.40).

RLT: Story. Context. Lots of performers will show up and they have no idea what they are talking about. So for Deaf people it can be frustrating. . . . Making sure that the audience can understand what you're saying is more important than the show, the dancing, the moving, the lights, the flash. It's like yeah it's great but nobody can understand you so that means your signing sucks. So always make sure that what you're doing is clear and understandable and that it makes sense, has context, it has a story, has a point. Otherwise it's frustrating.

Another thing I would like to see improved is the first 30 to 60 seconds of songs is just the music and then there's a voice that comes up. So in that introduction a lot of interpreters tend to sign "music music music," and then for a Deaf person who can't hear anything, who doesn't have an idea of the feeling, the experience of what the music is doing, and that person saying "music music music." The hearing people are hearing it and they know what it's building up to or they know the genre. Or it's their parents' wedding song, oh I recognize that, and it's bringing back a memory, those things happen instantaneously. Or maybe it feels like the song is going to make me sad or the music is going to make me want to get up and dance, so these are things that people know right away, in 15 or 30 seconds where the music is headed. And that is missing when someone is signing "music music music," so it is not an equal experience.

I did experiment with one of my workshops where I turned on my favorite song, "She Drives Me Crazy" by Fine Young Cannibals. So I turned on the music and for a good 15 seconds I was doing different things before I started the lyrics, and it stopped and I asked the interpreters, the students, professional interpreters, all of them could hear—well, maybe ten were deaf—but I asked them what? What came up when you heard this? And some had never heard it before, they are too young, I guess, I'm old school, they said feels like old 80s. I said okay. What does that make you think of, what kind of musician? Maybe big hoops, wild clothes, maybe driving in the car going somewhere. That was in the first 30 seconds, so they are already ready to go with the 80s genre, and like you can tell it was lighthearted, it felt funky, all of these things. And that's what is missing for Deaf people when they want to experience the music, because the interpreter is going music music music, but that does nothing. So that's frustrating. Because it is the experience part, the context, that history, the memories, the emotional part of music. So I would encourage more analyzing how to capture that feeling, that experience, so people can imagine what is happening when it comes to the translation.

Raven Sutton mentions the importance of non-linguistic visual elements, including costuming and hairstyling. She also emphasizes the importance of matching the prosody of the original song (▶ Video Example 2.41).

RS: If the artist is doing a long note going on and on and on and then it is finished. That is something I want to show with my body. I want to make that movement extended like don't leave me, so then I would have to sign and stretch it out to match how long they are holding each note.

I can feel the voice, the vocals as well. And I follow the count because vocals are an instrument as well. If they are talking about the mouth movements, I will ask my friend what that sounds like. Is it long or short? So when I have my interpretation about the emotional part I will ask what do you hear, how do you interpret the sound? What is the artist singing? And there is a lot of research and a lot of study and memorization and a lot of pairing that happens with some of the music videos that you will see. Also the style and what kind of video it is. Sometimes I like to try to copy that and match the colors what I am wearing and maybe my hairstyle whether I pull it back or leave it down. I would try to copy whatever they are doing.

Paris Glass felt that facial expressions were crucial for musical expression, which is at the heart of their sign language music covers (▶ Video Example 2.42).

PG: When I am watching, when I'm consuming the content, I look at facial expressions. That is the number 1 thing that I look for in expression like that, is I want to see on your face what you are feeling. Because as expressive as sign language is with gesturing and all of that, it is your face that gives everything you're feeling. And that is another reason that Deaf people tend to be so much better at expressing music through sign, is because we are already used to showing not our hearts on our sleeves, but our faces.

So when I am consuming the content it is very much about the face and the expressiveness. I want to feel what you are feeling. That is why I am watching. In the same way that most people would want to feel what the singer is feeling. It is the exact same kind of transaction there. In terms of what I want to put out, I guess it would be the opposite. I want other people to be able to feel what I am feeling. That is why I am taking my heart out and posting it on social media.

Finally, Harmony Baniaga expressed that the beat and rhythm were of primary importance to her own music covers. Like Glass, she also emphasized the importance of facial expressions for conveying affect and meaning (▶ Video Example 2.43).

HB: I would say using your body to show the beat, and follow with the rhythm of the song. And again trying to clearly sign the concepts of the song. So that Deaf people can understand clearly what the song is about. It's important to use facial expressions too. Because if you can't understand the expressions you can't really understand the music. If it's a happy song or if it's a sad song, like you know a heartbreak song and you've got a smile, it doesn't really make sense. So, compared to someone who is just stonefaced the entire time, no facial expressions. It's like, What are you trying to say? I don't really understand. I think it's important to have something like, for example, for WAP, I was saying more like in a hip-hop style, not just like standing still, signing to a camera. So making sure you have body movements that also match with the music, and then adding some style to it too.

The Future of Sign Language Music

New innovations are constantly emerging in sign language music. I asked what each Deaf musician felt was the future of sign language music.

Teresa Blankmeyer Burke was hopeful for the future, noting that current students at Gallaudet have more fluid and open relationships with the worlds of music and sound (▶ Video Example 2.44).

TBB: I do notice that our students now tend to have a more fluid sense of the relationship to sound than the students that I had seventeen years ago when I started working at Gallaudet. And I think a nice analogy for that is gender fluidity. Just as our students seventeen years ago were a little more rigid about gender categories and the students today are much more fluid about it, I'm seeing something also in relation to music and sound. There are Deaf people, I've had students who have told me this, and colleagues

who have said, "Music, what for? What's the point?", and use it as a way
of sort of asserting their—if they do not engage with music at all as a Deaf
person it's like they're, they use that to assert their centrality as a Deaf
person in the community. I also know many many many people who are
from multi-generational Deaf families who love music. So I don't think it's
a cut-and-dried thing.

Raven Sutton and Paris Glass emphasized the importance of highlighting
Deaf artists and Deaf talent in order for sign language music to thrive
(▶ Video Example 2.45, Video Example 2.46).

RS: Personally my goal and what I would like to see in general, is I want artists to have either a personal interpreter or a Deaf person at the ready to interpret their music. . . . And I also want to see more Deaf representation. Not
necessarily related to us being Deaf, if that makes sense. Like on Netflix let's
say there is a drama, Deaf U. Kind of like Gallaudet. Okay, fine. That kind
of exposure is nice and a little educational. People can learn about the Deaf
community. But I want to see us doing more of normal everyday things and
things that we enjoy doing and things that other people—not having to do
with being labeled Deaf. Just Deaf people enjoying the many things that
hearing people enjoy. Like, knowing that a lot of Deaf people enjoy music,
Deaf people like going to concerts. So let's have interpreters set up at the ready.
    I also would like to see Deaf artists in the spotlight. And I would like
to see Deaf people talking about that, and hearing people as well. We are
providing information that Deaf people can do signed music. And being
able to spotlight people for their skills and knowledge. That is really what
I would like to see.

PG: I would hope that the future of signed music is primarily Deaf. I really
want more Deaf representation in the media, in social media, in absolutely
everything. And there is this idea that Deaf people don't enjoy music. I understand where it comes from but Google is free. So I really want to see
more Deaf people feeling comfortable and safe expressing themselves like
that. Because it's such a good feeling. So I just hope that the future of signed
music is primarily Deaf.

Rosa Lee Timm and Marko Vuoriheimo both point out the importance
of creating curricula that are inclusive of sign language music, while Matt

Maxey discusses how sign language music has entered the commercial sphere (▶ Video Example 2.47, Video Example 2.48, Video Example 2.49).

MV: At Deaf schools there's usually no music classes and everybody says you're Deaf you don't understand this, and Deaf people think, okay music is just a hearing person thing. But I think that music fits everybody. I have been traveling around the world quite a lot, also in Finland, and giving presentations. I'm not a researcher by any means but I think I try to be a little bit careful when I'm telling about my opinion regarding the structure of music. I have said very carefully, though, that Deaf children should be taught how the music is constructed. There's intro, there's verse, there's bridge, and refrain. All these different parts, etc. So if you're taught, if you know parts of the music, and how you can play with them and exchange them, and you get the clue of how to tell the story in music. . . . And if you are teaching this to Deaf children about music I'm 100% certain that later on when these children grow up and they're looking for jobs or writing a budget etc., whatever text they write, they will be much clearer. They have this kind of idea of how the story goes and how things are presented. And I think, when you're writing emails or stories, or whatever text that Deaf people are writing that sometimes just needs a little bit of editing, I think you could use this kind of a music education also, when you learn how the music is structured.

MM: The fact that companies are working more with sign language and music now. Definitely it's becoming more, I guess the power of TikTok, and Snapchat, Instagram, etc. I feel so old talking like this, but, just really the fascination of sign language and music has opened that door for companies to really try to apply it to their agenda. Whether it's for DEI, diversity, equity, and inclusion, or just more for marketing proposals, where, hey, we're inclusive, they're still trying to be more inclusive of the sign language and music than ever before. I feel like in the last five years, I see it far more than I've seen in the first maybe twenty-five years growing up, and that alone it just kind of blows my mind because it's, again, I've never thought it was possible. I never thought it would be something where I'm looking on TV, I'm watching the basketball game and they've got music playing in the background for a Deaf commercial about CODAs. Huh! Okay, this is cool, this is new. And then we have Verizon commercials. We have Broadway plays, we have Snapchat ads, all of this. It's just cool to see the times shift into more of yes, we can do music too, yes, we're trying to defy the stereotype of, "Deaf people listen to music? Why would that person go to a concert?" This is why, and to see most hearing and Deaf organizations come together to defy that has been a pleasure to watch.

RLT: I think we are just beginning to scratch the surface of what signed music can do. Just a scratch. I think it is just the beginning, it's something we are starting to talk about and starting to be researched. Maybe ten years from now it is going to be part of our curriculum, maybe music education will be taught to Deaf people, maybe in elementary through college, maybe there will be a formal music theory education, maybe a series of classes on genres and studying each of them more deeply. This is what I feel like the future will be: more sophisticated rhythms, more structure. Like ASL poetry already has this, there is lot of criteria and different kinds of poetry, whether it is hand shape, alphabet poetry, all the different kinds. But signing music, I feel like we are on track now to become more sophisticated and the value of that is we will be able to preserve ASL better. Meaning, more qualified interpreters, performers, to be more accessible to audiences, and it will be a human experience for a Deaf person. So I think all of that is going to be so great, I think the possibilities are expanding and they are there and I am very excited.

2.4 Conclusion

As I document in Chapter 1, Deaf musicians have historically encountered significant resistance from the hearing world when creating and performing music. The interviews I conducted with contemporary Deaf musicians, however, reveal the resilience of Deaf music-making, and of sign language music in particular. In the present day, sign language music is rich and varied, encompassing a wide range of genres, mediums of distribution, and perspectives. Signing musicians also come from a variety of backgrounds, including people who were born Deaf, became Deaf in childhood or later in life, as well as people who identify as hard-of-hearing or CODAs. They perform sign language music for a variety of reasons: some are professional musicians, some are interested in teaching and mentoring future generations of signing musicians, and others post their videos for their families and friends to enjoy. While some signing musicians are experimenting with the possibilities of social media platforms such as Instagram and TikTok, there remains a vibrant community of signing musicians who perform live as well. In all my conversations with signing musicians and lovers of sign language music, one message was clear: the future of sign language music is bright, and it is Deaf.

PART II

ANALYSIS

A Note on Notation

The second part of this book explores several key parameters of sign language music: voice; rhythm and meter; melody; and meaning and form. Before delving into the techniques used by sign language musicians, though, we must determine how sign language music can be notated. Several problems arise when it comes to devising a notation system for sign language music, stemming from the fact that, as Pizzuto, Rossini, and Russo observe, "until now, none of the SL [sign language] used in the world has autonomously developed a written form" (Pizzuto, Rossini, and Russo 2006, 1).[1] While there have been many attempts to create systems for writing signs, the authors note that there is no certainty that these writing systems "will lead to a real evolution of written SL" (Pizzuto, Rossini, and Russo 2006, 1). The difficulty of creating a system for writing sign language is compounded by the artistic modifications of sign language in musical performances.

The most recent and successful sign language writing systems include SignWriting, designed by Valerie Sutton, and Stokoe Notation, designed by William Stokoe. Stokoe-based notation systems are efficient at notating single, decontextualized signs, but as Pizzuto, Rossini, and Russo note, Stokoe notation "cannot be used for segmenting and transcribing individual signs and signs' sequences occurring in the actual flow of signed conversation, with all the morphological modifications noted in discourse" (Pizzuto, Rossini, and Russo 2006, 3). Furthermore, Stokoe-based notation cannot easily accommodate information about movement direction, speed, rhythm, or emphasis. Thus, it is not well suited to representing sign language music, which involves extensive modifications of signs in a musical context.

---

[1] See also Boutet and Garcia (2006); Garcia (2006, 2010); Di Renzo et al. (2006).

Valerie Sutton's SignWriting provides a more promising avenue for notating sign language music (Sutton 1990). SignWriting provides extremely detailed information on how signs look, it is easy to read and does not require prior knowledge of a signed language in order to be comprehensible to a reader, it shows facial expressions well, and it can include information about expression and other nonmanual markers. However, the typical vertical orientation of SignWriting makes it difficult to align with music notation, and it still does not show the rhythmic placement of signs or their relationship to a given meter.

In developing a notation system for sign language music, I considered using a system for dance notation, such as Labanotation or DanceWriting. While these systems excel at showing movements of the dancer's whole body in relation to a background meter, they are not as adept at showing the detailed movements of the face and hands that are the primary objects of focus in sign language. I therefore chose to focus on adapting SignWriting to a musical context by combining SignWriting, glosses, and music notation.[2] The result is an analytical notation that reveals important aspects of how signs look, how they relate to the background beat and the vocalized English layer, and what those signs mean.

Example II.1 shows a single sign written using the Sutton SignWriting system. This is the sign representing the English word "signing." In Example II.2, we can see the handshape used in each hand, which is a "1" handshape (the square represents the closed fist and the single line represents the index finger). The orientation of the hand is shown from the perspective of the signer: in this case, the half-filled glyph indicates that the signer sees the hand from the side.[3] The glyph is unbroken across the knuckles, which means that it is oriented vertically (parallel with the wall plane), rather than horizontally or parallel with the floor, which would be indicated by a breaking the sign with a white band through the knuckles. We can further see that both hands move: the movement of the right hand is indicated with a black arrow, the movement of the left hand with a white arrow. The right hand starts near the body (thick line) moving downward in a forward-back circle parallel with the side wall, while the left hand starts further from the body (thin line)

---

[2] A gloss, written in uppercase letters, conventionally shows the basic meaning of a sign in a written language such as English.

[3] If the signer sees the palm of the hand, the glyph is unfilled, while if the signer sees the back of the hand, the glyph will be filled.

Example II.1 The Sutton SignWriting symbol for the word SIGN.

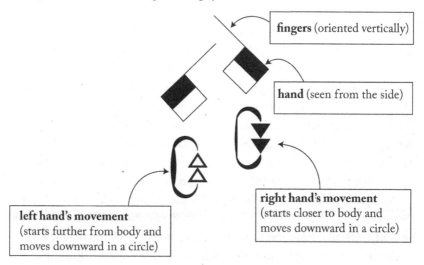

fingers (oriented vertically)

hand (seen from the side)

right hand's movement
(starts closer to body and
moves downward in a circle)

left hand's movement
(starts further from body and
moves downward in a circle)

Example II.2 The letters of the ASL manual alphabet in SignWriting.

a b c d e f g h i

j k l m n o p q r

s t u v w x y z

moving upward. As indicated by the two arrows, the hands complete two circles.

There is a great deal of highly detailed information presented in a single SignWriting glyph. Much more information can be represented as well: details of the movements of fingers, hands, and arms as well as the types of contact between parts of the body; details of the signer's facial expressions, head position, posture, and body movement; information about expression (such as speed or emphasis of movements) and punctuation; and infinite information about directionality and type of movement. SignWriting can represent not only any grammatical utterance in American Sign Language (ASL), but virtually any movement in any sign language. A detailed explanation of how to construct utterances in SignWriting is thus outside the scope of the present chapter. However, watching the video examples on the companion website alongside the SignWriting symbols should elucidate the meanings of the symbols, and any less intuitive symbols are explained in writing. Example II.2 presents the SignWriting symbols for the ASL manual alphabet for reference purposes.[4]

Example II.3 shows a single line of a signed hip-hop track by Warren "Wawa" Snipe, "Only ASL One," notated in SignWriting. The excerpt should be read vertically, from top to bottom. This notation shows detailed information about the visual appearance of the signs and their relationship to one another, showing for example how the head turns from facing forward on the first sign, to facing left on the second sign. However, critical musical information is missing from this transcription, including information on the rhythmic relationships between signs, the relationship between the signs and background beat, and the relationships between the signed layer and the vocal layer of the track.

The notation system used in this book combines typical Western rhythmic notation with a gloss and symbols from SignWriting. The passage from Snipe's "Only ASL One" shown in Example II.3 is recreated in Example II.4 using my notation system. I indicate important rhythmic aspects of the signed layer using different kinds of noteheads in the rhythmic transcription: regular noteheads indicate a single-movement or stationary sign, or the beginning of a multi-part sign; "x" noteheads indicate internal repetition that occurs within a sign; and triangular noteheads are used to indicate parts of multi-part signs where the parts of the sign occur on different parts of a beat or on different beats.

There are some obvious disadvantages to this notation system: namely, that it requires watching the video alongside the transcription. However, it clearly shows the rhythmic placement of individual signs and important parts of signs, as well as information about holds and repetition. It also shows the metric placement of signs and their relationship to the sounding

---

[4] For more detailed information on the SignWriting system, see Sutton (1990).

Example II.3 Warren "Wawa" Snipe, "Only ASL One," opening, transcribed using Sutton SignWriting. The lyrics rapped by Snipe in English are: "Her hearing aids were purple, moving hands in a circle." Each sign is accompanied here by an English gloss in uppercase letters that summarizes the sign's meaning.

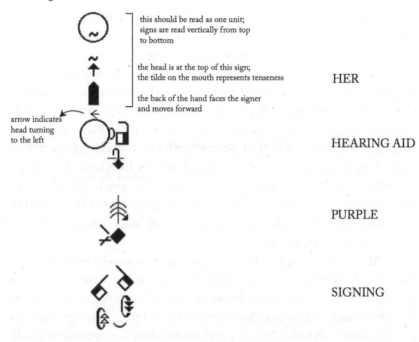

Example II.4 Wawa, "Only ASL One," opening, transcribed using the sign language music transcription system.

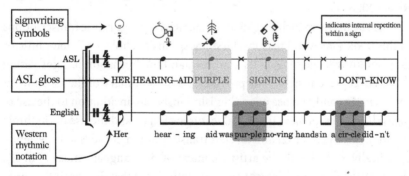

layers of the music, if any are present. Finally, the use of the gloss is helpful for non-signers to understand the meaning of the signs. Thus, it is better suited than SignWriting for understanding the rhythmic aspects of sign language music, but worse than SignWriting for understanding how an individual sign looks.

As Example II.4 shows, my notation system makes use of ASL gloss, which conventionally shows the basic meaning of a sign in capital letters. ASL gloss uses several symbols to represent grammatical elements. For example, a line above a sign or series of signs labeled "q" indicates a question, using the yes-no facial expression with eyebrows up. Dashes between signs show that a sign is accomplished in a single gesture. Some other symbols include t (topic); wh-q (wh-type question); rh-q (rhetorical question); neg (negative); nodding (nod head); fs (fingerspelling); * (emphasis); IX (point); co (conversation opener); cs (cheek to shoulder); # (fingerspelled loan sign, e.g., J-B = JOB); +++ (repeat); arc (sign in an arc); pow, ooo, puff cheeks, mmm, pursed lips, sta, cha (mouth morphemes); (2h) (two hands); (2h) alt (two hands alternating); CL (classifier); rt, lf, ctr (right, left, center); cond (conditional) (Liversidge 2021).

As Pizzuto, Rossini, and Russo point out, it is crucial to understand that glosses "are always an *ancillary* device that *does not replace, but accompanies,* in a reference language known to the author and the reader of a given study, *an independent representation of the language data object of inquiry*" (Pizzuto, Rossini, and Russo 2006, 4, emphasis original). They therefore criticize the use of glosses in sign language research where there is no independent representation of the signs, noting that "any so-called transcription of SL data via labels of this sort cannot be defined a 'transcription' in any appropriate sense of the term" (Pizzuto, Rossini, and Russo 2006, 4).

It will be useful to include glosses in the sign language music transcriptions in this book for several reasons. First, most music scholars will have little or no prior knowledge of ASL, its grammar, and the formation of signs. Using a gloss to represent signs thus provides a basic summary of the meaning of each sign. Second, the use of an English translation, in addition to the use of SignWriting to represent the visual features of signs and the use of rhythmic notation, provides a rich and layered transcription method that is designed specifically to deal with the artistic context of sign language music. Finally, this notational system is meant as an analytical tool that, like any other analytical representation of musical information, must be read and interpreted alongside the performance.[5] To create the glosses in this book, I enlisted the help of Deaf native ASL user who is also fluent in English, Dr. Anne G. Liversidge. As Liversidge emphasized in our correspondence, ASL glossing "has traditionally been used to translate fairly simple sentences and short scripts in ASL to help ASL students 'read' and interpret ASL. Glossing is not a high art form. ASL doesn't have a written form, but ASL GLOSS is the closest it gets to a written form" (Liversidge 2021). She also noted that all glosses may be open to different interpretations. While ASL gloss is not a perfect tool, it is a useful one when it comes to representing sign language music, especially to readers unfamiliar with ASL.

While this notation system is an analytical tool created for music-theoretical application, it may be of interest to other readers as well. The fact that the notation system incorporates multiple forms of notation (SignWriting, glosses, and rhythmic notation) alongside the video as the original text means that those who are not experts in understanding ASL or in reading music notation can still follow along. With multiple means of perceiving the material, this notation system is designed to be accessible to groups with differing dis/abilities.

---

[5] Transcribing and analyzing non-notated music presents music analysts with significant challenges. Like other popular music, signed music does not use a score or other abstractions—the only authentic musical objects with which one can engage are recordings or live performances (for a discussion of authenticity in popular music, see Zak [2001]).

3
The Signing Singing Voice

3.1 Introduction

In the musical television series *Zoey's Extraordinary Playlist*, the titular character (played by Jane Levy) discovers that she can perceive the innermost thoughts of others in the form of pop songs. In an episode entitled "Zoey's Extraordinary Silence," Zoey encounters a Deaf character, Abigail, played by Deaf West Theatre's Sandra Mae Frank. Upon meeting Zoey, and being told by her father that she cannot travel to Kenya alone, Abigail bursts into song—Rachel Platten's "Fight Song," specifically. The song's spoken English lyrics are, however, supplanted by the sound of a solo cello, and Abigail does not orally produce the melody; instead, she signs it. By framing Abigail's signing in this way, the show's writers suggest not only that Frank's character possesses a signing voice, but that the signing voice can be a *singing* voice as well.

The "Fight Song" scene brings up a number of important issues. First, it suggests the existence of a signing voice that sings: a "signing singing voice." While the locution does present something of a tongue twister, it also highlights an important point: just as there is a difference between the orally produced spoken voice and singing voice, so too is there a distinction between a signing voice in a conversational register and a signing singing voice. Thus, the locution "signing voice" does not quite go far enough in describing the character Abigail's rendition of "Fight Song"—while the term "signing voice" encompasses all registers of signing, from conversational to poetic to musical, the term "signing *singing* voice" refers exclusively to musical signing. Second, the scene reflects a subtly uncomfortable hearing lens on the signing singing voice. Although the show's writers and producers eliminate Rachel Platten's voice in the sounding music of "Fight Song," they insert a cello melody as a kind of surrogate singing voice in its stead. At the same time, there are no subtitles provided. In an interview with the *Daily News*, show creator Austin Winsberg explains that he "thought most people would know the melody of 'Fight Song,'" so that despite the "barrier to entry ... the

Seeing Voices. Anabel Maler, Oxford University Press. © Oxford University Press 2024.
DOI: 10.1093/oso/9780197601976.003.0004

audience would be smart enough to figure it out" (Feldman New York Daily News, April 4, 2020). Intelligence aside, the presence of the "Fight Song" melody and ASL singing without captions bars access for those who are Deaf but do not sign, or who do not know ASL specifically. It furthermore frames the signing singing voice as incomplete and in need of supplementation, in the form of the aurally perceived surrogate voice produced by the cello. I spoke with one of the signers featured in the scene, Harmony Baniaga, who told me that she had a positive experience working with the other Deaf artists and dancers, and with the choreographer, Mandy Moore. However, it became clear that the show's artificial framing of the signing voice caused issues for the performers as well:

> During that project it was interesting for me, because we were signing music without the lyrics. So I felt a little bit overwhelmed because I prefer having the song in the background with the voice and the music. We, the Deaf people who were making that project, we were working with each other: we would have cues on what the next lyric was, we tried to practice and memorize with each other before that day.

While the depiction of the signing singing voice in "Zoey's Extraordinary Silence" has flaws, it nevertheless points to the cultural significance of the voice, and to the importance of exploring vocal delivery across modalities. As Victoria Malawey writes in the introduction to her study of the popular singing voice, "the importance of vocal delivery in pop music is undeniable"—in other words, "voice matters in pop" (Malawey 2020, 2–3). Indeed, the voice seems central to any definition of song, not just popular song: in the encyclopedia *Grove Music Online*, for example, "song" is defined as "a piece of music for voice or voices, whether accompanied or unaccompanied, or the act or art of singing" (Chew et al. 2001). Songs, as we typically understand them, are *sung*, and singing necessarily involves the voice. In the introduction to this book, I gave an example of a percussion song, "Boat, Drink, Fun Enjoy," a piece of music that is understood within Deaf culture as a *song*. If this song—and other songs that fall within the general category of "sign language music"—is understood and performed *as a song*, then it ought to involve the voice in some capacity. In my interview with ASL performer Paris Glass, they emphasized the importance of voice and singing in their conception of signed music:

For me personally I do view [signing music] as a kind of singing. That is another opinion that will vary wildly, depending on who you ask. . . . And there will be Deaf people who do not think they are on the level—the same level for one reason or another. I personally do connect it with singing.

We must begin any study of signed vocal music, then, with an understanding of the singing voice. But, as the example of "Zoey's Extraordinary Silence" suggests, the singing voice need not always involve an audible voice. In other words, the singing voice may not be produced exclusively through the vibration of the vocal folds in the human throat, although it is often understood that way. Nina Eidsheim characterizes this overwhelming focus on the orally produced voice as the result of our "fetishization of sound." The vocal cords, in other words, tend to "get all the attention" in studies of voice (Eidsheim 2015, 111). This fetishization results in what H-Dirksen L. Bauman has called "a nearly maniacal obsession with the voice," which, as Bauman points out, undergirds the still-widespread educational system of oralism, which privileges speech over language, comprehension, and culture (Bauman 2008, 43). In sign language songs, the signing performer may rarely or never produce any audible vocal sounds, and yet these pieces of music are unquestionably vocal. We must therefore pose the central question: what constitutes a signing singing voice?

Malawey compellingly argues for a "systematic model for interpreting vocal delivery" that specifies what we are hearing and provides "comprehensive language of how to describe what we hear" (Malawey 2020, 4). The model for interpreting vocal delivery in pop music provided by Malawey comprehensively addresses most of the aspects associated with vocal delivery using the vocal cords, covering the areas of pitch (including range, intonation, and vibrato), prosody (including phrasing, metric placement, motility, embellishment, and consonantal articulation), and quality (including timbre, intensity, harmonic spectrum, phonation, and changes in sound).

Watch Rosa Lee Timm's interpretation of the chorus of "Come What May" in ▶ Video Example 3.1. This is clearly an expressive vocal performance—Timm's is a voice that *moves*, in every sense of the word. But while some of Malawey's analytical parameters for vocal delivery are applicable to Timm's performance (those associated with prosody, for example, which is an important part of sign languages as well as spoken ones), it is clear that many of the parameters associated with pitch and quality are not useful in analyzing Timm's signing singing voice. Instead, aspects of Timm's performance like her mouth movements, facial expressions, eye gaze, and body movements contribute to the expressive qualities of her signed vocal delivery.

In this chapter, I investigate the concept of the signing singing voice in greater detail. I begin by outlining some of the philosophical and musicological underpinnings that support the notion of a signing voice, building upon the work of Mladen Dolar, Brian Kane, Nina Sun Eidsheim, Annette Schichter, H-Dirksen L. Bauman, Alexis MacIntyre, Jessica Holmes, Amanda Weidman, and others. I also explore concepts of voice in Deaf culture, including the abuses of voice associated with oralist educational practices in America. I then turn to the different aspects of vocal delivery as they pertain to the signed voice, focusing on prosodic elements as well as mouth movements, facial expressions, eye gaze, body movement, and collectivity.

3.2 What's in a Voice?

Voice studies has recently grappled with the idea that the singing voice is material and embodied, introducing what Nina Sun Eidsheim and Annette Schlichter call "friction between the material and the metaphorical dimensions of the vocal" (Eidsheim and Schlichter 2014). As Amanda Weidman points out, the voice lives a double life—that is, the voice is "both a set of sonic, material, and literary practices shaped by culturally and historically specific moments and a category invoked in discourse about personal agency, cultural authenticity, and political power" (Weidman 2014).

But as Alexis MacIntyre and Jessica Holmes have cautioned, recent efforts to formalize the voice, to confine its location to the vocal folds, run the risk of limiting it to a phonocentric concept that exclusively involves, in the words of Adriana Cavarero, "sonorous articulation[s] that emit from the mouth" (MacIntyre 2018; Holmes 2016; Cavarero 2005). MacIntyre argues that voice studies' fascination with the sounding voice specifically results in inaudible voices becoming "pathologized or ignored" by the dominant hearing culture. While Cavarero's work most obviously privileges the sounding voice to the exclusion of non-sounding voices, this attitude is present in less obvious ways in most studies of the voice that assume the primacy of voices that emit from the vocal folds. In response to the overwhelming focus on the sounding voice in the field of voice studies, MacIntyre suggests that "drawing Deaf voices into the fold may not only clarify the conceptualization of the voice, but hone the persistent friction of mind–body dualism" (MacIntyre

2018, 168). By pursuing a detailed exploration of Deaf voice, we may be able to clarify some of the persistent puzzlements of voice studies more broadly.

Voice studies' fixation on the sounding voice typically excludes members of the signing community as well as members of the nonspeaking community. This exclusion takes a variety of forms, some more extreme than others. Cavarero, for example, locates identity explicitly in the sounding voice, which makes the "deep body" accessible to another (Cavarero 2005). By contrast, Nina Eidsheim draws attention to the multisensorial aspects of music, reimagining sound as "event through the practice of vibration" (Eidsheim 2015, 3). Other scholars, like Mladen Dolar, meanwhile, focus on the psychoanalytical dimensions of voice, including the "unheard" or "aphonic" voice. None of these scholars, however, engages explicitly with signing voices, or with the concept of voice as it pertains to nonspeaking communities more broadly.

In her exploration of communication technologies for nonspeaking persons, Meryl Alper argues that communication technologies "that purport to 'give voice to the voiceless'" must be understood within a complex network of culture, law, and policy, and that these technologies are "still subject to disempowering structural inequalities" (Alper 2017, 2–3). Alper ultimately argues that "voice is an overused and imprecise metaphor" that oversimplifies the human experience of disability (Alper 2017, 2–3). For Alper's interlocutors—nonspeaking children and their parents who use an iPad and the app Proloquo2Go as their primary mode of communication—voice is much more than a sonorous articulation emitting from the mouth.

The concept of voice is similarly complicated by the signing community, which includes not only Deaf persons, but also some hearing people. Adrean Clark and John Lee Clark have argued that the signing community consists of those who share a signing identity; this can include hearing Children of Deaf Adults (CODAs), relatives, and "adopted 'Deaf-heart' friends" (Clark and Clark 2016). In their video "CODA BROTHERS: CODA VOICE," the comedic duo the CODA Brothers, Ben and Andy Olson, humorously discuss the CODA voice, a kind of audible vocal delivery based on the grammar and idiomatic expressions of a signed language (in this case, ASL) that is only legible to other CODAs (Olson and Olson 2007).

It should be clear that, in nonspeaking and signing communities, either the concept of voice does not involve the mechanisms of the otolaryngological voice, or, if does involve audible vocalization, that voicing is informed and transformed by the cultural context and bodily orientation of the speaker. Any definition of voice must therefore take these perspectives into consideration. In searching for a conceptual footing for this definition, I now consider philosophers and musicologists who may provide such a foundation to my approach.

In his Deaf reading of Derrida's critique of phonocentrism in *La voix et la phénomène*, H-Dirksen L. Bauman proposes that "there are new possibilities of a theory of the voice no longer beholden to sound, but to the gesturing body that may speak outside the reach of phonocentrism" (Bauman 2008, 51). Bauman's work, which critiques the logocentrism and phonocentrism that have led to hearing culture's "maniacal obsession with the voice," extends Derrida's notion that deafness "sets *différance* in motion" and argues that signed language "needs to be read alongside the ideas of writing, supplementarity, and trace" (Bauman 2008, 50; 2006, 357). In Bauman's reading, writing and speech are both forms of sign—at the heart of both is gesture, or "making meaning through movement" (Bauman 2008, 50). Similarly, MacIntyre conceptualizes vocality "as a rhythmic action" of the moving body, resonating productively with Eidsheim's definition of the voice as "the action of the body" (Eidsheim 2015, 130).

As MacIntyre, Eidsheim, and Bauman all suggest (using different methodologies and frameworks), the signing singing voice must be understood in terms of the movements of the body. How, then, can we reconcile this notion of the voice with other theories of the voice that have been foundational within musicology and music theory? Mladen Dolar, for example, proposes a Lacanian, psychoanalytic understanding of voice that presents the voice and body in a tenuous and strained relationship in which the "body implied by the voice, disembodied as it may seem, is enough to be cumbersome and embarrassing" (Dolar 2006, 60). This tension between the voice and the body from which it emerges leads, as Dolar points out, to the problem of what Michel Chion calls the acousmatic voice: "a voice whose source one cannot see," a voice without a body (Dolar 2006, 60–61).[1] Yet a signing voice cannot exist without a body—it exists only through movement of the body, perceived through vision and/or touch (it can, however, be acousmatic, an idea to which I shall return momentarily). A large portion of Dolar's *A Voice and Nothing More* is devoted to reducing the voice, separating it from "empirical voices that can be heard" and finding instead the "unheard voice, an aphonic voice, as it were" (Dolar 2006, 73). As Brian Kane explains, for Dolar,

---

[1] For more on the acousmatic voice, see Brian Kane's monograph *Sound Unseen* (Kane 2014).

the voice must be distinguished from its sonorousness, "from the meaning-fulness of its statement and the source from which it is emitted" (Kane 2014, 214). The philosophical foundation for the aphonic voice established by Dolar has promising implications upon which we might base a preliminary understanding of nonspeaking voices, including signed voices. The concept of the aphonic voice suggests that vocality is not inextricably tied to sono-rousness after all. The exact nature of the signing voice requires, however, a more thorough explication than Dolar provides in his theorization of the aphonic voice.

Kane (2015) provides a model for understanding the voice that, with a few modifications, may serve as a theoretical underpinning for my conceptuali-zation of the signing voice. Kane understands voice (*phoné*) as constituted by sound (*echos*), meaning (*logos*), and site (*topos*). *Logos*, or meaning, refers to the content of utterances. Since, as has been well established since William Stokoe's publication of *Sign Language Structure* (1960), sign languages are natural languages with grammatical structures, the concept of *logos* needs no modification to be legible in the context of the signed voice. *Topos*, or site, refers to the site of the emission of the voice. In the case of the signing voice, the *topos* is always a visible or touchable body—as MacIntyre notes, the signed voice, which is utterly corporeal, is "inalienable from the body" (2018, 168). However, as with the audible voice, the site of the voice may not, in fact, be the body of the speaker. Finally, *echos*, or sound, refers to the sound of the voice, its "purely sonorous aspect." This aspect of the voice is the one that must be set aside in any consideration of a signing voice, for signing voices do not typically produce sound.[2]

What takes the place of *echos* in the signing voice? I propose that, in place of the purely sonorous aspect of voice, the signing voice is constituted in part by *motion*: the way in which one's body moves. I have purposefully avoided naming the third aspect of the signing voice as involving seeing, since signed languages can be voiced and understood through two modalities: sight and

---

[2] Simultaneous communication, or SimCom, is an exception. SimCom involves using a spoken language and a signed language simultaneously, but it is not a widely accepted practice in Deaf cultures, since it inevitably causes one of the two languages to suffer grammatically, as it is not pos-sible to simultaneously communicate in two different languages at the same time without resorting to pidgin (see Shannon [2016] for more information on SimCom). The language that suffers is typ-ically the speaker's second language, whether that is the voiced or signed language. Austin Andrews argues that using SimCom can also interfere with development of a child's ASL identity in the case of CODAs (Children of Deaf Adults) (awti 2014).

touch. The motion that constitutes the third aspect of signed vocality is that which is in excess of *logos*, or meaning creation.

Kane identifies a fourth term, *technê*, as a necessary supplementary aspect of his model, defining it as the technologies and techniques that disturb the circulation of the voice, *phoné* (Kane 2015, 674). Blocking out the site of sound, *topos*, by the reduction of vision or through technology, is one example of *technê* and creates the "acousmatic voice" discussed by Dolar. Technologies and techniques can similarly be used to disturb the circulation of the signing voice. Take, for example, video relay services, or VRS. VRS allows a signing person to communicate with someone who does not sign through the telephone, by using a VRS CA (communication assistant) who interprets between the signed language and spoken language. The audible voice that a hearing person perceives on one end of a VRS call is doubly acousmatic: the source of the speaking is hidden, of course, but more than that, the source of the signing person's *voice* is hidden. We can understand how the signing voice can become acousmatic through the slightly more straightforward example of face-to-face sign language interpretation, as well. In the case of face-to-face sign language interpretation, a signer's voice is translated into speech through the *technê* of sign language interpretation. Thus, while the source of the speech may be visible to the hearing person (the source of speech being the interpreter), the source of the *voice* is not legible to the hearing person (the source of the voice being the signer).

Sound artist Christine Sun Kim discusses this particular form of acousmatic voice in terms of "leasing" the voices of her interpreters, noting that using an interpreter is akin to borrowing or leasing their voice (Schwaiger 2015). Kim also emphasizes the unique challenges that come with the acousmatization of her voice through the voices of interpreters:

> I think the practice of borrowing voices also has a lot to do with trust. It's a lengthy progress to develop trust between myself and collaborators/ interpreters. I've noticed that I cannot work with certain sign language interpreters for too long as my voice can easily get lost in their voices. (Mansfield 2015)

At the same time that the acousmatization of the signing voice poses challenges, it also affords Kim artistic opportunities to try on different interpreters and "guid[e] people to become [her] voice" (Mansfield 2015).

To summarize, the signing voice exists at the crossings of meaning, site, and motion, all of which can be disrupted and mediated by *technê*. However, the concept of voice as it pertains to the signing community—and in particular to deaf persons—must also be understood within the context of hearing ideologies of voice that have oppressed (and continue to oppress) signing voices and caused vocal trauma within the Deaf community.

3.3 Oppressive Voicings

In Amanda Weidman's review of anthropology and voice, she defines ideologies of voice "as culturally constructed ideas about the voice," including "theories of where the voice comes from; . . . the relationship between the voice and the body; what constitutes a "natural" voice; and who should be allowed to speak and how" (Weidman 2014, 45). Our cultural ideologies of voice "set the boundary for what constitutes communication, what separates language from music, and what constitutes the difference between the intelligible and the unintelligible" (Weidman 2014, 45). As Jessica Peritz eloquently states, "voices are sites where bodies of ideology have been buried" (Peritz 2022, 3). Our dominant ideology of voice in Western culture privileges the audible voice and understands the voice as emerging from the human mouth. Bauman argues that this phonocentric ideology of voice has caused, and continues to cause, a great deal of harm in Deaf communities, leading to what Tom Humphries called "audism": "the notion that one is superior based on one's ability to hear or behave in the manner of those who hear" (Humphries 1975). Bauman thus proposes that phonocentrism is at the heart of the oppression of sign languages and Deaf persons (Bauman 2008).

Harlan Lane, in the foundational text *The Mask of Benevolence: Disabling the Deaf Community*, traces how "our current views of deaf people, our ways of talking about them, are a product of history" (Lane 1992, xi). In doing so, Lane reveals how bigotry and prejudice toward Deaf persons led to the oppression of sign languages through oralist educational practices, which continue to contribute to language deprivation in Deaf communities and the oppression of Deaf persons today.[3]

---

[3] For discussions of language deprivation syndrome and its harmful effects on deaf children, see (W. C. Hall 2017; M. L. Hall et al. 2017; Skotara et al. 2012; Glickman 2007; Gulati 2019; W. C. Hall, Levin, and Anderson 2017; Cheng et al. 2019).

In revealing the tragic history of language oppression experienced by the sign language community, Lane quotes Johann Conrad Amman, a Swiss physician who pioneered teaching speech to deaf persons in German-speaking lands. In his 1901 overview of educational methods for teaching deaf persons, Thomas Arnold characterizes Amman's method of teaching as "wholly oral," noting that "his ideas had a very great influence in determining that subsequently followed in Germany" (Arnold 1923, 31). The quotations of Amman provided by Lane are notable in that they encourage the oppression of sign languages by recourse to the concept of *voice* specifically:

> In the Voice is the Breath of Life, part of which passeth into the Voice; for indeed the Voice is the Child of the Heart, which is the Seat of the Affections, and of Desire. Hence it is, that sometimes we are not able to keep back the impetuous Motions of the Affections; but out of the abundance of the Heart, the Mouth speaketh. . . . Therefore, to comprehend much in a few words, the Voice is an Emanation from that very Spirit, which God breathed into Man's Nostrils, when he Created him a living Soul. (Amman 1692, 4–6)

As Lane reveals, Amman draws upon the supremacy of spoken, audible voice in order to portray deaf persons as stupid, immoral, and incapable of thought, much like animals, and to justify the oppression of sign languages based on their inadequacy compared to spoken languages:

> How dull they are in general! How little they differ from animals! Especially if their parents and relations have neglected them, and taken no trouble by nods and signs to get rid of their natural incapacity and produce a certain manner of thinking. And even if their parents are most attentive to them, how inadequate and defective is the language of gestures and signs which they must use! To how few relatives and friends is their intercourse restricted! How little do they comprehend, even superficially, those things which concern the health of the body, the improvement of the mind, or their moral duties! (Amman 1873, 2–3)

Proponents of oral methods like Jean-Marc Itard used the notion of the superiority of the spoken voice in order to justify terrible experiments on deaf children in order to teach them oral skills, "applying electricity to the ears of some pupils," placing "leeches on [their] necks," piercing their eardrums, covering their ears "with a bandage soaked in a blistering agent," "fracturing the skulls of a few pupils," applying "a white-hot metal button behind the ear," and threading a string "through a pupil's neck" (Lane 1992, 212–213).

Lane goes on to reveal how the notion of the superiority of the audible and oral voice was a foundation of the strategy used by Giulio Tarra to suppress the use of sign language in deaf education. Tarra was elected president of the congress of educators that met in Milan in 1880 and would become known as the Milan Congress, an event that had a "devastating impact on deaf children and adults for over a century" (Lane 1992, 113) (see Chapter 1 of this volume for a more detailed explanation of oralism and its overall effects on Deaf music-making in the nineteenth and twentieth centuries). In his opening address, Tarra, like Amman, invokes morality and religion to elevate oral speech over sign languages:

> Oral speech is the sole power that can rekindle the light God breathed into man when, giving him a soul in a corporeal body, he gave him also a means of understanding, of conceiving, and of expressing himself. . . . While, on the one hand, mimic signs are not sufficient to express the fullness of thought, on the other they enhance and glorify fantasy and all the faculties of the sense of imagination. . . . The fantastic language of signs exalts the senses and foments the passions, whereas speech elevates the mind much more naturally, with calm, prudence and truth. (Quoted in Lane 1992, 114)

The impact of these efforts to venerate the spoken, audible voice over a signing voice has become clear over the century and a half that has elapsed since the Milan Congress, and they have resulted in a pattern of violent suppression of signing voices that continues to the present day. Lane quotes an "American deaf college student who attended high school in the 1980s," who reports: "If we tried to sign, we would get our hands slapped" (Lane 1992, 132). In the National Theatre of the Deaf's original work *My Third Eye*, produced in 1971, Joe Sarpy tells the following story about how the veneration of the voice led to a violent encounter with speech therapy:

> When I was small, my parents wanted me to attend oral school where children were not allowed to use the language of the hands—sign language or fingerspelling, but had to learn speech and lipreading. My parents are hearing. They wouldn't learn sign language. They hoped I would communicate with them in their way. The teacher said OK and started to teach me how to say different sounds. The teacher held my hand on my throat and

nose to feel the vibrations. The teacher wanted me to feel the vibrations that happen when I said M . . . M . . . M . . . and N . . . N . . . N. . . . And the teacher put a stick to hold down my tongue and it touched my windpipe, the teacher wanted to hear me say Ah . . . Ah . . . Ah . . ., and I almost vomited. (National Theatre of the Deaf 1971)

The proliferation of oral methods and the oppression of sign language communities relies upon the denial of the idea of a signing voice and elevation of the audible, oral voice. Musicological studies of voice have often reiterated and reinforced the denial of voice, and in particular *musical* voice, to Deaf persons. For example, in *Unsung Voices: Opera and Musical Narrative in the Nineteenth Century*, one of the foundational texts of the musicological study of operatic voice, Carolyn Abbate writes that "deafness has the capacity to deny music" (Abbate 1991, 130). Moreover, Abbate uses stereotyped ideas of deafness as "the place where one special interpretation of musical voices can begin," while simultaneously characterizing deafness as "the deepest imaginable antithesis to music, the one thing that a deaf person can never possess, a form of discourse unthinkable and unattainable" (Abbate 1991, 130). More specifically, it is the musical *voice* that Abbate thinks is inaccessible to deaf persons: "For the deaf man, all voices are unsung, not in one sense of the word—being unpraised or unrecognized—but in that they are undone, silenced, and dead: deafness means the end of music" (Abbate 1991, 131). Arguing that the voice is not merely absent from a Deaf person's world, but *dead*, denies not only the existence of signing voices, but also the experiences of those who have had the oral voice yielded against them as a weapon of audism.

The notion that the Deaf voice, and particular the Deaf singing voice, is unsung, nonexistent, or in need of therapeutic repair persists in contemporary storytelling about Deaf communities. The 2021 film *CODA*, for example, relies on precisely this stereotype. *CODA* tells the story of the titular Child of Deaf Adults (CODA), Ruby Rossi (Emilia Jones), who harbors a secret: a beautiful singing voice. As she pursues a singing career, she faces resistance from her Deaf parents, Frank (Troy Kotsur) and Jackie (Marlee Matlin), who are shown to have no interest in the world of music. In a revealing promotional message, the official Twitter account of streaming platform Apple TV tweeted: "Gifted with a voice that her parents can't hear, Ruby (Emilia Jones), a Child of Deaf Adults, finds herself torn between her family and her future." The logline betrays the audism at the heart of *CODA*, which centers on the notion that Deaf people cannot understand or enjoy music. At one point in the film, during a singing lesson, Ruby calls her family's Deaf voices "ugly," a moment that Deaf viewers cited as particularly traumatizing due to their experiences with oral methods. One member of the Deaf community, @rosshowalter, tweeted, "I went through 16 years of speech lessons only to be teased and ostracized, and so, to have a signing CODA call Deaf voices ugly just hit a nerve." In another telling moment, Frank, Ruby's father, touches her neck while she sings. Twitter user @LealaHolcomb wrote that "this is one of the worst possible scenes anyone can show in a movie about deaf people," and in response, user @ClaritySpacer added: "A cringe moment for me as well—remembering I had to do that with my speech therapist ugh." In the movie's final scene, when Ruby is driving away from her family home to begin her degree at Berklee College of Music, the speaking voice overcomes the signing voice when Frank speaks his only audible line of the movie: "go." These moments collectively reveal the persistent power of audist ideas about Deaf vocality: that Deaf voices are unattractive or ugly, and that the audible voice is ultimately more authentic or powerful than the signing voice.

3.4 The Singing Signing Voice

Voice is evidently a controversial subject as it pertains to sign language and deafness. But, as I have shown, there is a clear philosophical and musicological foundation for theorizing a signing voice, free of notions of orality and phonocentrism. As Eidsheim argues in *Sensing Sound*, the voice is not exclusive to one sense or another, but "multisensory physical activity—including vocal sounds and speech—is experience," and "affect and meaning are derived from that full experience" (Eidsheim 2015, 130). Therefore, in order to conceptualize a signing singing voice, we must be attuned to all aspects of that voice, "whether the result is audible to the ear through propagation in air or otherwise consciously or unconsciously sensed" (104).

I asked signing musician Rosa Lee Timm what she felt constituted her voice in her performances. In ⏵ Video Example 3.2, Timm describes several characteristics of the signing voice in her performance of the song "Come What May," including her use of shoulder positioning, hand shapes and movements, and facial expressions:

Yes, I think of it as a voice. You can communicate that through shoulder switches, facial expressions, hand signs. With the voice going up and down, that is what my signing is echoing, is that feeling when the voice is moving up and down, so it is echoing the singer. It's hard to explain, but picking signs that really reflect how the vocals are going up and down. It is not just English to ASL, it is so much more than that. Like for example [shows sign], in a perfect world, I'm trying to remember what the lyric was. This is what I signed: instead of signing WORLD I did the world spinning on axis, during that emotional part of it to have it make more sense. The regular sign WORLD is so flat, so picking signs that are going to capture that inflection.

In this chapter, I explore what I understand to be six key facets of the signing voice: prosody, facial expressions, mouth morphemes, eye gaze and movements, body movements, and communality. In conversation, these elements in conjunction act in the way tone of voice, or intonation, does in a spoken language, a notion supported by a number of studies on prosody and intonation in sign languages.[4] For example, to indicate that one is asking a question using a spoken language, one would make use of vocal pitch and tone of voice. The equivalent in ASL would involve facial expressions and/ or head movements. To ask a yes or no question, one raises one's eyebrows, widens the eyes, and moves the head forward. To ask a "WH"-question (i.e., WHO, WHAT, WHERE, WHEN, WHY, HOW, HOW-MANY), one furrows one's brows. To understand the signing voice, then, we must understand how these six elements function to express musical meaning and emotion. The roles of head movements, eyebrow raising and furrowing, shoulder tilts, and mouth movements are complex and differ across different sign languages.[5] In this chapter, I focus on how these elements are used expressively for musical purposes.

In the sections that follow, I will explore each of these elements as they are used by Rosa Lee Timm in her sign language covers of two songs. The first is "Come What May," written by David Baerwald and Kevin Gilbert, from the soundtrack to the 2001 film *Moulin Rouge*, and the second is "Blown Away," written by Chris Tompkins and Josh Kear and performed by Carrie Underwood.

---

[4] See Dachkovsky and Sandler (2009); Nespor and Sandler (1999); Padden (1990); Reilly, McIntire, and Bellugi (1990b, 1990a); Sandler (1999b, 1999a); R. Wilbur (2000).

[5] See, e.g., Antzakas and Woll (2001); Boyes-Braem and Sutton-Spence (2001); Veinberg (1993).

Prosody

As Malawey points out, "prosody—broadly conceived as the pacing and flow of delivery—is critical to vocal delivery" (2020, 69). Prosody in singing voices, she argues, fuses together musical prosody with speech prosody, "connecting inflection and phrasing with potential variable meanings of song lyrics" (70). In signed song, prosody is therefore of the utmost importance, as it helps convey the emotional content and meaning of the song through a visual medium.

In their work on Israeli Sign Language, Svetlana Dachkovsky and Wendy Sandler point out that sign languages have conventionalized ways of "(1) dividing utterances into prosodic constituents; (2) making signs more or less prominent; and (3) conveying intonational 'tunes,' tunes that are seen and not heard" (Dachkovsky and Sandler 2009, 288). Roland Pfau and Josep Quer have argued that in ASL, nonmanual markers, such as head movements, torso movements, blinking, mouthing, and other facial expressions, "participate in structuring an utterance prosodically," in addition to serving as an "essential part of the grammar of natural sign languages" (Pfau and Quer 2010, 397). In her exploration of ASL prosody, Elizabeth Winston points out that head and torso movements create spatial patterns and rhythms. In addition, some features of sign articulation can create prosody, such as "sign-internal movements, size of articulation, repetition, lengths of movements and holds both within and between signs, and height of the signs" (Winston 2000).

Consider, for example, how Timm uses elements of prosody such as repetition and movement speed in her interpretation of the first verse of "Come What May" (shown in Example 3.1, ⏵ Video Example 3.3). Note how Timm repeats the sign BEFORE to mark the end of the line "Like I've never seen the sky before," while the end of the following line ("I want to vanish inside your kiss") is marked by signing DIVE-DOWN/IMMERSE slowly, over five beats. In the prechorus, as the song starts to build toward the expressive and climactic chorus, Timm continues to make use of expressive timing, such as on the sign EXPRESS-to-you/give-my-heart-to-you, which lasts for nearly five full beats. This expressive use of timing and repetition is further heightened by Timm's use of the other five components of the signing singing voice.

Example 3.1 Rosa Lee Timm, "Come What May," verse 1.

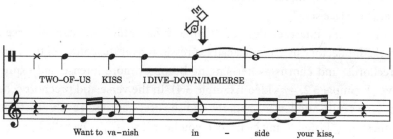

Facial Expressions

As I have already noted, facial expressions, such as raising or lowering the eyebrows or wrinkling the nose, play a crucial grammatical role in ASL. They are additionally important for expressing tone of voice and indicating emotion, including in the context of singing in sign. Indeed, as Dachkovsky and Sandler note, specific actions involve the eyebrows and eyes in sign languages function "much like intonational melodies of spoken language" (Dachkovsky and Sandler 2009, 288). In her discussion of Deaf sound artist Christine Sun Kim's *Face Opera II*, Jessica Holmes argues that "Kim and her collaborators defy the customary coupling of singing with audibility, and temporarily sever the related associations between the voice and vocal cords in order to 'sing' using silent facial expressions belonging to the American Sign Language (ASL) lexicon" (Holmes 2016). As Holmes describes, Kim and her eight collaborators use "a series of ASL facial expressions—without their accompanying manual hand shapes—as a mode of singing." But what makes the face sing?

In Timm's interpretation of "Come What May," we can observe a marked trajectory in Timm's facial expressions over the course of the verse, prechorus, and chorus as her singing becomes more intense and expressive (Example 3.2, ⏵ Video Example 3.4). In the verse and prechorus, her eyebrows raise and lower regularly, and she uses her raised eyebrows to ask a question ("Listen to my heart, can you hear it sing?"). Over the course of the prechorus, the tension rises and Timm's facial expressions become more expressive. For example, on the held sign EXPRESS-to-you/give-my-heart-to-you, which I noted above, her eyebrows are lowered and become slightly furrowed. In the chorus, her facial expressions become more expressive still as the music reaches a climax, her brow furrowing and nose wrinkling on the signs I DETERMINE-to LOVE YOU ("I will love you"). Her face then relaxes as the tension releases and the chorus comes to an end.

Mouth Morphemes

There are several different ways in which the mouth is used in signed languages. For example, "mouthings" are mouth movements that are borrowed from spoken languages, while mouth gestures are not borrowed from spoken languages (Boyes-Braem and Sutton-Spence 2001). J. Albert Bickford and

Example 3.2 Rosa Lee Timm, "Come What May," prechorus and chorus.

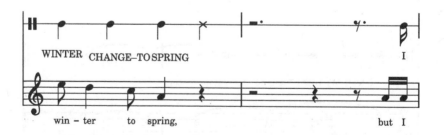

Example 3.2 Continued

Kathy Fraychinaud further distinguish between a use of the mouth that is "an inherent part of specific manual signs," and a use of the mouth that is "an independent morpheme" that may combine with different manual signs (Bickford and Fraychinaud 2006, 33). The authors also note that mouth morphemes may play different grammatical roles: they may function as adverbs, expressing degree, manner, and affect, or they may indicate "size, quantity, distance, relativization," or regulate conversation (Bickford and Fraychinaud 2006, 35).

Michiko Kaneko identifies three types of onomatopoeic mouth gestures or mouth morphemes that can be used in creative signing: iconic mouth gestures, where the source and target belong to the same sense; synesthesic, where the source and target forms belong to different senses; and metaphorical, where the source sense is used to refer to nonphysical concepts (Kaneko 2020). While Kaneko focuses primarily on poetic signing, these same onomatopoeic mouth gestures can be used to great expressive effect in musical signing as well. For example, in her translation of Carrie Underwood's "Blown Away," Rosa Lee Timm uses iconic and metaphorical onomatopoeic mouth gestures to express the song's emotional content.

In the song's opening line, Timm uses the PAH mouthshape iconically, in order to represent the lightning cracking across the sky—a visual experience represented by the explosive PAH shape (Example 3.3, ▶ Video Example

Example 3.3 Rosa Lee Timm, "Blown Away," verse 1.

3.5). She also makes use of the PUFF-CHEEKS mouthshape to iconically represent the wind blowing. This use of the PUFF-CHEEKS mouthshape quickly becomes metaphorical as well, though, representing the destruction that the singer wishes would be inflicted on her abusive father. Timm makes use of the CLENCHED-TEETH and HALF-LIP mouthshapes as well, which, according to Bickford and Fraychinaud, are associated with intensity and often used in signs like DISGUST, DIRTY, or DANGEROUS (Bickford and Fraychinaud 2006). Here Timm uses clenched teeth in order to metaphorically represent the sins that the singer wishes that the winds and rain would wash away. Over the course of the song, Timm's facial expressions become more intense, reflecting and augmenting the rising intensity of emotions in the music.

Eye Gaze and Movement

In ASL, eye gaze is used grammatically to express linguistic contrasts and mark verb agreement (Bahan 1996; Bahan et al. 2000; Neidle et al. 2000; Thompson 2006). While the important role of eye gaze in grammatical structures has been well established in the literature, the importance of eye gaze in musical expression has not been examined. However, eye gaze, in conjunction with blinking and other facial expressions, also plays an important role in the signing singing voice.

In her interpretation of "Blown Away," Timm uses eye gaze expressively at the very opening of the song. She begins with her eyes pointing downward before suddenly and emphatically looking up toward the sky as she signs LIGHTNING, blinking rapidly and emphatically to the rhythm of her signing. This sudden shift in eye gaze and movement is emphasized by Timm's lowered eyebrows and use of mouth morphemes at this moment as well (see the preceding discussion of mouth morphemes). Her eyes then widen, tracing the path of her hands as she signs STARE, showing the protagonist tracing the lightning strikes across the sky. Timm then looks to her right in order to indicate the object of the next sentence (storm clouds, signed TORNADO), but her eyes quickly turn to the center to show the storm clouds gathering in the protagonist's eyes. Timm's eyes are wide at this point, as the protagonist stares dumbstruck at the violent storm clouds. They quickly narrow as Timm turns to her right to sign about her father, a "mean old mister"—with her squinted eyes, tense face, and lowered corners of her lips, Timm indicates that the protagonist feels negatively toward the father. As she turns to her left to describe her mother, by contrast, "an angel in the ground," her eyes and face soften and relax, expressing her contrasting emotions about her parents.

Body Movements

Movement of the body, and especially of the shoulders, also plays an important grammatical role in sign language, often indicating a shift in object. Ronnie Wilbur and Cynthia Patschke have argued that body leans in ASL convey the notion of contrast at several levels. They argue that on this prosodic level, body leans mark "'stressed' in opposition to 'unstressed'"; lexically, they "reinforce the notions of actor 'involvement/non-involvement'"; and semantically, they mark inclusion (lean forward) and exclusion (lean backward) (R. B. Wilbur and Patschke 1998, 276). The prosodic use of body leans and shifting is of particular interest to our discussion of voice.

Timm uses body leans to great expressive effect in her rendition of "Come What May." While her shoulders remain mostly stationary in the first verse, in the song's prechorus, Timm leans forward dramatically when she signs EXPRESS-to-you/give-my-heart-to-you ("telling me to give you everything") (see Example 3.2). In the song's chorus, Timm uses subtle shoulder raising and lowering to express tension and release. Interpreting the line "come what way," she signs SHOW-UP FROM-NOW-ON with her right shoulder slightly raised, indicating tension and expressing that something negative may come later. She then signs NOT-MATTER, her shoulders relaxing once again, her face relaxing into a smile, and her head shaking back and forth to indicate that it does not matter what happens next. As she reaches the climactic moment of the chorus (I DETERMINE-to LOVE YOU), her shoulders rapidly lift then lower again, marking this moment as particularly expressive. The expressivity of this line of the song is further marked by the many other nonmanual signals used by Timm at this moment: her brows lower, her eyes squint nearly closed, her nose wrinkles, and her lips are pulled back. All these facets of Timm's signing come together to create her signing singing voice in her interpretation of "Come What May."

Communal Voice

As Paddy Ladd, Michele Friedner, and Stefan Helmreich have noted, collectiveness is an important aspect of Deaf culture and identity (Ladd 2003; Friedner and Helmreich 2012). I argue that the signing voice, and other nonspeaking voices, may be understood as collective or communal voices as well. For example, Alper discusses how the voice may be viewed as collectively constructed by nonspeaking communities who used technologies like the iPad in order to communicate. She notes that among her interlocutors, nonspeaking children and their parents, there was debate about whether "voice resided solely in the child's body or was distributed across multiple bodies ... particularly the bodies of mothers" (Alper 2017, 42) Some parents embraced the fluidity between their voice and their child's while others encouraged their children to view their iPad as constituting the child's voice exclusively.

In Pro-Tactile, a tactile sign language developed by and for members of the DeafBlind community in 2007, the singing voice may also be shared between bodies in a communal experience. For example, in a video shared on YouTube, DeafBlind community member Divya Goel performs the song "I Think You're Wonderful" by Red Grammer using Pro-Tactile. Her interpreter, Jason Eli Schwartz, uses touch to indicate when a new section of the song has begun, and when the song is coming to an end. Thus, the signing singing voice is shared between Goel and her interpreter, Schwartz.

Members of the Deaf community may also experience a sense of collective or communal voice when communicating through sign language interpreters. Christine Sun Kim has explored the idea of collective voice and identity in her work, noting her interest in "guiding people to become [her] voice" or an "extension of [her] identity." She notes that "the more [she] collaborate[s] with audiences and artists, the more sonorous [her] voice gets." However, she also laments that her voice "doesn't really exist without someone or something supplementing it," perhaps reflecting the dominance of phonocentric definitions of the voice (Mansfield 2015).

Of course, the acousmatic nature of sign language interpreting can also result in situations where the meaning of the signer's voice is lost. The anonymous Twitter account @DeafmemesExe jokes about such a moment in a tweet posted on December 10, 2020 (Example 3.4). The text of the tweet reads as follows:

Example 3.4 @DeafmemesExe tweet.

Interviewer: So, why do you want to work for Whole Foods?
Me: I love Whole Foods. I am a team player. I can lift more than 15 pounds.
   I want to get discounts.
Interpreted voice: I love 69. I am a team player. I can lift more 150 pounds.
   ·I want to get degraded.
Interviewer: [visible confusion].

In this joke, the potential for mistranslation when using a sign language interpreter becomes clear. Unlike Kim's experience of guiding others to become an extension of her voice and identity, many Deaf persons may find
their voice lost in translation even as it is transformed into an audible one.
In this sense, the shared or communal aspects of the signing voice are not always positive or beneficial to the signer.

3.5 Conclusion

As Nina Eidsheim points out in *Sensing Sound*, "the ontology of singing is masked by our fetishization of sound.... The singing body extends beyond that which we conventionally recognize as the vocal instrument" (Eidsheim 2015, 111). The signing voice, and especially the signing *singing* voice, ultimately reveals that studies of the voice have not provided an adequate framework for understanding signing voices. Moreover, I propose that the understanding of voice that I have developed in this chapter, which sees the voice as a fundamentally movement-based phenomenon, is essential for fully understanding the otolaryngological voice as well, the source of which is a body that *moves*. The face moves when we sing with the otolaryngological voice, as do the lungs, the ribcage, the diaphragm, the arms, the legs, the shoulders, the head. Other bodies move with us as well, as revealed by ProTactile signers, who point to the idea that not only is the voice not limited to a single place within a body, but that the voice is not limited to a single body. The signing voice affords an understanding of voice as moving through space, using the whole body, and emerging out of communal, reciprocal experiences between bodies. Only by understanding the voice in terms of moving bodies can we fully conceptualize what singing means.

This chapter provides a glimpse into what constitutes a singing, signing voice, and what parameters come together to create that voice in a signed song. There is a great deal more to say about the signing voice, but this preliminary definition offers a foundation for analysis. The signing singing voice is a complex and multifaceted phenomenon, just like the audible singing voice, and in order to analyze sign language music, it is crucial to understand how the different facts of the signing voice—including prosodic markers, facial expressions, mouth morphemes, eye gaze and movements, body movements, and collectivity—contribute to the overall effect of a piece of sign language music. Additionally, the singing voice interacts in productive and complex ways with the rhythmic movements of the signer's body, as well as with the melodic lines that the signer creates. All these elements together create musical meaning in a piece of signed music. Voice and vocality are at the heart of most sign language music, and thus the explication of the signing singing voice in this chapter provides a foundation for the all of the analyses that follow.

4

Rhythm and Meter

My perception of what music means is it's rhythm of the heart.
Rhythm of the Earth, the environment. Yes, there is rhythm in
sounds but that is such a small part of it—and for deaf people even
smaller still, the least important feature. There's visual rhythm, the
internal rhythm within us, there are many types of rhythm and
that is all music. It's all around us. But humans tend to focus only
on the auditory component, but music to me, is all of these—it's
rhythm.

—Ella Mae Lentz, Symphonious Odyssey

4.1 Introduction

Rhythm and meter, and the relationship between the two concepts, are two
of the primary objects of music-theoretical inquiry. Music theorists have developed robust frameworks for understanding the relationships between
rhythm, meter, accent, harmonic and tonal motion, and phrase structure.[1]
The parameters of rhythm and meter are generally understood to work together with the parameters of pitch, harmony, timbre, and texture in shaping
a musical work.

Consider what our existing theories of rhythm tell us about the song
"Boat, Drink, Fun, Enjoy," performed by George Kannapell in 1939 (Supalla
and Dannis 1994) (▶ Video Example 4.1; reproduced with permission from
DawnSignPress). The song uses the typical rhythmic pattern for percussion
songs shown in Example 4.1, revealing its place within a long-standing cultural tradition.

---

[1] See, e.g., Hasty (1997); Krebs (1999); Rothstein (1990); Schachter (1999); Cohn (1992); Lerdahl
and Jackendoff (1983); Cooper and Meyer (1963); Kramer (1988); Lester (1986); Yeston (1976).

Seeing Voices. Anabel Maler, Oxford University Press. © Oxford University Press 2024.
DOI: 10.1093/oso/9780197601976.003.0005

Example 4.1 A typical rhythmic pattern for percussion songs.

The song's lyrics, performed in American Sign Language (ASL), paint a picture of an enjoyable boat trip:

> BOAT BOAT
> BOAT BOAT BOAT
>
> DRINK DRINK
> DRINK DRINK DRINK
>
> FUN FUN
> FUN FUN FUN
>
> ENJOY ENJOY
> ENJOY ENJOY ENJOY

In addition to the rhythmic pattern, a spatial pattern emerges in the song as well: the body moves from left to right and back to left again with each sign, as follows:

> BOAT (left) BOAT (right)
> BOAT (left) BOAT (right) BOAT (left) (Cripps et al. 2017, 3)

Existing theories of rhythm take sound as a given, but the song "Boat, Drink, Fun, Enjoy" does not include any sounding elements—it is a song composed and performed purely in sign language. As Ella Mae Lentz urges us to recognize in this chapter's epigraph, though, there are many kinds of rhythm that do not involve sound: "there's visual rhythm, the internal rhythm within us, there are many types of rhythm and that is all music." In order to understand this song as rhythmic, and to understand whether it establishes a particular meter, we must understand how theories of rhythm and meter can apply to the visual domain.

In what follows, I first explore the concepts of entrainment, pulse (also known as beat or tactus), and rhythm as they pertain to sign language music. I argue that musical signers present visual rhythms using four movement types that are found in sign language poetry: hold emphasis, movement emphasis, movement size, and movement duration. The interaction of these four movement types creates the periodicity, accent, and flow that we understand as fundamental to rhythm in all kinds of music. I then turn to the creation of a metric framework in sign language music, showing how visual rhyme impacts the creation of metrical structures, and investigate the complex and metrically dissonant situations that arise when a spoken language and signed language interact. Finally, I turn briefly to the concept of phrase rhythm in sign language music.

4.2 Entrainment, Pulse, and Rhythm in Sign Language Music

While much of the existing music-theoretical literature on rhythm and meter focuses exclusively on rhythms as they sound in time, we can take from this literature some guiding foundational concepts for our study of a visual-kinesthetic form of music like sign language music. Jonathan Kramer's *The Time of Music* begins by stating: "Music unfolds in time. Time unfolds in music" (Kramer 1988). Music both moves through time and creates time as it unfolds, and this is equally true of sign language music. And, as Christopher Hasty argues, our ability to project a temporal span has a great deal to do with our bodily experiences of periodicity (Hasty 1997, 94). Another central aspect of musical rhythm is repetition. Elizabeth Margulis, in particular, focuses on how repetition shapes and permeates musical experience and practice. Repetition, she argues, makes music knowable outside of time (Margulis 2014).

Hasty argues that articulation is a key aspect of rhythm: that which is "homogeneous or lacking internal distinctions cannot be rhythmic." At the same time, Hasty emphasizes that parts and phrases must "flow together as a whole, diversified but unbroken" (Hasty 1997, 67). We can take from this statement that rhythm must involve discrete attack points, which are accented or unaccented, and which are grouped together.[2] Joel Lester identifies some of the factors that give rise to musical accent in tonal music: long durations (durational accents), new events (such as pitch change, harmonic change, or textural change), textural accents, contour changes, dynamics, articulation, and pattern (i.e., motive) beginnings (Lester 1986). Maury Yeston argues that these events can help to define a rhythmic stratum, and out of the

---

[2] On rhythm and grouping, see Lerdahl and Jackendoff (1983).

interaction of two differently rated strata emerges a sense of musical meter (Yeston 1976).

One of the most crucial aspects of rhythm for our purposes is the notion of entrainment, or the "process by which independent rhythmical systems interact with each other" (Clayton 2012, 49). As Eugene Montague (2019) documents, many biological and physiological studies of entrainment focus on long-term interactions between large-scale biological systems, studying, for example, cockroaches' entrainment to light cycles (Roberts 1965) or rats' entrainment to light-dark cycles (Goff and Finger 1966). The pathbreaking work of Mari Riess Jones focuses on what Montague terms the "short-term" model of entrainment, in which the receiver plays a greater role. Jones argues that human attention is "essentially rhythmic and periodic: it interacts with the external world through perceiving and locking into similar rhythmic patterns found in its environment" (Montague 180). Building upon the foundation of Jones's work, Justin London has argued that musical meter is based in bodily entrainment: meter involves the "synchronization of our movements to external rhythms" (London 2004, 12).

We typically understand these fundamental facets of rhythm as belonging to the realm of *sounding* pitches, but they are in fact organic to the world of sight and touch as well, as biological studies of entrainment to light patterns demonstrate. For the purposes of this book, we may wonder how humans entrain to patterned movements beyond just patterned sounds: if human entrainment to events perceived through hearing produces the phenomena of rhythm and meter, then can the same be true of human entrainment to events that are perceived through sight and/or touch?

In order to answer this question, we should explore whether the fundamental facets of rhythm, meter, and entrainment apply in the context of visually and haptically perceived movements as they do to aurally perceived ones. Movements, whether perceived aurally, visually, or haptically, exist in and through time. Just as a sound has a starting and ending point in time, so too does each movement of the body have a starting and ending point in both time and space. In "Boat, Drink, Fun, Enjoy," for example, each sign has a clear beginning, middle, and end: in order to articulate each sign, the body must move through both time and space. Indeed, signed languages have no written form—they *must* be produced over time, rather than frozen into an image.

Movements can also be periodic: they may recur at regular intervals. A simple example of this kind of periodicity is walking, which involves the regularly recurring movement of the legs and arms. Conducting is another

excellent example of periodic movement in a musical context. The periodicity of events in one's environment is key to human attention and entrainment: an attender "entrains to some relatively regular, prominently marked
time period within an event. . . . This period functions as an anchor or reference time level for the perceiver" (M. R. Jones and Boltz 1989, 470).

Movements can be repeated as well, another key component of entrainment. In "Boat, Drink, Fun, Enjoy," each movement occurs five
times. Movements may also be varied in their repetition, just as a series of
pitches may undergo variation. Movements can furthermore be articulated
into discrete attacks that flow together to create a whole. In "Boat, Drink,
Fun, Enjoy," we can see how each sign is individually attacked with the
punctuating movements of the arms, hands, and body, but at the same time,
the repeated signs together create a single flowing "line." Movements may be
accented as well, through duration, changes in contour, emphasis, articulation, and pattern beginnings. For example, the clapping at the start of "Boat,
Drink, Fun, Enjoy" creates a particular rhythmic pattern, and each time that
pattern begins again, the sign is accented.

Finally, movements may be polyphonic: they can create more than one musical stream (Roeder 2001). The separation of musical streams could occur between a signed layer and a voiced layer, as often occurs in genres like translated
songs (which involve the translation of an existing song into sign language)
or signed rap. Such polyphony could also occur between the signed layer and
elements of a background beat, or within the signing itself, between the two
hands, the body and the hands, or the face and the hands, for example.[3]

But can humans even perceive visual rhythms, much less polyphonic
ones? This is a relevant concern if we are to analyze visually and haptically
perceived rhythms in the same way as we analyze aurally perceived ones.
Studies on the perception of rhythm support the idea that listening to music
evokes a sense of motion in physical space (Clarke 2001; Shove and Repp
1995; Eitan and Timmers 2010). For example, Neil Todd suggests that the
sense of imaginary movement when we hear music is due to the interactions
of the auditory and motor systems (Todd 1999). In a recent synthesis of the
literature on rhythm perception, Todd and Christopher Lee argue for the
notion that "rhythm perception is a sensory-motor phenomenon": that the
vestibular system is of primary importance in rhythm perception, and that

---

[3] See Cripps et al. (2017) for more discussion of the potentially polyphonic aspects of signed music
and the difficulties in identifying polyphony in this context.

rhythm is also body-dependent (Todd and Lee 2015). Another study by Grace Leslie, Alejandro Ojeda, and Scott Makeig found that musical feeling can be communicate through rhythmic musical gestures alone, an effect that was supported by EEG brain activity (Leslie, Ojeda, and Makeig 2014). These studies suggest that rhythm is a bodily phenomenon, and while it can involve the sense of hearing, it does not exclusively rely upon a single sense. Indeed, already in 1921, Swiss music educator Émile Jacques-Dalcroze found that people who played or sang often had a difficult time keeping a consistent tempo, but when they walked or marched while playing or singing, they kept time perfectly (Jacques-Dalcroze 1973).

Rolf Inge Godøy has gone a step further in proposing that musical experiences are motor-mimetic in nature: that listening to music triggers visual images "by a simulation of sound-producing actions," and furthermore, that visual images can be translated into sound by "re-tracing the visual contours as sound-producing actions" (Godøy 2003, 318–319). If we can translate visual images of sound-producing actions into sound, can we also perceive visual rhythms? A study by Yi-Huang Su and Elvira Salazar-López on the perception of visual timing in structured dance movements suggests that we can indeed perceive a beat through a visual stimulus. The study revealed that visual timing is better perceived when the stimulus involves periodic trajectories that are marked by discrete contact points, and that this effect is not eliminated when a competing auditory stimulus interferes with the visual stimulus. The authors thus argue that beat-based timing underlies not only auditory musical rhythms, but temporally structured visual stimuli such as dance as well, and that the ability to perceive beats depends upon the use of discrete, periodic movements, rather than continuous ones. The authors also suggest that the parallelisms for processing auditory and visual rhythms could yield multisensory rhythmic information. In other words, sign language music presents a fascinating testing ground for understanding how humans process purely visual as well as multisensory (i.e., visual and auditory) rhythms.

Rhythm in sign language music is created through movement: movement of the hands, body, face, and head. In some sign language music, the rhythmic motion of the body exists at least partially in relation to sounding music, whether in the form of an existing song that is being translated by the signer, or in the form of an original rap performed simultaneously in a spoken and signed language. In other forms of signed music in which there is no sonic component, the movements of the signer's body in space may fully create the rhythm of the work. In ASL, nonmanual markers, such as head movements, torso movements, blinking, mouthing, and other facial expressions, "participate in structuring an utterance prosodically," in addition to serving as an "essential part of the grammar of natural sign languages" (Pfau and Quer 2010, 397). The most important nonmanual prosodic markers for the present discussion are head movements, torso movements, and sign articulation. In her exploration of ASL prosody, Elizabeth Winston points out that head and torso movements create spatial patterns and rhythms. In addition, some features of sign articulation can create prosody, such as "sign-internal movements, size of articulation, repetition, lengths of movements and holds both within and between signs, and height of the signs" (Winston 2000).

One starting point for understanding rhythm in sign language music is the literature on ASL poetry. Clayton Valli and Ceil Lucas broadly define rhythm in ASL poetry as created through "movement paths, assimilation, change of a sign, choice of a sign, handedness, alternating movement, movement duration, and movement size" (Valli et al. 2011, 188). Alec Ormsby has further identified some of the most important structural features of poetic signing, which will be useful for our discussion of sign language music. First, ASL poetry exhibits more "planned coincidence of like phonemic features" than conversational ASL. Second, poetic signing features a "general balance and fluidity," whereby the signing duty is divided between the two hands rather than mainly using the dominant hand, as in conversational signing. The third important facet concerns flow: the flow of poetic signing is "regulated so that it appears smooth and particularly graceful," and it is generally "slower and more fastidious" than regular signing. Fourth, ASL poetry will intentionally move outside the conventional boundaries of the signing space, a technique used in sign language music that I explore in more detail in Chapter 5. Fifth, ASL poetry tends to preserve sign structure, and sixth, features of signs are often blended in poetic ASL in order to "enhance the overall grace of articulation" and to "create expressive new signs" (Ormsby 1995, 228–229).

Many of the features identified by Ormsby in poetic ASL are used in musical ASL. Most crucial for our understanding of *rhythm* in musical ASL are the planned repetition of like phonemic features, which we can understand as rhyme; the balance between the two hands; and the use of a regulated flow. I will argue that in musical ASL, however, the flow is not always more smoother or more fastidious: instead, the importance of making a recurring beat perceptually evident to the audience encourages the use of discrete, periodic movements in musical signing. There is some evidence to suggest that the flow of musical ASL is indeed *slower* than usual, though; a study I conducted with Heather Mangelsdorf and Jason Listman showed that when watching an ASL song performed as a poem and as a piece of music, both Deaf/hard-of-hearing participants and hearing participants found the signs in the musical version to be slower than in the poetic version (Mangelsdorf, Listman, and Maler 2021, 169).

If poetic ASL and musical ASL share many elements in common, one might ask whether we can or should distinguish the two art forms from one another and whether they should be called music rather than poetry. In response to the first question, whether we can distinguish between the two, we might observe the features of musical ASL that are clearly distinct from poetic ASL: musical ASL tends to use more repetition, more obviously periodic movements tied to a beat (whether visual or aural), and more articulated movements. With respect to the second matter, we must recognize that music is defined by and through human culture: if a community understands musical ASL as music, then it is music by definition. As the discipline of ethnomusicology has shown, the cultural artifact we call "music" has different meanings in different cultures and may have little to do with the categories we understand as natural and essential to its existence (Bohlman 2002).

Even beyond accepting that rhythm can be a visual and kinesthetic phenomenon, I propose that the motor and visual aspects of rhythm, especially in the context of sign language music, are crucial to understanding why rhythm is such a central element in the human musical experience more broadly. Rhythm creates shared, communal experiences through engagement with our bodies. Our bodies help us to keep time, and keeping time with each other through moving our bodies helps us to create social cohesion and bonding (McNeill 1995; Freeman 2000). From infancy, rhythmic coordination and entrainment is essential for bonding and communication between mother and child (Jaffe et al. 2001; Dissanayake 2000). Rather than being peripheral to the study of musical rhythm, then, analyzing the embodied rhythms of sign language music is central to our understanding of human musicality and what I am calling the "resilience" of music.

Rhythm, Pulse, Groove

We can understand the pulse, or beat, as "the most comfortable rate at which one readily 'entrains' . . . to a musical rhythm via body movements such as hand claps or foot taps" (Câmara and Danielson 2020, 276). As Guilherme Câmara and Anne Danielson observe in the context of groove music, the beat is often expressed by instruments like the snare drum or bass. However, in the absence of these percussive instruments, a pulse or beat can still emerge in the presence of "longer, cyclically repeating rhythmic patterns" (Câmara and Danielson, 277). Moreover, subdivisions of the beat are necessary for establishing a sense of "groove" in music. Although the concept of groove is difficult to pin down, Câmara and Danielson understand it to involve patterns, to invoke pleasure and appeal to movement, and to exist as a state of being.

Let us return to the percussion song "Boat, Drink, Fun, Enjoy," which I briefly discussed in the introduction to this chapter (transcribed in Example 4.2). I noted that it makes use of the traditional rhythmic pattern for percussion songs, as well as a spatial pattern that moves periodically from left to right and back to left again.

How is the pulse established in a percussion song like this one? In some percussion songs, like Gallaudet University's "Bison Song," a drum is used to create and reinforce a sense of pulse. In others, like "Boat, Drink, Fun, Enjoy," the pulse is established purely through signing. In "Boat, Drink, Fun, Enjoy," a repeating rhythmic pattern is established from the beginning of the song, through Kannapell's clapping. The pattern of clapping includes events on each beat, as well as on subdivisions of the beat, creating the following rhythm: ♪♪|♪♪♪♩|. When the song begins, Kannapell uses the same repeating rhythmic pattern to guide his signing: each visual beat is associated with a discrete contact point in the signing space. With some signs, like BOAT,

Example 4.2 "Boat, Drink, Fun, Enjoy."

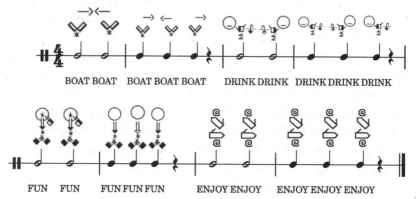

the contact point is a point in space, on the left or right side of the body. With other signs, like FUN, the point of contact is on the hand. Notice that in "Boat, Drink, Fun, Enjoy," both hands are used equally, much like in poetic ASL. Each hand strongly articulates its movements through emphasis at the point of contact. The alternating hands flow rhythmically through the signing space, creating discrete, periodic, repeated motions, separated by points of rest or holds.

Songs like "Boat, Drink, Fun, Enjoy" are striking in that they do not merely align signs to some preexisting, auditory beat but use different types of movements—such as holds, specific movement paths, movement emphasis, and different movement durations—in order to actually create a sense of rhythm and meter for the viewer. These movements are fundamental to creating rhythm in signed poetry as well. Rachel Sutton-Spence has observed that "rhythm in sign language poetry can be described in terms of the changes that occur within signs or in the transition between signs ('movements') and periods of no change ('holds')" (Sutton-Spence 2005, 45). Clayton Valli has further established four fundamental movement types that can create poetic rhythm: the first is hold emphasis, which can involve long pauses, subtle pauses, or strong stops; the second is movement emphasis, which can involve long, short, alternating, or repeated movements; the third is movement size, which can involve an enlarged movement path, shortened movement, reduced movement path, and accelerating movement; and the fourth is movement duration, which can be regular, slow or fast (Valli 1993). These movements and holds create a sense of pulse or beat and also allow for the creation of distinctive rhythms and rhythmic patterns.

Some genres of sign language music use percussive elements to create a sense of groove, in addition to visual rhythms. For example, the genre of signed hip hop or "dip hop," a term coined by Deaf rapper Warren "Wawa" Snipe in 2005, typically involves a Deaf or hard-of-hearing artist simultaneously performing vocalized and signed rapping over a looped background beat. In her thorough exploration of the history of dip hop, Katelyn Best contextualizes the emergence of the genre as part of a broader social movement within Deaf culture, associated with the Deaf President Now and Deaf Rights movements of the late 1980s (Best 2015/2016). Dip hop presents a unique format for hip-hop music, as artists rhythmically convey lyrics in two languages simultaneously. As Best observes, the very fact that in signed rap the lyrics are "performed bilingually, in both manual and aural languages" facilitates the "opportunity to break down stereotypes of music and deafness" (Best 2018, 4). The unique format of signed rap—which involves simultaneous rapping in two natural languages in different modalities—thus engenders unique rhythmic strategies and paradigms.

In non-signed rap music, there is often a notable relationship between the lyrics and the backing track, colloquially referred to as a "beat."[4] Kyle Adams describes several examples of rap tracks in which the rhythmic delivery (or "metrical techniques of flow") is influenced by rhythmic characteristics or motives of the background beat (Adams 2008). Ohriner (2016) expands upon this premise in describing an example of rapper T-Mo emphasizing a triple-meter aspect of the beat for OutKast's "Mainstream" by employing three-beat rhymes more frequently than expected. Robert Komaniecki similarly describes rappers' flows mirroring aspects of the background beat, analyzing a rhyme scheme in which rhyme changes and chord changes correspond (Komaniecki 2017).

Signed rap also presents a specific relationship to the background beat. As Jeannette Jones explains, "feeling vibration is a key part of the deaf experience of music," and that vibration is often experienced through the bass. One of Jones's interlocutors, Ed Chevy (bass guitarist of the all-Deaf band Beethoven's Nightmare), describes the need to "[increase] the volume or the bass so that vibrations are felt or certain frequencies can be heard" in order to feel the beat (J. D. Jones 2015, 61). In correspondence with Katelyn Best, dip-hop artist Darius "Prinz-D The First Deaf Rapper" McCall has also expressed his love for "any genre that has a lot of boom in the bass drums"— indeed, Best has identified the use of "low frequency bass patterns for its beats" as one of the primary features of dip hop alongside the use of sign language for its lyrics, creating "a flow between the two that is both visual and tactile" (Best 2015/2016, 72–73). The bass line and percussion are thus essential and defining aspects of the background beat for dip-hop artists, and the relationship between the signed lyrics and the bass drum is particularly strong in signed rap.

The excerpt from Sean Forbes's "A Song for My Haters" in Example 4.3 demonstrates how percussion may structure the flow of the signed rap (⏵ Video Example 4.2). Here, Forbes aligns signs that are emphasized through holds, repetition, or movement duration with events in the bass

---

[4] In hip-hop scholarship, the term "beat" can refer to the backing musical track over which a rapper performs, or it can be used in its more traditional sense, describing location(s) within a given measure, depending on context.

Example 4.3 Sean Forbes, "A Song for My Haters," verse 2.

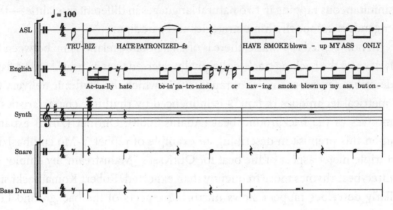

drum and snare. The first and last letters of the fingerspelled P-A-T-R-O-N-I-Z-E-D, for example, align rhythmically with notes in the bass drum and snare and are signed emphatically by Forbes.[5] The signs blown-up and HAVE in m. 2 are similarly emphasized. We can see a similar relationship with the bass drum and snare in the sign HATE in m. 5, HAVE NONE in m. 5, and DON'T WANT, BULLY, and HATER in m. 6.

In dip-hop tracks like "A Song for My Haters," the groove is thus established both through the visually perceived signed rhythm and through the presence of a background beat. Through movements and holds, Forbes creates a unique visual surface rhythm with his signing, which itself establishes a pulse. This visual pulse is reinforced by the strong percussive elements of the snare and bass drum, creating a sense of groove.

In an interview with Molly Mackin for *Ability* magazine, Forbes suggests that this focus on the bass and percussion is indeed a crucial part of his creative process:

> Every time I listen to a new song, or even an old song I know, I always try to follow the different rhythms that happen throughout it. Bass and drums are pretty simple for me to follow, but sometimes I'll be in a situation in which I'll have a different point of reference when I'm listening to something, and I'll be able to pick up the guitar or the piano line, and follow that rhythm. (Mackin 2011, 11)

Forbes goes on to describe how following the melody is "pretty hard" for him, which he accommodates by asking coworkers or family members about the melody. By contrast, "rhythm is something that is born inside you" and is a foundation of Forbes's compositional process (Mackin 2011, 11). Leyland "Lee" Lyken (aka DJ SupaLee), a Deaf nightlife promoter and DJ, echoes this sentiment in an interview with Diane Nutting:

> I believe as a DJ I take a unique approach because I am really focusing on the beats and rhythms—primarily the bass levels because many deaf people need and want that to sync with the music experience. I don't always understand the words of a song, but I feel the beats and use that to create the

---

[5] Fingerspelling is the practice of spelling out an English word using the letters of the ASL manual alphabet. This practice is commonly used to spell names and other words that cannot be conveyed using an existing sign.

blend. As a DJ, my job is to feel out the crowd and pick the best music to move them. (Nutting 2019)

Lee also argues that "a deaf person connects to music as a form of energy and expression, even if they don't understand all the lyrics." He believes that "a slow beat will make them feel more mellow, an upbeat song will make them feel like dancing" (Nutting 2019). Both as a creator and perceiver, then, Lee foregrounds the importance of pulse in Deaf musical experiences.

4.3 Visual Meter

Richard Cohn understands the concept of meter to involve a sound-based stimulus, in which the mind "seeks and identifies patterns," which patterns are in turn expressed by the body (Cohn 1992, 208). More specifically, Cohn defines meter as a set of pulses, or "an inclusionally related set of distinct, notionally isochronous time-point sets" (Cohn 1992, 210). The sense of meter thus involves the existence of a series of approximately evenly spaced, or isochronous, time points, organized into a set of at least two pulses, in which "each time point of the slower pulse is also a time point of the faster one."

Cohn exclusively defines musical meter in terms of sound-based pulse streams, but as we have already established, a sense of pulse can be perceived visually or haptically. The existence of visual beat patterns, rhythm, and groove suggests that meter can similarly established through vision and/or touch. In "Boat, Drink, Fun, Enjoy," there are three pulse streams created by the surface rhythm of two slower signs followed by three faster signs and a brief hold (♩♩|♪♪♪♪), represented in Example 4.4 by a series of dots. These pulse streams meet Cohn's isochronous condition, in that they are approximately evenly spaced, and his inclusion condition, in that each time point of the slower pulse layers is also a time point in a faster one. The purely signed pulse streams in "Boat, Drink, Fun, Enjoy" thus meet the criteria for a three-deep duple meter according to Cohn's definition.

The flow of the signing in "Boat, Drink, Fun, Enjoy" is further segmented into two-bar phrases based on repetition of movements (i.e., BOAT BOAT / BOAT BOAT BOAT) and contrast. Each of these two-bar phrases exhibits internal contrast as well: the first measure involves slower, larger movements, while the second measure features faster, smaller movements.

Example 4.4 Pulse streams in "Boat, Drink, Fun, Enjoy."

We might also note that while the signs BOAT and DRINK establish a pattern of alternation between the right and left hands and the right and left sides of the body, that pattern is somewhat altered in the third and fourth sections of the song, on the signs FUN and ENJOY. The sign FUN is signed twice on the right side of the body for the first measure of the phrase (m. 5 of Example 4.2); then, in m. 6, the sign is abbreviated and the two hands alternate right-left-right. For the sign ENJOY, the opposite is true: in m. 7 it is signed on the right of the body, then on the left, and in m. 8, it is signed three times only on the right side of the body. We can thus see a broader binary form emerge over the course of the song, where mm. 1–4 form one unit, while mm. 5–8 form a second, slightly contrasting unit.

Rhyme and Repetition

One crucial aspect of metrical perception is repetition: through repetition, we can perceive patterns in a stream of rhythms, which allows us to perceive the pulse streams that define meter. As Elizabeth Margulis notes, musical repetition has other important effects as well: it establishes the basic parameters of a piece of music; it creates points of reference that bind events together, allowing perceivers to form expectations; it allows perceivers to shift their attention from lower to higher levels of musical structure; and it draws listeners into a participatory relationship with sound, encouraging them to entrain bodily to the music and making music more enjoyable (Margulis 2020). One type of repetition that features heavily in sign language music involves rhyme. Rhyming plays an especially important role in the genre of dip hop, where it helps to establish a metrical framework for the perceiver via repetition.

In non-signed rap, rhymed syllables are nearly always set to identical rhythmic motives in the same metric position (Komaniecki 2019). This happens with enough regularity that rhymed syllables being set to identical rhythmic motives can be identified as a norm of non-signed rap, while not setting rhymed syllables to the same rhythmic motives would be marked in that context.[6] Example 4.5, reproduced from Komaniecki (2019, 44), is a normative rhythmic setting of rhymed rap lyrics, in which every rhyming syllable group is also set to the same rhythmic figure. By contrast, Example 4.6, also reproduced from Komaniecki (2019, 46), is markedly atypical in that members of a rhymed pair ("Goodwill" and "good still") are set to different rhythms.

The concept of rhyme exists in sign languages as well, although it takes different forms due to the visual-spatial modality of sign language. Clayton Valli has identified four types of rhyme that may occur in ASL poetry: handshape rhyme (the repetition of the same or similar hand configuration), movement path rhyme (in which the same or similar movement is repeated inside successive signs), nonmanual signal rhyme or NMS rhyme (in which nonmanual signals such as facial expressions, eye gaze, or head orientation are repeated in successive signs), and line division rhyme (in which the terminal segments are similar in one of the preceding parameters) (Valli 1990). In her work on sign language poetry, Rachel Sutton-Spence expands this framework to include sign location as an important parameter. Sutton-Spence also points out, however, that while repetition of these parameters may loosely be called "rhyme," "the distinctions of rhyme, assonance, alliteration, consonance and others that are made in spoken language poetry are not directly applicable to signed poetry," and indeed, "there is no strong evidence for the regular occurrence of rhymes at the end of lines in most sign language poems" (Sutton-Spence 2005, 42–44). Dip hop makes use of the

---

[6] Repetition goes hand in hand not only with hip hop, but with popular music more generally. Margulis (2014) demonstrates that listeners rate music with repetition as more enjoyable, suggesting that repetition imbues music with a "social and biological role in the creation of interpersonal cohesion" (6) and that a listener's ability to anticipate musical activity can be directly correlated with their opinion of its quality.

Example 4.5 A transcribed excerpt of Cardi B's "Bodak Yellow" (2017, 0:14–0:44).

Originally published as Example 2.17 in Komaniecki (2019, 44).

Example 4.6 A transcribed excerpt of Kyle's verse in Donnie Trumpet and the Social Experiment's "Wanna Be Cool" (2015, 2:32–2:44).

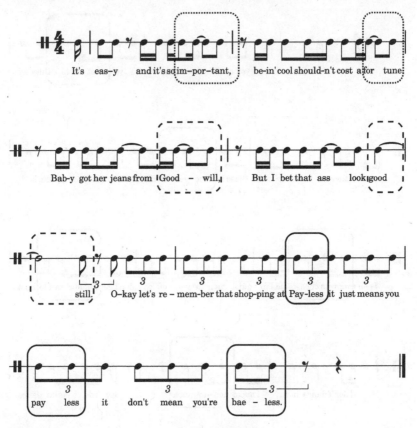

Originally published as Example 2.18 in Komaniecki (2019, 46).

kinds of poetic rhyme identified by Valli and Sutton-Spence, but it does so in conversation with the norms of the hip-hop genre more broadly. For example, dip-hop artists often do place rhymes at the ends of "lines," where we would expect them to occur in vocal rap. While this contrasts with the norms of ASL poetry, it makes a great deal of sense in the context of signed rap, which typically occurs simultaneously with vocalized rap. The use of rhyme schemes drawn from vocal rap also aligns with what Sean Forbes has said about his influences and creative process:

> I've been writing songs since I was a kid, and I grew up reading poetry and lyrics. I would often go on Bob Dylan's website and just read the lyrics. Over

time, just by looking at how any rapper rhymes words and fits syllables into verse, I got to a point at which meter and rhyme schemes became very natural for me. (Mackin 2011, 11)

This quotation suggests that the rhyme schemes and meters of non-signed rap were influential in shaping Forbes's rapping, which helps to explain why dip-hop artists often make use of devices like end-rhymes. We might therefore understand signed rap as an expression of bicultural experiences through music performance, utilizing both the conventions of hip hop and the techniques of ASL poetry in order to tell stories that shed light on Deaf identity and community (Davidson 2006, 221).

Given the typical alignment of rhyme and rhythm in non-signed rap, we might ask whether signed rap shows similar relationships between rhythm and rhyme. Dip hop instead presents a more varied landscape of rhyme-rhythm interactions, in which rhymed cells may or may not align rhythmically. The possibilities for rhyme-rhythm interactions in raps by Sean Forbes, Warren "Wawa" Snipe, and Marko "Signmark" Vuoriheimo may be represented as a quadrant based on the relationship between the signed layer and the spoken layer (Example 4.7). Rhymed cells in the signed layer may or may not align rhythmically, and at the same time, rhymed cells in the spoken layer may or may not align rhythmically.

The second verse of Snipe's "Faceless Man" combines types 1 and 2 (▶ Video Example 4.3). Example 4.8 shows that the signs for MILK HE and CALM DOWN are rhythmically aligned. They rhyme as well: the open 5 handshape that indexes the father in the song rhymes with the same handshape in CALM DOWN. Snipe also creates a spatial rhyme between the

Example 4.7 Rhythm-rhyme interaction types in dip hop.

Type 1	Type 3
Signed layer aligned Non-signed layer aligned	Signed layer aligned Non-signed layer not aligned
Type 2	Type 4
Signed layer not aligned Non-signed layer aligned	Signed layer not aligned Non-signed layer not aligned

Example 4.8 Wawa, "Faceless Man," verse 2.

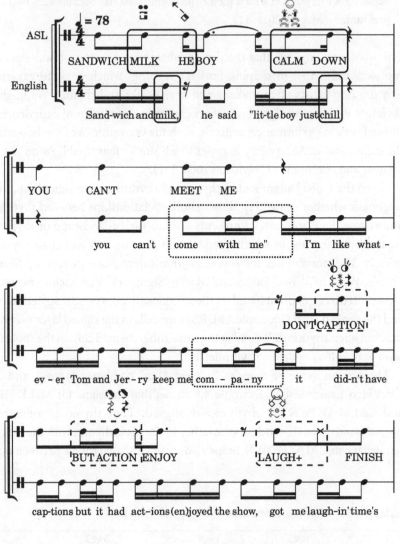

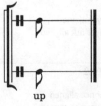

signs by signing them on opposing sides of his body. The repeated movement in the sign CALM DOWN creates the same rhythm as MILK HE, in approximately the same location in the second half of the beat. The same rhythmic alignment can be seen in the vocal layer as well. Rhythmic alignment in both layers represents type 1 in the quadrant of Example 4.7. Later in the same verse, the signs CAPTION and ACTION—which rhyme in their movement, orientation, and location—are not aligned rhythmically with one another, while the vocal layer maintains the rhythmic alignment of rhymed cells. However, the sign LAUGH+, which rhymes with CAPTION through the repeated use of pointed handshapes (the "one" handshape in LAUGH and the "nine" handshape in CAPTION), does align once more with CAPTION.

Snipe frequently plays with the alignment or misalignment of rhyming cells in his rapping. For example, the track "Only ASL One" tells the story of being a beginner signer in ASL class who struggles to communicate with his crush (Example 4.9). In an interview, Snipe informed me that "Only ASL One" was written by his producer, DJ Nicar, who is hearing. He relayed that the song is meant to represent the experience of DJ Nicar as well as others who come into the Deaf community for the first time. He explains that when people who are just learning sign language meet someone who is fluent and signs rapidly, they might feel nervous or uncomfortable, and the song is meant to reflect that nervousness and awkwardness (▶ Video Example 4.4).

In the first verse, Snipe creates an obvious, even simplistic alignment between the rhyming signs PURPLE and SIGN through heavy-handed repetition within each sign, thus rhythmically conveying the slowness of a beginner signer. The sign for SIGN continues for longer than expected, though, due to the slow repetition within the sign, emphasizing the slow, awkward signing of a student. This rhythmic character is mirrored in the vocal layer of his performance: he raps a mostly unvaried stream of sixteenth notes, with the fourth beat of every measure predictably containing an end-rhyme.[7] His signing becomes faster and more fluent as the song progresses, and he begins to play with the alignment of rhyming cells. The lack of alignment between the rhyming cells FUNNY and CLUMSY (which rhyme through palm orientation, handshape, and nonmanual markers) conveys the clumsiness of the character in a comedic way. The mismatch between movement types in

---

[7] Condit-Schultz (2016) and Ohriner (2016) have demonstrated that most rhymed syllables in vocal rap appear on beat 4, something to which listeners are likely subconsciously attuned.

Example 4.9 Wawa, "Only ASL One," first verse.

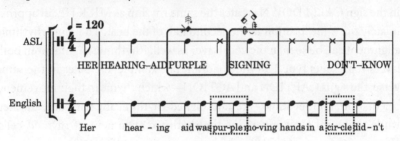

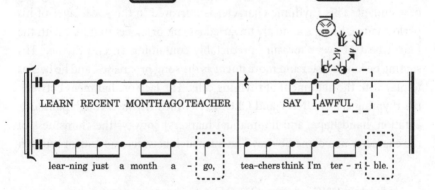

CLUMSY and AWFUL, in which the sign CLUMSY is emphasized through repetition and AWFUL through a strong stop, further compounds the joke—now the cells are rhythmically aligned, but they use contrasting movement types, palm orientation, and handshapes.

In the track "Two Blown Speakers," Sean Forbes presents an example of the third type, in which the signed layer is aligned and the spoken layer is not (Example 4.10, ▶ Video Example 4.5). As Example 4.10 shows, Forbes uses the same rhythmic cell for each rhyming sign (PROCESS, WAYS, ENOUGH, SHOW-up). PROCESS and WAYS rhyme in handshape, location, and movement, while ENOUGH and SHOW-up have a location, handshape, and palm orientation rhyme. However, the verbal layer does not show the same strong rhythmic alignment between end-rhymes. In fact, if one were to judge this track solely on the vocal flow, it would come across as basic (one-syllable rhymes, rhyming "way" with "ways") and possibly even sloppy, since the rhymed syllables occur in nearly the same metric location, but not quite at the exact same place as the other syllable in the couplet. The signed layer, by contrast, is tight and emphatic.

In "I'm Deaf," Sean Forbes provides an example of the fourth type, in which neither the signed layer nor the spoken layer has rhymed cells that align rhythmically (Example 4.11, ▶ Video Example 4.6). Here, Forbes creates a signed rhyme between CAN on the second beat of the first line with CAN (repeated) on the second beat of the second line, while rhyming "keys" and "-ing" within the last beat of each of the spoken lines. Contrary to expectations from non-signed rap, the second rhyme in each couplet arrives in a different metrical location.

Marko "Signmark" Vuoriheimo's "The Letter" shows how even when the signed and spoken layers feature rhythmic alignment between rhymed cells, the signed layer can have a great deal of variety and interest in the relationship between rhymes and rhythms. Example 4.12 (▶ Video Example 4.7) shows how Vuoriheimo makes use of rhythmic holds, repetition, movement, and movement duration to emphasize rhythmic alignment of rhymed cells. For example, while WORLD and WHAT are not precisely aligned in terms of the length of the sign, they have a similar long pause effect, emphasized through their shared enlarged movement size, slow speed, and handshape rhyme. The signs LOST and MESSED-UP rhyme in their movement and handshape and last for the same

Example 4.10 Sean Forbes, "Two Blown Speakers," verse 2.

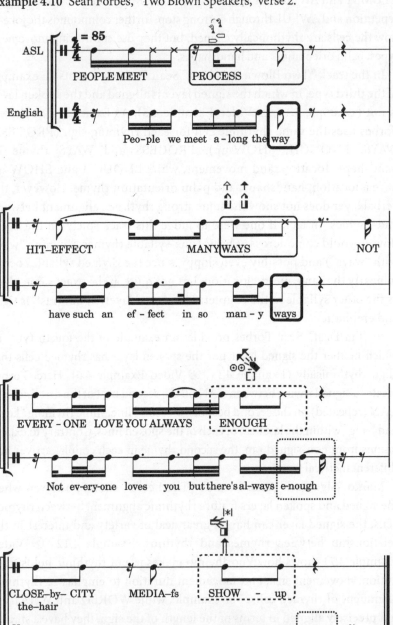

Example 4.11 Sean Forbes, "I'm Deaf," verse 3.

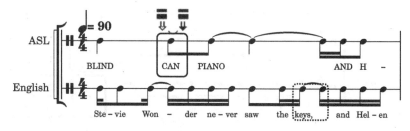

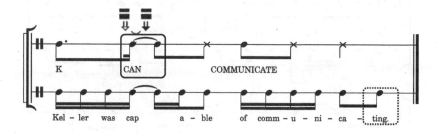

amount of time, but do not occur in the same part of the measure—this only serves to emphasize the sign WRONG, which should have rhymed with MESSED-UP but emphatically does not. Here, Vuoriheimo's choice of WRONG and MESSED-UP, which do not rhyme, drives home the wrongness of Emma Agnew's murder in 2007, the subject of the track. By contrast, the signs for FAMILY, FOREVER, TOGETHER, and SEND throw-to-you are aligned rhythmically—the first two through holds and the second two through repeated movements. The rhythmic alignment of these rhymed cells reinforces the message of solidarity and support for Emma's family, physically representing the Deaf community coming together after her loss.

In an interview, Vuoriheimo explained the origins of the song and its importance. He explained how Emma Agnew had been a fan of his music. They met only once, in July 2007, at a gig Vuoriheimo played in Madrid, Spain. They took a few pictures together, and only months later, in November 2007, Vuoriheimo received the news that Agnew had been murdered. Vuoriheimo's music was played at her funeral because, in Vuoriheimo's words: "Emma had told her friends, 'One day when I die I don't want any church music, I want Signmark's music at my funeral.' And that's why I decided to write this song, 'The Letter'" (▶ Video Example 4.8).

Example 4.12 Signmark, "The Letter," verse 2.

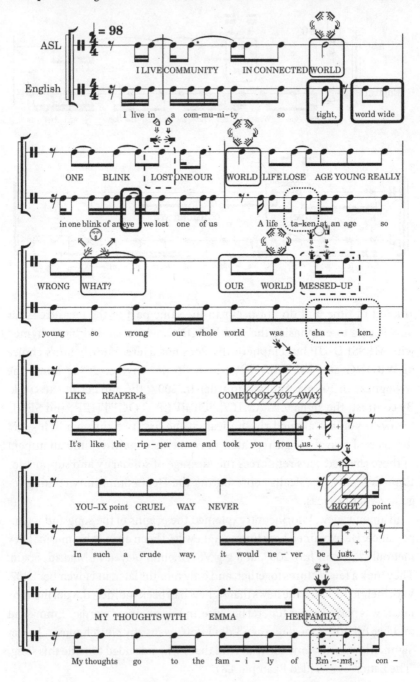

Example 4.12 Continued

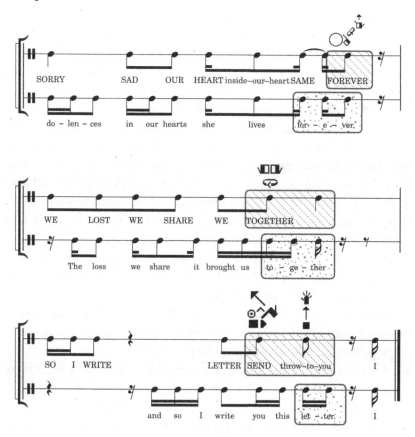

Multiple Metric Streams

In dip hop, a visual-spatial signed language and a spoken language are performed simultaneously. The simultaneous use of two different language modalities means that two rhythmic streams emerge in the music. ASL, like all signed languages, is a natural language completely distinct from English, with its own grammar and formational parameters for each sign.[8] As a result, the signed layer and voiced layer of signed rap often do not align metrically with one another. Indeed, Wawa has discussed how using two language

---

[8] Stokoe (1960) identifies three main formational parameters for signs: location, movement, and handshape.

modalities often means he is "working to tell the story twice," once in English and once in ASL. In English, he focuses on "the message and word play within the rap," while in ASL he focuses on "the visual aspects of how to tell the story" (Nutting 2019). When he performs live, he signs in ASL against a track of his voice rapping the words, resulting in some listeners not believing that Wawa's own voice is the one heard on the recording.[9]

The simultaneous use of two distinct language modalities can result in complex metrical situations. For example, the signed layer of rap may begin before or after the non-signed layer, thus creating two distinct relationships with the background beat. In the second verse of "Watch These Hands," Sean Forbes creates a sustained metrical dissonance between the signed and non-signed raps beginning in m. 3 of Example 4.13 (▶ Video Example 4.9).[10] Here, the signed layer gets one eighth note ahead on YOU ASK ME in m. 3 and continues in this manner through m. 4. The two layers briefly align on SHORT ("short"), but the signed layer moves quickly to fingerspell B-U-S an eighth note before it appears in Forbes's non-signed rap. Beginning in m. 6, the two layers are fully aligned once again.

The opening of the second verse of Forbes's "Watch These Hands" provides a simple example of another kind of contrast between signed and vocalized rapping. This passage, shown in Example 4.14 (▶ Video Example 4.10), features a signed layer that is twice as slow as that of the vocal layer. A more sustained example of this rhythmic technique occurs in the track "I'm Deaf," in which Forbes uses two signed couplets within the space of one spoken couplet to create a quasi-polymetric effect, in which the implied meter of the signing is twice as fast as that of the spoken rap (Example 4.15, ▶ Video Example 4.11). Here, Forbes emphasizes the rhyme between CAN'T and the F of the fingerspelled C-L-E-F to create a pointed handshape and movement rhyme, further emphasizing the rhyme with his entire body by raising his left foot off the ground and leaning forward. He then rhymes EXPECT with DEAF/GIVE UP, perhaps to express his frustration and also create a highly marked movement and handshape rhyme with EXPECT.

---

[9] That audiences do not initially believe that Wawa uses his own voice to rap brings up broader issues of the role of the voice within Deaf culture. The use of the voice is often associated with the oralist educational movement, which suppressed sign language in favor of promoting speech and lipreading (for more discussion of oralist philosophies see Baynton 1996, 1992). In fact, Wawa has discussed how attitudes about the voice have shaped his reception within Deaf culture, stating that he was heckled and labeled "hearing-minded" or "trying to be hearing" in his early rap performances (Peisner 2013).

[10] See Krebs (1999) for more detailed discussion of metrical dissonance in the music of Robert Schumann. The present dissonance would be characterized by Krebs as a displacement dissonance.

Example 4.13 Sean Forbes, "Watch These Hands," verse 2.

Example 4.14 Sean Forbes, "Watch These Hands," opening.

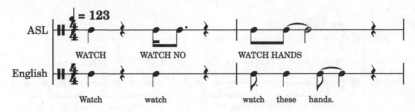

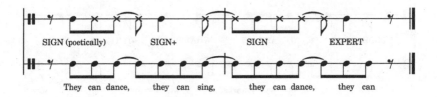

Example 4.15 Sean Forbes, "I'm Deaf," verse 3.

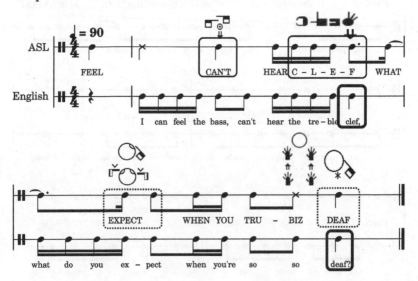

Jason Listman provides an example of a similar rhythmic technique outside of dip hop, in his interpretation of Bruno Mars's "Just the Way You Are" (Example 4.16, ▶ Video Example 4.12). In this video, Listman uses movement emphasis involving his head and body, as well as holds and repetitions of signs, in order to create a rhythmically distinctive signed layer. The sign EYES, for example, is marked by Listman opening his mouth. Listman marks the

Example 4.16 Jason Listman, interpretation of "Just the Way You Are."

Example 4.17 Chart showing alignment of ASL signs and English lyrics in Listman's "Just the Way You Are."

1	x	y	z	2	x	y	z
			Oh	--	her	eyes	her eyes -- make the
			HER	EYES		EYES	STARS
stars	look like	they're not	shining.	Her	hair	her hair	falls
SHINE-into	--	SHINE-into	--	HER	HAIR		FINISH
perfect-	-ly with-	out her	trying.		She's so	beauti-	-ful
--	PER- -FECT	--	-- FINISH	YOU		BEAUTIFUL	--
	and I	tell her	every	--	day.		
--	--	--	--	I TELL YOU		DAILY	
--	--	Yeah	--				
		YEAH					

1	x	y	2	x	y
		HER	EYES	EYES	
STARS	SHINE-into		SHINE-into	-	HER
HAIR		FINISH	--	PER- -FECT	--
	FINISH	YOU	BEAUTIFUL	--	--
--	--	--	I TELL YOU		DAILY
--	--	--	YEAH		

entire phrase STARS SHINE-into by suddenly turning his head upward and to the left, and he marks the repetition of SHINE-into by once again turning his head, this time to his right. HAIR is once again marked by Listman's open mouth, and the signs PERFECT and BEAUTIFUL are both marked by holds.

As a result, some of the signs emphasized by Listman's holds, movement, and nonmanual markers imply a triple meter, although the original music is in a quadruple meter (see Example 4.17). By combining the natural flow of sign language with the sounding music, Listman achieves a layered, contrapuntal effect through the interplay of the signed and sung words, an effect that can only be understood by experiencing the visual music and the heard or felt music in tandem.

The signed layer may also have a special relationship with the background beat that is not mirrored by the vocal layer. For example, at the opening of Forbes's "Watch These Hands," the signed layer does not correspond exactly with the non-signed layer; the signs in the first two measures, for example, create a more syncopated, complex rhythm than the relatively straightforward one found in the vocal layer. The addition of the sign NO in beat 3 of m. 1 creates a feeling of intensification through rhythmic acceleration. Furthermore, each iteration of LOOK-AT becomes more intense through the use of non-manual markers (Example 4.14).

We can see another example of rhythmic intensification of the signed layer in the third verse of Forbes's "I'm Deaf" (Example 4.18, ⏵ Video

Example 4.18 Sean Forbes, "I'm Deaf," verse 3.

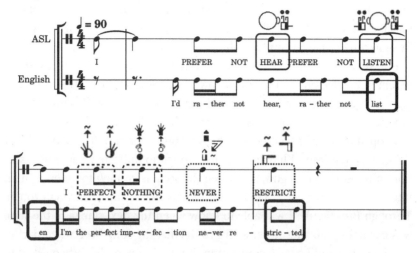

Example 4.13). In this excerpt, enjambment in the non-signed layer creates a sense of continuity and increased urgency as the first phrase spills over a metrical boundary into the second phrase. The enjambment in the non-signed rap is mirrored through the increased density of rhymed couplets in the signed rap. Forbes creates this sense of increasing density by avoiding emphasis through lack of movement holds, reduced movement path (indicated by tildes in the SignWriting symbols, which represent tense movement), and very regular movement durations among the rhyming cells.

4.4 Phrase Rhythm in Musical Signing

The rhythmic techniques I have discussed thus far can be used to define phrases and phrase goals in sign language music as well. Signers can create rhythmic closure, for example, by resting or holding a sign after performing several in quick succession. We observed this phenomenon in the percussion song "Boat, Drink, Fun, Enjoy," shown in Example 4.2. In that case, pauses at the ends of two-bar sections indicated a formal break. A change in the established pattern of movement directionality also worked to create a formal boundary on a larger scale, between the two halves of the song.

Signers may also use movement holds or movement emphasis in order to articulate phrase boundaries. For example, in the track "The Letter" (see

Example 4.12), Vuoriheimo ends the first phrase of his rapping with the sign for WORLD, which he signs slowly over two beats. He uses movement emphasis at the end of the third phrase, ending with the sign SHOCKED, which he signs forcefully and emphatically.

Phrase delimitations can also be achieved through the medium of touch. In a video entitled "I Think You're Wonderful—Protactile American Sign Language Version," Divya Goel performs the song "I Think You're Wonderful" by Red Grammer using Pro-Tactile (PT), a tactile sign language developed by and for members of the DeafBlind community in 2007.[11] Her PT interpreter, Jason Eli Schwartz, uses touch to indicate when a new section of the song has begun, and when the song is coming to an end. In an interview with Schwartz, Goel says: "I experience music through touch. Through Pro-Tactile, I was able to know when the next stanza of the song was occurring. Furthermore, with Pro-Tactile, the song becomes a part of me. The song and I have a connection. It rests in my body." When asked to describe the DeafBlind experiences of music, she further explains: "With the DeafBlind community, wow, it is a completely unique experience. We experience the music through touch. DeafBlind individuals can have equivalent experiences to anyone else. Through Pro-Tactile we feel the beat, the flow of the stanzas, whether the music is continuous or has pauses or so forth. This way we can *literally* embody the music" (emphasis original) (Goel and Schwartz 2019).

4.5 Conclusion

Rhythm, pulse, and meter are foundational elements of all music, including sign language music. In this chapter, I have shown that in musical signing, the signer can create a sense of pulse and groove using movements and holds of their hands and body—this pulse may be perceived solely through vision or touch, or it may interact with a background beat created by percussive instruments. I have further shown that the pulse streams created by these movements and holds may be organized into a robust, visually or haptically perceived metrical structure. Within that metrical structure, there can be a great deal of play between the rhythms of the signer's body and the underlying beat, as well as between rhythmic cells and rhyming cells. The rhythms

---

[11] For a thorough explanation of the principles of Pro-Tactile ASL, see granda and Nuccio.

of the body can also help to create musical phrases, demarcated through holds, pauses, or emphasis.

The examples in this chapter—from the 1939 performance of "Boat, Drink, Fun, Enjoy," to Marko Vuoriheimo's "The Letter," to Divya Goel's Pro-Tactile performance of "I Think You're Wonderful"—reveal the resiliency of rhythm in human musical life. Rhythm, pulse, and meter can be heard, seen, and felt, and can be transmitted from performer to audience through sounds, movements, and touch. A video posted by the Perkins School for the Blind shows how rhythm, even more than something that is transmitted from performer to audience, is something that is created together within communities (Perkins School for the Blind 2018). The video shows Jaimi Lard, a DeafBlind woman, learning the Cupid Shuffle. One PT interpreter in front of her and one behind, they create the rhythm and the steps with their bodies, moving gracefully and joyfully to the music. As Divya Goel put it, the music rests in their bodies—the rhythm becomes a part of them.

5

Melodic Techniques

5.1 Introduction

Melody, like rhythm and meter, is typically considered one of the foundational elements of music. As one of the most accessible and familiar aspects
of music, though, melody often eludes our music-theoretical grasp. In their
encyclopedia definitions of melody, both Alexander Ringer and Harold
Powers provide an initial definition that seems straightforward: melody
is "pitched sounds arranged in musical time," or "a coherent succession of
pitches" (Ringer 2015 [1980]; Powers 2015 [1986]). But both definitions
then become complicated by the association of melody with voice; as Powers
writes, melody "is ultimately vocal," and "the line between speech and song is
sometimes very hard to draw" (Powers 2015 [1986]). The concept of melody
is thus intimately linked with the vocal, and with the embodied musical
gesture.

Melody has been of some interest to music theorists since the eighteenth century, playing a central role in the theoretical treatises of authors
like Heinrich Koch, Johann Kirnberger, Johann Mattheson, Joseph Riepel,
and Jean-Jacques Rousseau. For theorists like Riepel, Kirnberger, and Koch,
melody was intimately tied to the concept of phrase structure, punctuation, contrast, and rhythm (Baker 1976). But despite the interest in melody
evinced by these eighteenth-century theorists, Jean-Phillipe Rameau's dec-
laration in the 1722 *Treatise on Harmony*—that "a knowledge of harmony is
sufficient for a complete understanding of music" (Rameau 1971, 3)—nevertheless resulted in the deep neglect of melody in favor of harmony and
form (Samarotto 2009, 1). Following the widespread neglect of melody in the
nineteenth century, however, a handful of theorists have prioritized melody
over harmony.[1]

For Ernst Kurth, music was "melodic-genetic rather than harmonic-
genetic" (Rothfarb 1988, 13). As Lee Rothfarb has noted, Kurth's emphasis

---

[1] For an excellent summary of historical perspectives on melody, see Trippett (2019).

Seeing Voices. Anabel Maler, Oxford University Press. © Oxford University Press 2024.
DOI: 10.1093/oso/9780197601976.003.0006

on melody was both "a reaction against the nineteenth-century overemphasis on harmony" and a response a more general renewed interest in melody around 1900 (Rothfarb 1988, 13). Kurth's theory of melody is, moreover, fundamentally tied to the concept of *motion*. Kurth conceives of melody in terms of a linear path of motion, supported by "a force Kurth calls 'kinetic energy.'" For Kurth, the purest melodies convey "a sense of kinetic energy and dynamic continuum" through sounds, and this type of melody is best exemplified by the music of Baroque composers such as Bach (Rothfarb 1988, 31).

While Kurth's ideas about melody were rooted in psychology and the notion that melodic motion is a "sonic embodiment of psychic energy" (Rothfarb 1988, 41), Leonard Meyer took a major step forward by approaching the topic of melody from the perspective of implication and realization (Meyer 1956, 1973). Building on Meyer's work, Eugene Narmour attempted to ground the implication-realization model within the scholarship on human perception and cognition. His work seeks to explain the principles by which "listeners perceive, structure, and comprehend the vast world of melody" (Narmour 1990, 3) by taking a bottom-up, universal approach, avoiding reference to tonality or to specific musical styles. Narmour's theory rests on two simple hypotheses, based on likeness and difference: that when two elements of a melody (such as form, intervallic pattern, or pitch elements) are similar, the listener will infer repetition, and when form, intervallic patterns or pitch elements of a melody are different, the listener will infer change (Narmour 1990, 3). For Narmour, melody consists essentially and simply in the intervals between successive pitches. As Zbikowski has pointed out, this definition is rather mechanistic and vague, in that it includes any series of pitches, even the arpeggios that open the first prelude in Book I of Bach's *Well-tempered Clavier* (Zbikowski 1993, 179).

All the preceding definitions and theories of melody have one feature in common: they are based on the fundamental notion that musical melody involves pitches, and the intervals between pitches. But what of sign language music, created and perceived in a visual-kinesthetic modality, that does not necessarily involve sounding pitch—is the concept of melody still useful or informative for understanding and analyzing this music? Given that melody is a central component of vocal music, and that melody is closely tied to the concepts of form, phrasing, gesture, and the musical line, it seems that the notion of melody must be central to any theory of sign language music.

5.2 Melody and Sign Language

The pitch-focused nature of most definitions of melody poses challenges when attempting to apply the concept to sign language music, even in the case of simple songs like "Boat, Drink, Fun, Enjoy." Indeed, this has caused problems for scholars like Cripps, Rosenblum, Small, and Supalla, who list the primary elements of Western music—rhythm, timbre, melody, texture, and harmony—and, using Clifford Geertz's Thick Description Model, attempt to find their correlates in signed music (Cripps et al. 2017). The authors draw on Catherine Schmidt-Jones's definition of melody as "a series of notes (of particular pitch and duration) together, one after the other," which leads them to conclude that "music in the signed modality should have organized pitches" (Cripps et al. 2017, 5). In their analysis of the song "Eyes" by Janis E. Cripps, the authors identify pitch as Cripps's hands moving "up and down with rhythmic beats expressed at varying speeds with the two layers of movement," but it is not entirely clear why this type of movement in visual music equates to pitch in auditory music (Cripps et al. 2017, 10). They go on to admit that "identifying fixed pitch and melody was difficult in this clip" (Cripps et al. 2017, 11). The definition of melody as pitch-based causes other issues for the authors in their analysis of "Eyes," as they identify the overlapping of hands as an important element of the second clip they analyze. They wish to make a comparison to "polyphony within the signed modality" but note that "polyphony cannot be further analyzed" because the foundational concepts of melody and harmony have not been adequately identified in signed music (Cripps et al. 2017).

It seems clear that defining melody in terms of pitch is not remotely helpful when it comes to theorizing melody in sign language music; in fact, it hinders our ability to make interesting analytical observations about this music. Instead of focusing on pitch, then, I propose that we return to some more fundamental features of melody that *do* resonate with the visual-kinesthetic modality of sign language music. For while not all parameters of sounding music are relevant to the analysis of sign language music, and vice versa, I nevertheless believe that some concept of melody is indeed present in this context. The melodies of sign language music are distinct from the melodies found in sounding music, however; signed melody does not involve sounding pitches or intervallic patterns, or any one-to-one translation of those concepts into the world of gesture. To better understand the nature of melody in sign language music, we might begin with the popular or everyday definition of melody, as defined by Gino Stefani (1987). We can also explore the broad concepts of conceptual metaphor, embodiment, and the kinetic line, as they apply to both sounding melodies and visual ones. Finally, we ought to understand the distinctions between melody and speech in signed languages, so as to define the limits of what constitutes melody in sign language music.

Gino Stefani identifies a "musicological disease" at work in our existing definitions of music, which either focus entirely on melody as a "succession of pitched sounds" and do not "give an account of most melodic experience," or "slip towards totality" by defining melody as "an amalgam of all musical components" (Stefani 1987, 21). Stefani's cure is to return melody to everyday culture, defining it simply as "that dimension of music which everyone can easily appropriate in many ways: with the voice by singing, whistling or putting words to it; with the body by dancing, marching, etc." (Stefani 1987, 21). Melody, in other words, is "what everybody sings or whistles" (Stefani 1987, 23). This definition is necessarily culturally specific and relies on populations possessing a "*common melodic competence*" (Stefani 1987, 22). In the case of signed music, then, it does not really matter whether existing, hearing-centered definitions of melody accommodate signed melodies; instead, what matters is a shared understanding of what "singable music" is within a given cultural context—in this case, the context of Deaf culture. The features of such "singable music" need not be pitch-based at all; instead, Stefani highlights features such as "easy to listen to, to recognize, to memorize and repeat; a line, a single voice; a figure against a background, a prominent element; something gratifying, sweet, involving emotions" (Stefani 1987, 23).

A crucial element of melody is thus the vocal, the singable. We have already established that there exists a signing voice, and most important for our understanding of melody, a signing voice that *sings* (see Chapter 3). The remaining step we must take is to reimagine what Stefani calls the "oral matrix of melody" for a signing singing voice, rather than an oral one. Stefani outlines four elements of oral behavior (utterance of a single voice, periodic duration of breathing, curve or normal oral emission [rise-growth-fall], and continuous movement in the space between pitches) and six elements of the singing voice (constancy of pitch within a syllable, medium register, limited range, flowing line, relatively slow movement, ease, euphony) as making up the "oral matrix of melody" or "melodic vocal minimum" for oral singing. Some of these may apply, with few modifications, to a signing singing voice as well. We might define the four elements of signing melodic behavior as follows: utterance of a single voice, periodic duration, curve (rise-growth-fall), and continuous movement in space. Five of the elements of the singing voice are easily translated to the signing voice as well: medium register (normal signing space), limited range, flowing line, relatively slow movement, and ease. Stefani further identifies the motive, "the smallest melodic unit," as a crucial element of creating popular melodies, and this concept is also relevant within a signed musical context.

Let's return for a moment to the song "Boat, Drink, Fun, Enjoy." This song is usually described as a classic example of what Bahan calls "percussion signing," which often uses the rhythmic pattern "one-two, one-two-three." But, as I noted in Chapter 4, there is more to this short example than its rhythmic pattern. The directionality of the movement and location of signs in the signing space create a sense of musical line, or the progression of one musical object to another. In ASL poetry, space is often discussed in terms of the line, which Bauman argues "carries a generating capacity, an expressiveness all its own whose speed, tension, length, direction and duration construct and disperse a particular energy" (Bauman 2006a, 104). These lines "gesture through time and space, controlling and dispersing energy as a dancer does" (Bauman 2006a, 107). In sign language music, kinetic lines play an especially important role, since the signer produces not only what Bauman calls "precise grammatical and visual images" through sign, but musical images as well (Bauman 2006a, 107). The musical image produced by the artist depends on how she manipulates the signing space through movements and holds.

In Western acoustic music, we already use spatial metaphors to describe pitch relationships, as Zbikowski has pointed out in his work on musical metaphor (Zbikowski 2002). Using words like "high" and "low" to describe pitch, for example, reflects the conceptual metaphor PITCH RELATIONSHIPS ARE RELATIONSHIPS IN VERTICAL SPACE. We might therefore understand one of the conceptual metaphors at work in signed music as involving a blend of the domains of physical signing space and melodic lines. The resulting conceptual metaphor is MELODIC RELATIONSHIPS ARE RELATIONSHIPS IN SIGNING SPACE. It's important to note that the relationships in signing space may not be vertical relationships—in fact, I have observed that while hearing signers do privilege relationships in vertical space to represent musical pitch, Deaf signers make use of the vertical plane *and* the horizontal plane, thus taking advantage of the entire signing space.

This type of cross-domain mapping, in which the target domain (music) is different from the source domain (physical space), is foundational to our understanding of melody, as Steve Larson has argued (Larson 1997–1998). Specifically, Larson explores the metaphor of "musical forces," which he views as a combination of two metaphors: "first, that MUSIC IS MOTION; and second, that MUSIC IS PURPOSEFUL" (Larson 1997–1998, 57). These fundamental conceptual metaphors for understanding melody align neatly with my own definition of music, outlined in the Introduction to this volume, as "culturally defined, purposeful movement." The concept of music as rooted in motion also resonates with Ernst Kurth's melody-centered, kinetic theory of music. The notion that we experience music as purposeful motion means that understanding how signers embody melodic lines in their music is not only important, but truly fundamental to our understanding of human musical experiences more broadly.

It will also be important to understand what distinguishes "melody" from "speech" in sign language music. There has been a great deal of interest in the relationship between melody and speech, and how these are processed by the human brain. As Diana Deutsch's speech-to-song illusion makes clear, a listener's identification of a stimulus as either speech or melody does not necessarily depend upon some stable set of characteristics (Deutsch, Henthorn, and Lapidis 2011). Taking this notion a step further, Edwin Li, in his development of the concept of a "speech-melody" complex in Cantonese popular songs, proposes that instead of asking *what* speech and melody are, we can profit from "a hermeneutic approach that asks *when* they are" (Li 2021, 2.9). In asking and answering the questions "when is speech?" and "when is melody," Li thus urges us to consider not the stable properties of speech or melody, but "what they had been doing as sound before they became speech/melody, and what they together do and will do, with and to oneself, and what one brings to them" (Li 2021, 2.9). In my analysis of sign language music, I take up Li's perspective of prioritizing the context and impact of signing, rather than attempting to define some properties of signing as speech-like and others as melody-like. In a study conducted by Listman, Mangelsdorf, and myself, it became clear that the context and viewer's interpretation of a signed performance had an enormous impact on whether they interpreted the signing as poetic or musical in nature (Mangelsdorf, Listman, and Maler 2021). In that study, we showed participants both translated signed songs (performed as music) and translated signed lyrics (performed as poetry). The hearing participants rated the signed songs as more musical than the signed lyrics, but the Deaf and hard-of-hearing participants rated both the signed lyrics and the signed songs as more musical than the hearing group. This suggests that musicality is defined differently by these different groups, and that the context and interpretation of the perceiver is crucial.

Nevertheless, there are some aspects of signing that are not melodic in nature. As I have already established, melody in sign language music involves the directed and purposeful movement of the body through the signing space. This movement might involve any part of the body. Not all movements are directed in signed music, however; for example, facial expressions that accompany signs and express affect are not directed movements, and they are thus better understood as a component of vocal quality or expressivity than as a component of melody. The same is true of eye gaze, which tends to be steady rather than dynamic and moving.

In sum, melody in sign language music is distinct from melody in sounding music, and is defined within the cultural context of Deaf and signing culture more broadly. It involves the directed, purposeful movement of the body through the signing space, which uses movements and holds to create dynamic, kinetic lines.

5.3 Melody in Signed Performances of "The Star-Spangled Banner"

To make clear the nature of melody in sign language music, we must know what defines common melodic competence: what, in a signed song, is that which everybody sings? In the preceding section, I proposed that most of the elements that Stefani lists in his oral matrix of melody might form the basis of a signed matrix of melody. But it remains to be seen whether these elements are, indeed, shared among a community of signers and that melodic lines in sign language music are created by the body's movement through the signing space. If there is indeed a concept of melody in signed songs—that which is shared, a common melodic competence—then we ought to be able to see some shared features across multiple versions of the same song. Furthermore, these performers ought to involve intentional use of the physical signing space in order to convey melodic relationships. Whatever features of the singing signing voice are shared across those versions would represent a common melodic competence.

One song that has been signed many times, by many performers, over many years is the US national anthem, "The Star-Spangled Banner," making it an excellent test case for the concept of melody in signed music. "The Star-Spangled Banner" was first filmed in American Sign Language in 1901. In fact, one might argue that this performance of "The Star-Spangled Banner" represents the first time that music of any kind *ever* appeared on film, given that its filming preceded the sound era of film. In the early 1990s, there began a tradition at the annual Super Bowl of including a signed performance of "The Star-Spangled Banner" alongside the oral performance. Beginning in 1992, therefore, we have a fairly large corpus of thirty unique signed performances of a single song for comparison. Unfortunately, however, we do not have access to many of the full signed performances, due to mainstream television networks typically highlighting the oral performance at the expense of the signed one, often showing only brief clips of signed performances. There are, however, extended videos available of many of these performances, as well as additional interpretations of the song that have been independently posted to websites like YouTube by Deaf musicians outside the context of the Super Bowl.

Just as Deaf performers are often pushed aside by mainstream television networks in their Super Bowl broadcasts, so too have they been largely overlooked in musicological commentary on the history and cultural connotations of performances of the US national anthem. One fascinating example of this erasure appears in the liner notes to the two-CD set "Poets & Patriots: A Tuneful History of 'The Star-Spangled Banner,'" written by Mark Clague (Clague 2014). The CD set's cover features a photo of seven boys and girls, shown in the midst of signing. The CD booklet identifies the photo's subjects as follows: "students from St. Rita's School for the Deaf (Cincinnati, OH) perform the *Banner* in sign language, 1918" (Clague 2014, 1). Yet the liner notes make no mention of the signed performance of "The Star-Spangled Banner" featured on the cover, nor of any other signed renditions of the work. The tokenizing of signed performances in this way is an insidious form of erasure, implying that there is little to say about the tradition of signed performances of "The Star-Spangled Banner" or other songs.

Signed performances of "The Star-Spangled Banner," which form a rich vocal tradition, deserve equal critical attention to their orally performed counterparts. When we think about oral performances of "The Star-Spangled Banner," we recognize that there are enormous variations across performances. One might compare, for example, two performances of the national anthem by Marvin Gaye in 1983 and Renée Fleming in 2014. In most respects, these two performances could not be more dissimilar: they contrast dramatically in their style (funky as opposed to operatic), tempo, orchestration and size of ensemble, rhythms, and vocal embellishments. At the same time, we can still recognize that these performances share a common melody: that which everyone sings.

Now let us consider three signed performances of "The Star-Spangled Banner." In ⏵ Video Example 5.1, you can see three videos playing simultaneous performances: the performer on the bottom left is Rosa Lee Timm, in the center is Marlee Matlin, and on the bottom right is Warren "Wawa" Snipe. Each performer is singing the same section of the national anthem, beginning with the line "And the rockets' red glare." Like their oral counterparts, these performances vary in tempo, meter, embellishments, ensemble size, style, and so forth; yet, as I will demonstrate, they share a common melody. Each performer has their own style of performance, and their performances are often influenced by the style of the oral performer when they are signing the anthem at the Super Bowl.[2] However, we can still observe commonalities in their use of the signing space to create dynamic horizontal and vertical melodic lines.

In the following, I compare ten different signed performances of "The Star-Spangled Banner" for which full videos are available in an effort to define the principal features of melody in signed music. The ten performers are Marlee Matlin (Super Bowl 1993), Heather Whitestone (Super Bowl 1995), Phyllis Frelich (Super Bowl 1998), John Maucere (Super Bowl 2013), Treshelle Edmond (Super Bowl 2015), Aaron Loggins (Super Bowl 2019), Christine Sun Kim (Super Bowl 2020), Warren "Wawa" Snipe (Super Bowl 2021), Candace Jones (Atlanta Area School for the Deaf, 2018), and Rosa Lee Timm (Texas School for the Deaf, 2018). I first explore the elements that characterize signing melodic behavior before identifying the elements that define a melodic signing voice.

---

[2] It is also important to note that the context of the performance may impact aspects of the signing: since these performances take place in large stadiums, the movements of the signers may be exaggerated compared to a performance that takes place in a smaller venue.

Elements of Signing Melodic Behavior

I have already identified four elements of signing melodic behavior based on Stefani's oral matrix of melody: utterance of a single voice, periodic duration, curve (rise-growth-fall), and continuous movement in space. All the performances of "The Star-Spangled Banner" listed above have one signing performer, and thus meet the criteria "utterance of a single voice."[3] We must, therefore, explore whether these performances indeed feature periodic duration (akin to Stefani's periodic duration of breath), a rise-growth-fall curve, and continuous movement in space.

Periodic Duration

Sign languages are not limited by the periodicity of breathing, as they do not involve the use of the oral voice, but like all languages, they make use of patterns of stress, intonation, and rhythm—in other words, prosody.[4] Prosodically marking an element of a signed language might involve making changes in timing, including pauses, while intonational elements are conveyed using facial expression and head position (Sandler 2010). One might imagine, then, that the marking of phrases in sign language music would involve changes in timing, such as slowing down, pausing, or holding signs.

All ten performers use changes in timing in order to create a sense of periodic duration, or phrasing, in their interpretations of "The Star-Spangled Banner." Specifically, they often sign more slowly and expansively at the ends of phrases. For example, at the end of the first line of the song, "O say can you see," Whitestone signs SEE over four beats, while each preceding sign took only one beat to perform (▶ Video Example 5.2). At the end of the phrase "whose broad stripes and bright stars," Matlin, in her 1993 performance, signs STARS much more slowly than the preceding signs in the phrase (▶ Video Example 5.3). Kim's interpretation in 2020, while grammatically very different from Matlin's, also slows down at the end of this phrase as she deliberately signs CL-5-(claw): "stars on flag" to indicate the many stars on the American flag (▶ Video Example 5.4). In Snipe's interpretation in 2021,

---

[3] There have been Super Bowl performances of the national anthem using ensembles, and there are many examples of signed music performed by multiple performers, but it is generally possible to identify which is the prominent melodic line. In ensemble performances at the Super Bowl, all of the signers tend to perform in unison.

[4] For more on prosody in signed languages, see Dachkovsky and Sandler (2009); Nespor and Sandler (1999); Sandler (1999a, 1999b, 2010); Winston (2000).

he signs WATCH very slowly, representing those watching the battle over the ramparts (◉ Video Example 5.5).

Often, when performers slow down, they do so by holding a single, moving sign. This is true in all of the preceding examples of holds: in each case, the performer signs the necessary movement more slowly than they perform the other signs in each phrase. Performers may also hold a non-moving sign, as Frelich does when representing people watching over the ramparts (◉ Video Example 5.6).

The most extreme form of phrase marking is the pause: instead of moving slowly and fluidly through a single sign, or holding a stationary sign, a performer may choose to stop signing briefly for emphasis. All ten performances I studied reserve this form of phrase marking for the climactic lines, "and the rocket's red glare, the bombs bursting in air / gave proof through the night that our flag was still there." Loggins, for example, pauses dramatically on the word "there" in the English text, on the sign HERE, or while indexing the flag, as do Kim, Frelich, Snipe, Maucere, and Edmond. Timm also pauses on HERE, and additionally pauses on the sign STAY (◉ Video Example 5.7). The exceptions are Matlin, Jones, and Whitestone, who both slowly hold their sign for the waving flag instead of pausing emphatically.

Rise-Growth-Fall Curve

While orally produced melodies can be understood metaphorically as involving movement up and down in vertical space, the use of space in sign language is not limited to the vertical dimension. Rather, sign languages are three-dimensional, and signers can move horizontally as well as vertically within the signing space. In order to identify the particular melodic pattern of movement that characterizes a given signed piece of music, then, we ought to look at patterns of movements up and down, right and left, and forward and backward (i.e., away from the signer and toward the signer) in the signing space.

Indeed, the interpretations of "The Star-Spangled Banner" I studied use similar movement paths to navigate the signing space. This can partially be explained by the grammatical use of space in ASL, which uses body, head, and eye gaze shifting in order to index different pieces of information, or different characters in a story. In the case of "The Star-Spangled Banner," for instance, the flag is almost always signed to the signer's right, and the battle between the British and the Americans is often represented by shifting from left to right (Maucere's and Edmond's interpretations are exceptions, placing the flag to the left instead of the right). Not all the similarities between interpretations have solely grammatical explanations, though, indicating that the use of space is still an important element of melody in sign language music.

Typically, signers begin the song by signing in front of their body before moving to the right on SEE, indexing the flag. The different interpretations of the phrase "the dawn's early light" often include the depiction of the sun rising, a sign in which the right arm sweeps from the left side of the signing space to the right. The hailing of the flag similarly takes place to the right of the signer's body. Most signers represent the "twilight's last gleaming" as the sun setting, which reverses the direction of the sign for "sunrise." We can thus see a gentle, consistent movement between the right and left sides of the signing space in the opening of the song—they are fairly evenly represented.

When signing about the flag, as I have already mentioned, most signers use the right side of the signing space, as exemplified by interpretations of the lyrics "whose broad stripes." "Bright stars" is usually placed more toward the center of the signing space, representing where the stars on the American flag are located from the perspective of the signer. In interpreting the "perilous fight," most signers expand their signing space and move between the right and left, dramatizing the fight between the British and the Americans.

The signing space continues to expand with the lyrics "O'er the ramparts we watched," where most signers start to incorporate motion forward, toward the audience. Most signers move from left to right as they represent the watchers looking over the ramparts, before turning to the right to represent the flag "gallantly streaming."

At the climactic line "And the rocket's red glare, the bombs bursting in air," most signers begin to expand the signing space diagonally and vertically, with the rockets moving from left to right and from the bottom of the signing space to the top, and the bombs usually bursting in air higher in the signing space. The signer's eye gaze typically traces the paths of the rockets and bombs, looking upward in space. The line "gave proof through the night that our flag was still there" typically involves motion across the entire signing space, left to right, as well as forward.

At the penultimate line of the song, the right side of the signing space typically wins out, with the star-spangled banner clearly indexed to the right, and with the eye gaze following. For the final, triumphant line, signers typically return to face the center, moving outward and upward, often dramatically, on the sign BRAVE.

To summarize, in typical interpretations of "The Star-Spangled Banner," the signer's movements take up more of the signing space (in all three dimensions) over the course of the song. Signers typically start and end the song by signing toward the center, and move smoothly between the right and left sides of the signing space in the middle of the song. The signers' movements also tend to become larger in the second half of the song. In her interpretation of the song's final line, for example, Kim even crouches to make the movement from low to high on BRAVE more dramatic and expansive (⊙ Video Example 5.8). Similarly, Snipe leans forward as he begins to sign BRAVE, repeating it as he slowly rises back up and triumphantly raises his fists into the air and holding the sign (⊙ Video Example 5.9). Of course, these observations are generalizations across ten different signed performances of the song, and there are naturally variations across the performances as well. Nevertheless, there is a clear pattern of rise-growth-fall across all performances, in which the signing space opens up slowly until the climactic and expansive line "And the rocket's red glare, the bombs bursting in air," before settling back into the right side of the signing space, and finally returning to the center of the signing space for the song's final line. Furthermore, all of the performers move continuously through the signing space, the final necessary element of the signing melodic voice.

Is this a melody? If I were to combine sections of an orally produced melody, transposing them to be in the same key and octave, the melody would act as a through line that tied the performances together. One might ask whether the same is true of a signed melody. ⊙ Video Example 5.10 combines several different performances of "The Star-Spangled Banner," revealing a consistent melodic shape throughout these varied instantiations of the same song.

Elements of the Melodic Signing Voice

In Chapter 3, I argued that there is a clear philosophical and musicological foundation that underpins the notion of a signing singing voice, and I identified six key facets of a signing voice: prosody, facial expressions, mouth morphemes, eye gaze and movement, body movements, and communality. All these elements contribute to what we might call the popular signing voice, the other half of our signing matrix of melody, which is characterized by medium register (normal signing space), limited range, flowing line, relatively slow movement, and ease.

Most of the ten performances of "The Star-Spangled Banner" I have analyzed thus far do not seem to best exemplify these characteristics, given that they frequently include movements outside the signing space. However, it is important to note that these live Super Bowl performances took place in large stadiums, and while their orally singing counterparts were aided by the use of microphones, most of the signed performances were not afforded the same technological aid. Thus, many of the performers used larger and more exaggerated movements in order to be visible to their audience. I will therefore focus on the performances that were broadcast using picture-in-picture (Whitestone, Frelich), where the signer was placed next to the vocal performer (Matlin), or where the performance did not take place in the Super Bowl setting (Jones, Timm), which exemplify a more typical melodic signing voice.

Medium Register

Typically, in sign languages developed within Deaf communities around the world, signs take place on or in front of the body, "in the area between the waist and the head" (Bauer 2014, 123), which Klima and Bellugi define as the "signing space" (Klima and Bellugi 1979). As Anastasia Bauer notes, this space extends vertically "from the waist to the space above the signer's head and transversely from the elbow to elbow when both arms are kept loosely bent" (Bauer 2014, 123).[5] The use of the signing space is grammatically important in sign languages, since as Carol Padden notes, "the space around and on the signer's body is exploited at all levels," including contrasting similar signs by location, marking verb agreement, and distinguished discourse topics (Padden 1990, 118).[6]

Sign language music exhibits the same use of the signing space as everyday signed discourse. In the signed interpretations of "The Star-Spangled Banner" by Whitestone, Frelich, Matlin, Jones, and Timm, the signers make use of the vertical space between the waist and just above the head, and the horizontal space from elbow to elbow. We can note that, for the most part,

---

[5] There are variations in the use of signing space across different sign languages, as well as across dialects of the same sign language. For example, the signing space of Black American Sign Language appears to be larger than that of ASL more broadly (McCaskill et al. 2011).
[6] See also Liddell (1990, 1995).

the signers keep their elbows loosely bent to stay within the normal signing space, without fully extending their arms in any direction.

At the same time, melodic signing does sometimes move outside the conventional boundaries of the signing space for expressive purposes, as does poetic signing (Ormsby 1995). For example, when signing the lines "And the rocket's red glare, the bombs bursting in air," Whitestone moves outside the conventional signing space and into the space above the head. The same is true when she signs FREE on the line "O'er the land of the free": she extends the sign outward to the right and left, expanding the horizontal signing space. Finally, as is typical of most signed performances of "The Star-Spangled Banner," Whitestone extends her arms fully upward on the final sign BRAVE, fully expanding the upward portion of the signing space and moving well beyond the conventional signed space (▶ Video Example 5.11).

The expressive use of non-conventional signing space seems typical of sign language music historically as well, based on the available recordings of signed music from the early part of the twentieth century. The first recording of "The Star-Spangled Banner," filmed in 1902 and performed by an unknown Deaf woman, shows the signs for FLAG and ROCKET moving above the signer's head, extending the vertical signing space in a manner very similar to more recent interpretations of the song (▶ Video Example 5.12). We can see a similarly expansive use of the signing space in a recitation of the song "Home Sweet Home" by Johanna H. McClusky, filmed in 1930 at a convention of the National Association of the Deaf in Buffalo, New York, revealing that this phenomenon is not exclusive to the specific melodic shape of "The Star-Spangled Banner" but was a melodic technique that was broadly used in signed music.[7]

Limited Range

While musical signers do sometimes move outside the normal signing space for expressive purposes, they nevertheless tend to stay mainly within the normal signing space. This has the effect of limiting the range of melodic signing as well. However, we can also understand "limited range" to refer to a limited range of movement types within a particular song. As I have already discussed, the interpretations of "The Star-Spangled Banner" heavily feature transverse movement in the signing space throughout the song,

---

[7] See the following archival video in the Gallaudet video archives: https://ssl.gallaudet.edu/video library/?embed=19198 (at 07:00).

while climactic moments feature vertical movements from low to high in the signing space. Movements from high to low, for example, are not typical of the melody of "The Star-Spangled Banner."

Flowing Lines and Ease

In ASL melodies, flowing lines may be understood to emerge from fluency in ASL and fluidity in how signs are produced and in the transitions between signs. Linda Lupton identifies several features that characterize fluency in ASL: use of ASL word order (as opposed to English or English-like grammatical structures); ability to "create a picture" in signs; smooth, steady, and clear transitions between signs (as opposed to choppy, hesitant, or jerky movements); relaxed, good posture; and use of facial expression, body movement, and eye contact (Lupton 1998). In signed music, we can thus surmise that fluency of signing and fluidity of movement through the signing space will be important for the creation of flowing melodic lines. We can note this fluidity in signed performances of "The Star-Spangled Banner," such as the one performed by Jones (▶ Video Example 5.13). Note how, at the opening of the song, each sign moves smoothly into the next, without any hesitation or jerky movements. We can also note how Jones uses open, smiling facial expressions to convey a sense of awe or wonder when portraying the American flag, contrasting with her furrowed brow as she represents the "perilous fight." Her relaxed posture contributes to the sense of a flowing line, as well to as a general sense of ease in the performance.

Johanna McCluskey's 1930 performance of "Home Sweet Home" provides an historical example of the importance of flowing lines in signed music. In her performance, each sign flows smoothly and fluidly into the next. She also uses many circular motions that move side to side in the signing space, as well as emphasizing movements forward (away from her body) and back (toward her body). These fluid circular movements create a gentle rocking effect in her melodic signing.

Relatively Slow Movement

The final element that characterizes the melodic signing voice is relatively slow movement. Ursula Bellugi and Susan Fischer found that, in a comparison between spoken English and ASL by Children of Deaf Adults (CODAs), a sign in ASL takes longer to produce on average than a word in a spoken language, but a proposition takes about the same amount of time to produce in either language (Bellugi and Fischer 1972). But is melodic signing typically produced more slowly than conversational signing in ASL? Ormsby notes that poetic signing is typically produced in a "slower and more fastidious manner" than regular signing, and it appears that the same is true of melodic signing (Ormsby 1995). As I noted in Chapter 4, a study conducted by Mangelsdorf, Listman, and Maler suggested that, when watching a piece of signed music performed either as a poem or as a piece of music, both Deaf and hearing participants found that the signs in the musical version were slower than in the poetic version of the song (Mangelsdorf, Listman, and Maler 2021).

5.4 Case Study: Rosa Lee Timm, "Blown Away"

Having established that melodic lines exist in signed music, and that they are based on the directed, purposeful movements of the signer through the signing space, we can now embark on a more thorough analysis of a performer's use of expressive melodic lines in a single piece of signed music: Rosa Lee Timm's interpretation of Carrie Underwood's song "Blown Away." The song tells of a tornado bearing down on the protagonist's "sin-filled" house in Oklahoma, where she lives with her alcoholic father (described as a cruel figure), as her mother is deceased. The story is told in the third person, and the song's form is typical of the popular genre, consisting of an instrumental introduction, two verses, and several iterations and fragmentations of the chorus, which increases in intensity each time it is repeated.

Timm's interpretation of the song begins with her facing the camera directly, as indicated by the first SignWriting symbols in Example 5.1 (▶ Video Example 5.14). Although her head is lowered at first, she soon raises it to sign directly toward the audience, embodying the story's protagonist. As she signs LIGHTNING come-through-skies her eyes gaze upward, and as she signs LOOKING her eyes follow her hands, moving right to left and slowly downward until she is staring directly into the camera. She points to the right side of the signing space to index the tornado, before moving the sign, and her eye gaze, to the center once more, staring directly at her audience. Timm thus establishes that the song's main character signs to the front, while the tornado is indexed to her right side. When she describes the character's father, a "mean old mister," she signs toward the right side of the signing space, with the corners of her mouth turned down, while the signs about her mother, "an

Example 5.1 Score of Rosa Lee Timm's cover of "Blown Away" (Carrie Underwood), verse 1.

angel in the ground," are located to the left side of the signing space, and her expression turns to one of longing. At the end of the first verse, the sign Timm uses to indicate the destructive tornado is again signed to her right.

The beginning of the prechorus is marked by Timm turning to face the camera directly again as she signs NOT ENOUGH RAIN O-K-L-A ("there's not enough rain in Oklahoma") with a neutral facial expression (▶ Video Example 5.15). She then turns to the right, the signing space of the father, and her facial expression turns to one of disgust (lips pulled back and down, nose wrinkled, brows lowered and furrowed) as she signs CLEAN SIN + OUT-of HOUSE ("to wash the sins out of that house"). Timm repeats this pattern for the second pair of lines in the prechorus, facing forward to repeat NOT ENOUGH RAIN O-K-L-A and to her right to sign WIND take-nails-out PAST/long-ago.

In the chorus (Example 5.2, ▶ Video Example 5.15), Timm begins by facing the camera once again, but now her facial expressions are no longer neutral: her brow is furrowed, her eyes wide and intense, and her mouth opens as if screaming as she signs SHATTER EVERY WINDOW UNTIL ALL house-CRUMBLE. She continues to locate signs about the crumbling house to her right side, associating them with the signing space she established for the father in the first verse. As the chorus builds to a climax, Timm expands the signing space, her signing beginning to take over the left side as she signs BLOW-AWAY TWISTER. She seems almost to be embodying the storm, sweeping away the previously established signing spaces for FATHER, MOTHER, and even the protagonist herself. Timm's dramatic and intense facial expressions, and freer use of the signing space, contrast markedly with the more reserved use of signing space seen in the verse. We can also see a slightly expanded use of the vertical dimension, as Timm crouches slightly on the sign BLOWN-AWAY. We are left, however, with a mere echo of the voice as the chorus comes to an end, and consequently Timm's signing dies down without fully taking over the signing space.

The second verse finds the protagonist making the decision to leave her father passed out on the couch while she locks herself in the cellar, allowing the wind and rain to destroy the house (▶ Video Example 5.16). Timm begins by facing the camera, now with her eyes round and wide as she notices sirens coming closer: HEARD SIREN + getting-CLOSER/NEARER *looks around*. She looks to her right and behind her, indicating that emergency services are approaching from that direction. Her facial expression is apprehensive and unsure as she looks around. She indicates that the protagonist

Example 5.2 Score of Rosa Lee Timm's cover of "Blown Away" (Carrie Underwood), chorus.

Example 5.2 Continued

begins to run forward, a panicked expression on her face (RUN-with-legs), before noticing her father passed out on the couch (FATHER DRUNK PASSED-OUT) on her left side. She looks to her left with concern for a moment, but her expression quickly changes: she faces the camera resolutely, her face showing her disdain for the father and sudden resolve. Her expression changes to a smile as she signs I GO-AHEAD BASEMENT KEY-locked (she locked herself in the cellar). Her movements are now precise and calm, her signing space restricted, indicating that she feels in control on the words I CALL-it SWEET REVENGE.

The second verse is followed immediately by the chorus, without an intervening prechorus (⯈ Video Example 5.17). In this iteration of the chorus, Timm's facial expressions intensify: on the signs BLOWN-AWAY/ DESTROYED GO-AHEAD ("'til it's all blown away"), her eyes squeeze shut, her nose wrinkles, and her upper lip and the corners of her mouth pull back as her clawed hands squeeze into fists. Timm begins to expand the signing space during the chorus as well. She expands the vertical dimension of her melodic line by looking up and tilting her head back on iterations of BLOWN-AWAY/DESTROYED. When she mimes *blow on hands 'til nothing there,* she also expands the signing space to the right side: we can imagine, as perceivers, the line of her signing extending from her mouth and off into the distance on her right. Finally, on the line EVERY TEAR, DRINK, PROBLEM BLOW-AWAY/disappear-into-the-wind ("Every tear-soaked whiskey memory blown away"), Timm's hands move so far to the right that they extend beyond the reach of the camera, a dramatic expansion of the horizontal line of her melody.

The chorus is followed by a prechorus-chorus pair, after which the chorus begins to fragment into repetitions of the words "blown away." The intensity of the sounding music builds slowly throughout this final section. As the chorus builds in intensity and begins to fragment, the melody becomes more melismatic, prompting Timm's gestures to become more expansive and dramatic; her movements begin to take over the left side of the signing space, where she located the father's signs in the second verse. Eventually, Timm not only uses the sign for tornado to encompass the entire signing space twice over, she also transforms her body into a twister, twirling wildly as the music's intensity rises (▶ Video Example 5.18). Timm also expands the vertical space of her signing even more, by alternately raising her signs and tilting her body backward to expand the upper range of her signing (on the sign TWISTER), and crouching to lower the normal signing space (e.g., on the signs HOUSE CRUMBLE). The dramatic expansion of Timm's horizontal and vertical lines cannot adequately be explained by referencing the narrative arc of Underwood's song. These changes occur over repeated iterations of the chorus with no further narrative developments, but the audience nonetheless experiences a marked increase in the intensity of the music, both heard and seen.

At the end of the song, Timm's TORNADO sign seems to shrink, until her hands are pressed close together, once again compressing the vertical dimension that she had previously expanded (▶ Video Example 5.19). Her facial expressions move from intense anger and ecstasy, as we saw in the verses and choruses, to an expression of horror. Just as she expanded her horizontal and vertical lines while the song's intensity increased, Timm now closes them off as the protagonist seems to realize what she has done, staring out at the viewer as the music abruptly ends. Timm thus uses the signing space in a rich and multifaceted manner to create musical lines that increase in intensity over the course of the song, and that leave us with a new interpretation of the song's ending. While the second and final verse of the original song ends on an exultant note, calling the protagonist's actions "sweet revenge," Timm's cover of "Blown Away" suggests instead that the protagonist feels horror and remorse at her actions. Timm's melodic lines in "Blown Away" are furthermore completely independent from those of Underwood: they have a shape and character of their own, and need not be experienced alongside the sounding music to have an enormous emotional impact on the viewer.

5.5 Signed Polyphony

If there is melody in sign language music, as I have argued thus far, then it stands to reason that there may also be the concept of counterpoint, or polyphony more generally. Cripps, Rosenblum, Small, and Supalla raise the question of polyphony with respect to the song "Eyes" by Janis E. Cripps, in which they identify the overlapping of hands as a potential "allusion to polyphony within the signed modality" (Cripps et al. 2017, 12). They note, however, that they cannot analyze this polyphony further because melody has not yet been adequately defined in this genre. However, with our new understanding of melody in the visual-kinesthetic modality, perhaps we can begin to better understand the polyphonic aspects of a piece like "Eyes." The authors describe how, between 00:01:26 and 00:01:49, Cripps uses "5" handshapes in two layers: one further away from her body and one closer to her body that also involves her face. In the first layer, in black and white, her "palms face down and away from her as they rise and fall," while in the second layer, in color, her "5" hands face outward, "then towards her and then outward and inward again" as she gazes at her hands (Cripps et al. 2017, 11). Based on the preceding discussion of the elements of signed melody, one could certainly argue that the use of different movement types, movement paths, use of space, and use of nonmanual markers (i.e. facial expressions) in each layer does indeed suggest there are two distinct visual melodies at work in this clip, thus creating an effect of visual polyphony.

We can see a straightforward example of signed polyphony in an archival video of the Gallaudet University Christian signing choir The Joyful Sign, entitled "A Time for Music." In their interpretation of the 1981 song "Love Is Spreading over the World" by Neil Sedaka, a soloist signs in the center of the stage on a podium, supported by two backup singers who are placed behind her. In front of her, on ground level, are two choruses, each consisting of four signers. The soloist signs the main melody, while her backup singers either sway back and forth or reinforce the soloist's melody. When the soloist signs the lyrics "hear it in the trees as the breeze is blowing," the chorus of four signers on the soloist's right does not sign the same melody as the soloist. Rather, two of the female signers hold the sign for TREE, a central male signer holds up his rounded arms above his head to represent the sun, and the final female signer signs BLOW, as if she is the wind blowing through the trees. As the soloist signs the lyrics "see it in the fields where the grass is growing," the chorus to her left also signs a new melody. The male signers on the outside edges of the group hold out their flat forearms, palms down in a closed 5 handshape, to represent the fields, while the two female signers stand between them and show the grass growing upward from the fields, using flat O handshapes, with the palms facing inward, moving upward and spreading their fingers into open 5 handshapes as in the sign for GROW.

The choral setting of "Love Is Spreading over the World" performed by The Joyful Sign reflects the communal and reciprocal aspects of signed music more broadly. Even the straightforward "Boat, Drink, Fun, Enjoy" is a fundamentally communal, choral piece of music, where the audience's participation is a welcome and expected element of the performance.

5.6 Conclusion

Although it is a fundamental parameter of many kinds of music, melody seems difficult to analyze in a visual-kinesthetic modality because visual instantiations of melody are generally undertheorized. This chapter situates the signed melody within Stefani's notion of "common melodic competence," as well as theories of embodiment and kinetic lines. Ultimately, I define signed melody as the directed, purposeful movement of the body through the signing space, which uses movements and holds to create dynamic, kinetic lines. I then establish a "signed matrix of melody," based on Stefani's "oral matrix of melody," which is characterized by four elements of signing melodic behavior (utterance of a single voice, periodic duration, curve, and continuous movement in space) and five elements of the popular signing voice (normal signing space, limited range, flowing line, relatively slow movement, and ease). By comparing different signed interpretations of one song in the visual-kinesthetic modality, I reveal how these shared characteristics work to define a signed melodic line. Finally, I show how we might use our understanding of these shared melodic features to analyze more complex melodies, to show how signed melodies can express meaning, and to understand how signed songs can make use of polyphony as well as single-line melodies.

The melodies created in signed music are independent of those that appear in sounding music. One might assume that, in the case of a signed song that is based on an existing piece of sounding music, like the national anthem or Carrie Underwood's "Blown Away," the peaks and valleys of a signed melody would correspond with those of the sounding melody. As I have demonstrated, however, this is not the case: signed melodies have their own shape and momentum, regardless of the presence of a sounding melody.

The development of a robust theory of visual and kinesthetic melody is important not only for furthering our knowledge about sign language music, but for our understanding of melodic music more broadly. The features of signed melody that I have identified may be adapted to understand other kinds of visual-kinesthetic melodies that do not make use of a signed language, such as in visual scores or dance.

6

Meaning and Form

I always use the same three elements: rhythm, texture, and timbre,
meaning how I express myself with the music. So I do that by using
my language, like my facial expressions, positioning, my body language, handshapes, to reflect those elements.

—Rosa Lee Timm

6.1 Introduction

Music moves us. In other words, music expertly elicits emotional responses
in those perceiving it, and the meaning of music is thus intimately tied to its
affective capacity. Moreover, the music's ability to move us, to invoke emotional responses, is grounded in our embodied experiences: in "forcing an
encounter between mind and body," D. Robert DeChaine writes, music
creates a liminal space "charged with affect and fraught with tension"
(DeChaine 2002, 81).

Watching the performance of a signed song like "Boat, Drink, Fun,
Enjoy"—the melodic, rhythmic, and metric structure of which I have
explored throughout this volume—makes clear that signed music is a site
of encounter between mind and body that invites others to participate, to
move their bodies in making music together. The video focuses on two
main performers, but the audience sings or claps along with them, moved
by the music. But how does a song like "Boat, Drink, Fun, Enjoy" create
musical meaning for its performers and audiences? How does it act as a site
of affective engagement? In the video, one of the main performers, George
Kannapell, claps the rhythm of the tune, establishing both the metrical structure and the rhythmic contents of the song for the audience/participants. His
movements back and forth across the signing space create a melodic pattern
as well, and his joyful facial expression draws an affective response from his
audience—the mood is one of happiness and pleasure. It seems, then, that

Seeing Voices. Anabel Maler, Oxford University Press. © Oxford University Press 2024.
DOI: 10.1093/oso/9780197601976.003.0007

there are specific musical features, both rhythmic and melodic, that create musical meaning for those perceiving a song like "Boat, Drink, Fun, Enjoy."

In order to understand how sign language music creates affective meanings for its audiences, we must understand how movements of the body contribute to the creation of musical meaning. The topic of musical meaning is complex and often invokes semiotic theories of music.[1] The approach I take in this chapter is quite pragmatic, following Andrew Chung's definition of musical meaning based on J. L. Austin's idea of performative utterances. Chung argues that musical meaning should not be understood in terms of how musical structures, objects, or processes map onto extramusical or music-internal correlates. Instead, musical meaning is better understood as something that is used to "generate effects and to perform meaningful actions with meaningful consequences, to which we find ways to comport our listening, performing, or otherwise 'musicking' selves" (Chung 2019, 0.1.1). Chung emphasizes that for music to mean requires cooperation on the part of the perceiver to hear and interpret it as meaningful, emphasizing that music is an action that "interfaces with the goals, concerns, and activities of its practitioners" (Chung 2019, 0.1.6).

The perspective Chung outlines is useful in that in shifts our focus from mapping musical objects onto other objects, and toward what that musical object is doing. It also aligns with theories of affect, defined by Seigworth and Gregg in terms of "resonances that circulate about, between, and sometimes stick to bodies and worlds" (Seigworth and Gregg 2010, 1). Affect is thus very much embodied and relational in nature: a bodily capacity to affect and to be affected by encounters with others and the world.

Movements of the body help to convey emotion in musical contexts, and they can shape how we experience musical organization as well. Recent research has shown that both the visual and auditory modalities can convey structural and emotional information in the context of ballet performance (Krumhansl and Schenck 1997). Body movements in musical performances have also been shown to carry similar structural and emotional resonances for audiences, conveying important cues for the beginnings and ends of phrases as well as dynamic processes such as tension and release (Vines et al. 2003). The body movements of musicians can also convey specific emotional

---

[1] I.e., Kofi Agawu, Leonard Meyer, Naomi Cumming, Robert Hatten, David Lidov, Raymond Monelle, Eero Tarasti, and others.

intentions such as happiness, sadness, fear, and anger to perceivers (Dahl and Friberg 2007).

Research also suggests that music is closely connected to motion in other ways: merely listening to music evokes a sense of bodily motion and movement in physical space. Neil Todd suggests that this association between bodily motion and music is due to two mechanisms: a vestibulomotor mechanism and an audio-visuo-motor mechanism. In other words, music both urges us to move our bodies and evokes a sense of imaginary movement due to interactions between the sensory (vestibular, auditory, and visual) and motor systems (Todd 1999). Music does not only move us, however; it also touches us. As Zohar Eitan and Inbar Rothschild have demonstrated, tactile metaphors are strongly associated with musical parameters like pitch height, loudness, timbre, and vibrato, such that, for example, higher pitches are metaphorically understood to be sharper, rougher, harder, colder, drier, and lighter than lower pitches (Eitan and Rothschild 2010, 457).

Furthermore, humans of all ages are able to express emotional meaning through whole-body movement and dance. Thomas Boone and Joseph Cunningham have shown, for example, that children are able to encode the emotional meaning of music into the expressive movements of a teddy bear (Boone and Cunningham 2001). Misako Sawada, Kazuhiro Suda, and Motonobu Ishii further demonstrated that dancers can express specific emotions by altering movement characteristics, and that these emotions can be perceived by others (Sawada, Suda, and Ishii 2003). Several studies have also demonstrated that perceivers can make sense of the emotional meanings of dancing when presented with dances meant to convey emotions such as happiness, sadness, fear, anger, grief, joy, surprise, and disgust (Brownlow et al. 1997; Dittrich et al. 1996; Walk and Homan 1984).

Meaning and emotion are also physically expressed in sign language poetry. Authors such as Alec Ormsby (1995), Cynthia Peters (2000), Rachel Sutton-Spence (2005), and Sarah Taub (2001) have explored how ASL and BSL poems use metaphors and symbols in order to express meaning in signed poetry. Karen Christie and Dorothy Wilkins have also shown how ASL poets make use of themes and symbols of resistance, affirmation, and liberation in their poetry. These themes and symbols emerge not only from the linguistic contents of the poems, but also from the gestures of the performers, including eye gaze, facial expressions, rhyming, use of space, and other body movements (Christie and Wilkins 2007).

Several authors have elaborated upon the mechanism by which our embodied experiences connect with how we conceptualize music, drawing on Mark Johnson's theory of image schemata.[2] Lawrence Zbikowski argues that our understanding of musical concepts like tension and release is "grounded in repeated patterns of bodily experience," and these provide the basis for conceptual metaphors such as "COMPLICATED PHENOMENA CREATE TENSION, SIMPLE PHENOMENA CREATE RELEASE." We may then apply these conceptual metaphors to music through cross-domain mapping (Zbikowski 1997–1998, 7).

Zbikowski makes an important distinction between the mechanisms by which language and music express emotions: language largely makes use of symbolic reference, "in which the relationship between the token and the thing it represents is completely arbitrary," while music makes use of analogical tokens that make possible representations of "dynamic phenomena which range from inner psychological processes to the trajectory of bodies through space to the steps of a dance" (Zbikowski 2012, 128; 2017, 2–25). Zbikowski further suggests that the materials of music serve as prompts for perceivers to create what cognitive scientist Lawrence Barsalou calls "simulations" of these dynamic processes (Zbikowski 2010, 48). According to this perspective, emotional responses to music are simulations of already-experienced embodied emotional responses, which are shaped by our existing perceptual and conceptual knowledge (2010, 54; 2017, 78). These emotional responses are crucial in understanding how music is organized in time.

According to these perspectives, perceivers create simulations of dynamic, embodied processes based on the affordances of the music they perceive (including both visual-kinesthetic and auditory information), and these simulations structure music and create meaningful, affective responses. Several questions naturally arise with respect to how sign language music means. Namely, what are the affordances provided by sign language music? In other words, what analogical tokens are made available to perceivers encountering a sign language music performance? What simulations arise in those perceiving sign language music, as a result of these analogical tokens?

---

[2] E.g., see Brower (1997–1998); Saslaw (1996); Zbikowski (1997–1998); Gur (2008).

What impact do these simulations have on the meaning of the music: what emotions, bodily states, physical movements, or trajectories of objects in space are evoked by signing musicians in their performances, and how do these dynamic processes structure the form of the music?

In some ways, music in the visual-kinesthetic modality, such as sign language music, expresses embodied dynamic processes more immediately and directly than music in the auditory modality. While sign language music shares connections to both dance and poetry, it cannot be reduced to either, and thus we must understand how music-making in signed languages creates specifically *musical* meaning. In order to do so, we can turn to the fundamental parameters of signed music that I have already established: aspects of vocal production such as prosody, facial expressions, mouth morphemes, eye gaze and movements, body movements, and communality; pulse, rhythm, and meter; and aspects of melody such as periodic duration, curve, register, range, and flowing line. Sign musician Pamela Witcher has identified similar parameters as establishing meaning in her own signed music:

> Language is made up of sentences, words arranged in a particular way that convey meaning. Well dance is like that, but the words are your body, and the way you move creates meaning.... In sign [music] it becomes, like, the color of movement.... So with my signed music, I added in a separate dynamic element with sudden movements of the body, by adjusting the tempo, slow and fast, also by manipulating light and dark, movements up and down, or facial expressions with different tempos. (Canadian Cultural Society of the Deaf 2016)

In what follows, I explore how music and language interact to create musical meaning in signed music performances. Next, I delve into the topic of form in signed music, showing how signing musicians structure their performances. Finally, I analyze two works: Rosa Lee Timm's "River Song" and Jesse Jones III's "One World, Two Hands," revealing how each conveys musical meaning through simulations of dynamic processes, out of which emerges musical structure.

6.2 Sign Language Music, Words, and Meaning

The majority of sign language music involves linguistic as well as musical communication—in other words, as I noted in Chapter 2, sign language music most often takes the form of a song.[3] In order to understand how meaning is created in sign language music, then, we ought to look at how meaning is typically created in songs more broadly.

Scholars have written about songs in a wide variety of ways. Much of the attention in music-theoretical writing has been devoted to the nineteenth-century Lied. Kofi Agawu summarizes three competing models for the analysis of song, before proposing a fourth model of his own (Agawu 1992). The first is the assimilation model, originating in the work of Suzanne Langer, who argues that when words and music come together, "music swallows words." In the second model, there is instead an irreducible relationship between words and text, in which neither loses their identity. In the third model, the words provide access to meaning, while the music acts in a supporting role to the semantic meaning of the text. Finally, Agawu proposes a fourth model, which explains song as a confluence of three overlapping systems: words and music and song.

Zbikowski proposes another model for understanding how meaning emerges at the intersection of music and words, creating something that goes beyond the sum of its parts. Zbikowski's method of song analysis is based on the process of conceptual blending, a process by which "elements from two correlated mental spaces combine in a third" (2002, 245). In analyzing a variety of songs, from settings of Müller's "Trockne Blumen" to Harburg and Arlen's "Over the Rainbow," Zbikowski makes use of conceptual integration networks (CINs) in order to capture the process of conceptual blending that occurs when words and music meet in the form of a song. The notion of conceptual integration networks, developed by Mark Turner and Gilles Fauconnier (Fauconnier and Turner 2002), allows us to formalize the relationships between mental spaces that contribute to the conceptual blend, reveal the basic logic that allows the blend to take place, and describe the structure that emerges as a result of the blend. Zbikowski is careful to caution against understanding the CIN as a rigid, immobile structure; mental spaces are dynamic, and the CIN represents a mere snapshot of a moment in time, rather than a full accounting of the process.

The notion of conceptual blending presents an excellent starting point for thinking about meaning formation in signed songs that incorporate semantic meaning in the form of a signed text. Furthermore, it centers the idea that sign language music contains not only semantic meaning, but musical

---

[3] Some more recent signed music does not involve the use of words. See Cripps et al.

meaning as well—as with all songs, the music and text together create something that goes beyond either. By revealing how signing musicians create conceptual blends between the linguistic meaning of the signs and musical parameters such as vocal quality, rhythm, and melody, we can better understand how sign language music acts as a site of affective engagement for audiences. First, however, we should briefly examine how form emerges in pieces of sign language music.

6.3 The Form of Sign Language Music

The emotional effects of music have an enormous impact on how music is organized in time—in other words, its form. I have previously suggested (Maler 2018) that we can think about form in terms of what cognitive scientist Don Norman calls "affordances" in his work on material design (Norman 1988).[4] Affordances, which reflect the potential uses or actions latent in materials, are perceived based on physical attributes as well as the perceiver's past experiences. When a musical representation of a dynamic process, such as a simulation of an emotional state or physical movement, meets with a listener and her past experiences, out of that interaction emerges the formal function of a musical passage. Form can thus be understood as an emergent property of music through which a perceiver actively shapes musical meaning and thus musical organization, through the processes of object categorization and prospection and retrospection (Maler 2022). As I argued in the Introduction to this volume, musical meaning also emerges out of a perceiver's interactions with her environment, in addition to the affordances of the musical signal she perceives.

Object categorization involves the perceiver actively forming categories from a collection of musical objects. Some key aspects of categorization in music are similarity, dissimilarity, and repetition. Alexandra Lamont and Nicola Dibben provide an overview of two models in cognitive psychology for understanding similarity and its role in categorization: the first, prototype theory, is based on the relationship between an object and an abstract

---

[4] Caroline Levine extends the notion of affordance by applying it to literary forms, demonstrating that patterns in literature lay claim a specific range of potentialities.

prototype, while the second is based on background knowledge and conceptual models (Lamont and Dibben 2001).[5]

The processes of prospection and retrospection have to do with how listeners form expectations and react to events in musical time. Leonard Meyer argues that musical structures create perceptual expectations that can be manipulated by composers in order to communicate emotions (Meyer 1956). Importantly, Meyer notes that a musical style must "become part of the habit responses of composers, performers, and practiced listeners" in order to "be regarded as a complex system of probabilities," out of which arise the expectations upon which meaning is based (Meyer 1957, 414). A number of scholars have elaborated upon and tested Meyer's theories of expectation and meaning, including several studies that reveal how musical expectations influence the perception of music (Cuddy and Lunney 1995; Krumhansl 1995; Schellenberg 1996; Schmuckler 1989).

The subject of expectation also forms the basis of David Huron's "ITPRA" (Imagination-Tension-Prediction-Reaction-Appraisal) theory of expectation (Huron 2006, 16). Huron's work reveals how common musical devices make use of these basic psychological responses, arguing that expectation shapes many different aspects of musical organization, including patterns of repetition and form, motivic structure, and genre and style.

We can imagine that similar processes occur in sign language music: perceivers organize perceptual stimuli into categories based on repetition, similarity, and dissimilarity, and they form perceptual expectations, which may be manipulated by composers for affective reasons. Out of these interactions between the perceiver and the stimulus emerge motivic structures as well as formal patterns. In sign language music, these processes of categorization and expectation will be based on the parameters of rhythm, melody, and vocal quality.

In a song like "Boat, Drink, Fun, Enjoy," chunking the music into short phrases is relatively straightforward. As I noted in Chapter 4, the performers create internal phrase divisions by using holds at the ends of two-bar sections. The repetition of the rhythmic pattern (♫|♪♪♪♩) signals the start of each new phrase. There is repetition in the melodic pattern as well, in that each phrase consists of the same movement pattern: right, left, right, left, right. Finally, by

<hr>

[5] Zbikowski builds on the latter model of categorization in order to build a theory of how conceptual models are applied in different musical contexts. Other studies engaging with the concepts of repetition and similarity include Cambouropoulos (2009), Deliège (2007), and Margulis (2012, 2014).

Example 6.1 Stills from Russell Harvard, cover of Paula Abdul's "Straight Up," verse 1.

changing the movement pattern in mm. 5–8, the performers create a slight contrast, allowing the audience to perceive a binary form. The perceiver can thus make use of both melodic and rhythmic elements in determining the song's formal organization.

Russell Harvard's cover of Paula Abdul's song "Straight Up" reveals how similarity and dissimilarity can also help perceivers organize sign language music into categories, create expectations, and make sense of a work's formal structure. In the song's first verse, Harvard's movements are generally close to the body and confined to a fairly small signing space (▶ Video Example 6.1). His movements consistently alternate between the left and right sides of the signing space, perhaps representing the singer's confusion about "which way to go" (Example 6.1). His facial expression is mostly relaxed, although his brow is sometimes furrowed and his mouth open. Rhythmically, most of his movements last for one or two beats, with some signs, like CHILL, lasting for four beats.

The prechorus brings several important changes in melody, rhythm, and vocal quality (▶ Video Example 6.2). Harvard's facial expression becomes more tense and questioning, his brow remaining furrowed for the entirety of the section (Example 6.2). His movements become significantly faster, and for the first time, he faces the camera head-on, without alternating between the left and right sides of the signing space. Harvard's movements also become slightly larger, taking up more of the signing space than in the verse—his elbows, rather than being pressed into his body, move freely now. His movements are also much sharper and defined than in the chorus—one might describe them as "punchy." Finally, the prechorus exhibits significantly more whole-body movement to the beat than the verse did—a technique I have previously referred to as "pulsing" (Maler 2013).

Example 6.2 Stills from Russell Harvard, cover of Paula Abdul's "Straight Up," prechorus.

The onset of the chorus is marked by an enormous increase in the signing space as Harvard spins his entire body around, thus completing the progression from verse (most restricted space), prechorus (slightly larger space in front of body), to chorus (full use of the normal signing space and beyond) (▶ Video Example 6.3). His movements are also even more sharply defined than in the prechorus, heightening the sense of intensity in the chorus (Example 6.3). His face shows more dramatic changes in expression, from tense, pulled-back lips, and a furrowed brow to raised eyebrows and a rounded, open mouth. At the end of the chorus, Harvard again expands the signing space, with a large, repeated gesture that extends to his right and above his head.

The beginning of the next verse is clearly defined through its dissimilarity with the chorus and similarity with the first (▶ Video Example 6.4). Harvard's signing space quickly retracts and his movements suddenly become much smaller and less rapid than in the prechorus or chorus (Example 6.4). His movements also become less sharply defined and punchy, and he begins to alternate between the left and right sides of the signing space once more. These similarities allow the perceiver to understand this new section as a return to the "verse" category, which is dissimilar to the "prechorus" or "chorus" categories. The song's formal sections (verse, prechorus, chorus) are thus clearly distinguished from one another through dissimilarities in their rhythmic, melodic, and vocal properties, making the song's formal structure abundantly clear to the perceiver.

Harvard's use of similarly and dissimilarity to organize his cover of "Straight Up" into clear sections indicates that sign language music does indeed display formal organization. To make sense of the formal structure of

Example 6.3 Stills from Russell Harvard, cover of Paula Abdul's "Straight Up," chorus.

Example 6.4 Stills from Russell Harvard, cover of Paula Abdul's "Straight Up," verse 2.

a piece of sign language music, audiences draw upon the affordances of musical stimulus as well as their past experiences and embodied understanding. In doing so, they make determinations about object categorization and form expectations about how the music will proceed.

6.4 Musical Meaning in Two Original Signed Songs

Audiences may also make use of sign language music's affordances in making determinations about its meaning. In attending to features like vocal quality and expressivity, melodic lines, and rhythmic and metric techniques, a perceiver can make sense of a song's form, narrative, and affective meaning. In the sections that follow, I analyze how two signed songs—"River Song" by Rosa Lee Timm and "One World, Two Hands" by Jesse Jones III—construct musical meaning through the use of vocal techniques, melody, rhythm, and camerawork.

Rosa Lee Timm, "River Song" (2008)

Rosa Lee Timm's "River Song" is an original signed song with no auditory component. The song can be roughly divided into three verses, with an introduction, outro, and refrain. The song's lyrics tell of a day on a river. In ▷ Video Example 6.5, Timm introduces the song and what motivated its composition. In my analysis of "River Song," I focus on how Timm makes use of vocal techniques, melody, and rhythm in order to create musical meaning and distinguish between the song's two main characters, a large boat and a small boat.

In the song's introduction, the sun rises and its rays touch the current of a river. The river's meandering back and forth becomes a series of larger waves—this acts as a refrain, which returns between each verse. In the song's first verse, a little boat is carved out of wood, with a small flag placed inside. The little boat is approached by a much larger one, with a big flag and a smug personality. The two boats face off against each other, placed side by side in the river for a race. The verse is followed by an iteration of the refrain.

In the second verse, the boats both ride the waves, hoping and fighting to get ahead. The little boat is hopeful and determined, while the larger one is smug and dismissive of the smaller. The larger boat pulls ahead in the race, and despite the smaller boat's dogged determination, it capsizes. The larger boat laughs and the smaller one cries.

The third verse begins after a significantly shortened refrain. As we continue down the river, trees pass by on each side. Fish swim in the water; one is scooped up, much to its surprise. Other animals appear on each side of the riverbank; a frog hops by, a bird swoops low, a woodpecker pecks at a tree, a deer drinks from the river. The large, smug boat picks up the smaller one and sets it upright. After a final iteration of the chorus, the song's outro shows the little boat riding the waves once more as the sun sets over the river. The song's three verses can be broadly understood to represent two contrasting parts of a story: the first two verses tell of a tense competition between the larger boat and the smaller boat, while the third verse reveals the beauty of life on the river, which inspires the larger boat to help the smaller boat.

The text of "River Song" makes use of two conceptual blends, in which the two boats are portrayed as having human-like personalities. The CINs for these conceptual blends are shown in Examples 6.5a and 6.5b. The two input

Example 6.5 Conceptual Integration Networks for the text of "River Song," which anthropomorphizes two boats.

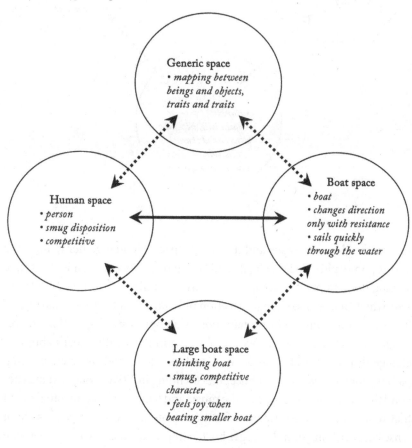

Example 6.5 Continued

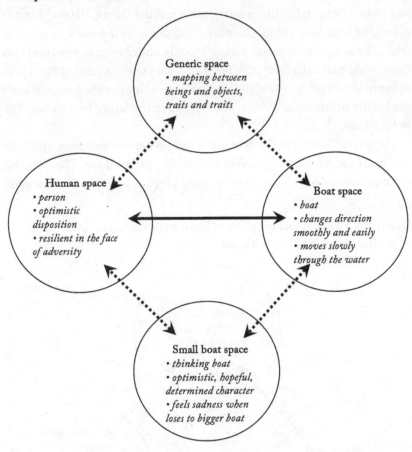

spaces, the "human" space and the "boat" space, blend together to form the anthropomorphized "large boat" and "small boat" spaces. Human traits like a smug disposition and competitive spirit are reflected in the larger boat's size, which allows it to change direction only slowly and with resistance, and its speed on the water. The human traits of an optimistic disposition and resilience in the face of adversity are reflected in the smaller boat's ability to change directly smoothly and easily, and its slower and more challenging path through the water. The conceptual blending in "River Song" extends beyond the text, as well—together, the music and text create a conceptual blend that represents a transformation from one state to another: from a state of tense competition, with the larger boat acting smug and uncaring, to a state of calm and happiness, with the larger boat transforming into a helpful and friendly character.

We can now turn to the musical features of "River Song" to reveal how the music and text blend to create the transformation from a competitive, unfriendly large boat to a kinder, friendlier one.

The song begins with a slow, metrically flexible introduction (▶ Video Example 6.6, Example 6.6). At first, Timm's face is relaxed and neutral as she signs that the sun is rising, and her body faces forward. As the rays of the sun touch the water, her facial expression changes briefly: her mouth purses and her eyes squint as the sun shines down, and as the rays make contact with the water her eyes widen and her mouth briefly opens to make a small "o" shape. Next, her face relaxes, showing contentment as she sings the song's refrain: her hands move back and forth, left and right across the signing space, as well as moving away from her body and toward the audience as she shows the meandering course of the river. The river's flow then becomes stronger and faster: Timm's cheeks puff out and her brow furrows, and her movements become larger and faster, taking up more of the vertical

Example 6.6 Stills from "River Song," introduction.

space and moving more rapidly away from her body. The river's flow then slows, her facial expression relaxing and transforming into an open smile as her hands flatten out and slow their movements, showing the river calming once again. Timm briefly implies a simple quadruple meter in the introductory section, but the ritardando that shows the river becoming calm then obfuscates the meter.

The introduction establishes a few key features of the meter, melody, vocal techniques, and rhythmic layers that Timm uses in the rest of the song. She briefly establishes a simple quadruple meter using the periodic movement of the waves on the river—this will be the meter for most of the song. She establishes one of the key repeated handshapes of the song as well: the 5 handshape. Finally, she establishes a recurring mouth shape, the small "o" shape, which is a facet of vocal technique. You can see her discussing her use of this recurring mouth shape in ⊙ Video Example 6.7.

The beginning of the first verse shows the smaller boat being hollowed out and confirms the simple quadruple meter suggested in the introduction (Examples 6.7, 6.8). In ⊙ Video Example 6.8, Timm describes how she was inspired to establish the song's meter using a melodic contrast between two sides of the signing space, and two different movement sizes and types. The smaller boat is located to the left of Timm's body, and she uses first her right hand, followed by her left hand, to show the little boat being created (⊙ Video Example 6.9). Both of her hands come together to show

Example 6.7 Stills from "River Song," verse 1.

Example 6.8 Notation of "River Song," verse 1.

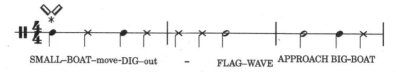

SMALL–BOAT–move–DIG–out   –   FLAG–WAVE   APPROACH BIG-BOAT

SPARKLE FLAG–WAVE LOOK–at–EACH–other LOOK–forward WAVE

Example 6.9 Stills from "River Song," verse 2.

the small flag being placed inside the boat as she pauses for a beat. Her facial expression is friendly and kind: her lips are slightly pursed and her eyebrows slightly furrowed, as if to represent the smaller boat's determined nature. The larger boat approaches from the right, and Timm accordingly moves her body to the right in order to represent its location with respect to the smaller boat. Her movements become firmer and larger, and her cheeks puff out, representing the boat's larger size. Her mouth opens and her eyebrows raise in a haughty expression. As the two boats face off against each other, her eyes narrow to represent the feeling of competition between them.

Timm also uses the first verse to establish another repeated handshape: the 1 handshape. In ⏵ Video Example 6.10, Timm describes the importance of these recurring handshapes, which form a kind of hypermeter in her signing.

The second verse opens by setting the stage of the boat race, showing how the boats move on the water (Examples 6.9, 6.12, ⏵ Video Example 6.11). Timm use her whole body to create circular movements

Example 6.10 Stills from "River Song," verse 2.

back and forth across the signing space, as well as moving vertically up and down. Her facial expressions express the same circular motion: her eyes widen and close, her cheeks puff out, and her mouth opens and closes slightly. Her body then continues its rhythmic motion back and forth across the signing space as she shows the larger boat looking at the smaller one and vice versa: she first moves her body to the right (the space of the larger boat) and turns to the left, before shifting her body to the left (the space of the smaller boat) and looking to the right. In this section, Timm's movements create a straightforward quarter-note rhythm, with one movement per beat.

As the competition gets more intense, Timm shows the smaller boat's increased efforts (Examples 6.10, 6.12). At first, her mouth forms a tense, small "o" shape, while her eyebrows are furrowed; then her mouth opens wider and she sticks her tongue out to the right and her eyebrows raise, showing the boat's intense concentration. Her stance is crouched, her shoulders hunched forward, representing both the smaller stature of the boat as well as its tense state. The little boat still experiences the joy of being out on the water, despite its efforts: as the flag waves back and forth, Timm's

Example 6.11 Stills from "River Song," verse 2.

expression changes to an open smile. The movements of the smaller boat are strong and full of effort: Timm's movements have definite starting and ending points in space and feature circular, repetitive motions. Timm then shifts her body to the right, standing straight once more, representing the larger boat. Her expression becomes haughty and smug: she rolls her eyes as she looks down at the smaller boat. Her movements as the larger boats are much less strong and pronounced: Timm stays quite still, and her movements are not circular or repetitive.

The tension rises as the competition heats up between the two boats, and Timm rapidly shifts between the two spaces (Example 6.11). She crouches, leans forward, and positions her body to the left to represent the smaller boat, using intense facial expressions: first her lips are pressed together with her brows lowered and eyes wide, then her bottom lip exposes her lower teeth and her brows become furrowed and raised and her eyes open even wider. By contrast, she stands up straight and tall with her body positioned to the right to represent the larger boat, with a relaxed and smug expression: her

Example 6.12 Notation of "River Song," verse 2.

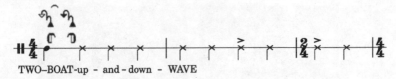

TWO–BOAT–up - and - down - WAVE

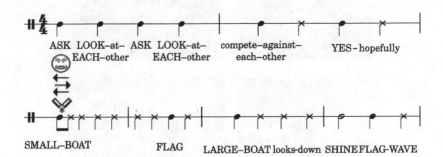

ASK LOOK–at– ASK LOOK–at–   compete–against–   YES – hopefully
EACH–other   EACH–other   each–other

SMALL–BOAT   FLAG   LARGE–BOAT looks-down SHINE FLAG-WAVE

BOAT-advances SMALL-BOAT–sails BOAT-advances BIG–BOAT–stands–looks–down

SMALL-BOAT–sails BIG–BOAT–stands SMALL-BOAT–sails SMALL-BOAT–tips–over

BIG–BOAT–looks–forward SEE–SMALL–BOAT LAUGH   SMALL-BOAT CRY

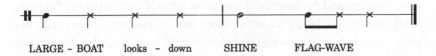

LARGE - BOAT   looks - down   SHINE   FLAG-WAVE

eyes are nearly closed and one corner of her mouth is turned up. The smaller boat then capsizes, and Timm's mouth opens in shock and disappointment. The larger boat laughs at the smaller and smiles as its flag waves, signaling its victory. This section makes extensive use of the 1 handshape that I pointed out in the first verse.

The third verse shows the life on the river, with many animals on each of the banks (Examples 6.13, 6.14, ▶ Video Example 6.12). The large boat sees each of these animals as it floats along the river. It remains haughty at first: Timm's lips are turned down, her eyebrows raised, her eyelids half shut. However, as the larger boat sees the calm, contented animals and trees passing by, Timm's expression changes, becoming more gentle: her brows relaxed and her eyelids nearly closed as her gaze swoops down from the upper right corner to the lower left, showing the larger boat spotting the smaller boat. Her shoulders move forward and she crouches down, showing the larger boat moving into the space of the smaller one. The larger boat lifts the smaller boat upright and rights its flag. The larger boat's movements are now much more purposeful, and Timm's facial expression mirrors that of the smaller boat earlier in the song: determined but kind. The rhythm of the

Example 6.13 Stills of "River Song," verse 3.

Example 6.14 Notation of "River Song," verse 3.

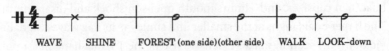

WAVE   SHINE   FOREST (one side)(other side)   WALK   LOOK–down

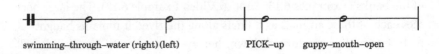

swimming–through–water (right) (left)   PICK–up   guppy–mouth–open

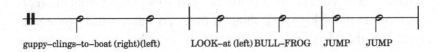

guppy–clings–to–boat (right)(left)   LOOK–at (left) BULL–FROG   JUMP   JUMP

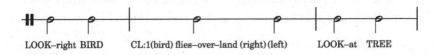

LOOK–right BIRD   CL:1(bird) flies–over–land (right) (left)   LOOK–at   TREE

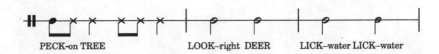

PECK–on TREE   LOOK–right DEER   LICK–water LICK–water

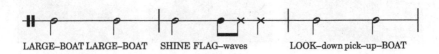

LARGE–BOAT LARGE–BOAT   SHINE FLAG–waves   LOOK–down pick–up–BOAT

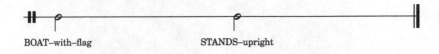

BOAT–with–flag   STANDS–upright

third verse is much slower and calmer; Timm's signs predominantly last for a half note each, lending this section a much more relaxed affect than that of the previous verse.

The text of "River Song" blends with several features of the music to create a transformation from one state to another: a state of tense competition transforms into one of friendliness and calm, and the larger boat's state of mind transforms from haughty and smug to helpful and kind (Example 6.15). Timm accomplishes this through the musical parameters of facial expressions, body positioning, use of space, and movement type and direction. While at first the two boats contrast in all these parameters, in the third verse the larger boat takes on several of the musical traits first exhibited by the smaller boat: a friendly facial expression, a crouched position, the lower left signing space, and purposeful movements. Timm is therefore able to

Example 6.15 CIN for "River Song."

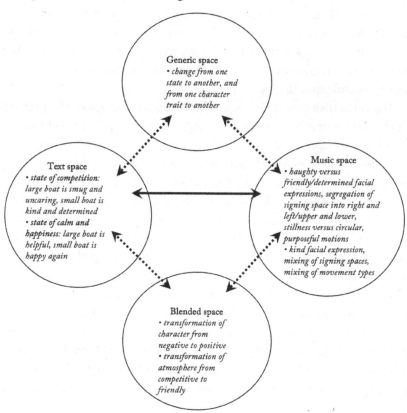

show the transformation from a negative state to a positive one by blending elements of the text and the music in "River Song." There is also a broader message in "River Song" of determination and hope against the challenges and setbacks of life, which is shown through the tenacity of the smaller boat. Timm confirmed this musical meaning in the interview I conducted with her (▶ Video Example 6.13).

Jesse Jones III, "One World, Two Hands"

The song "One World, Two Hands" is an original signed song, composed by Jesse Jones III and produced by Eric Calbert for a Deaf Awareness Day festival. While "One World, Two Hands" itself has no auditory component, it was inspired by the aural song "With My Own Two Hands" by Ben Harper. Jones's original song tells the story of environmental damage, with an inspiring message of hope for change. In the first verse, Jones depicts the world crying out for help: he first stands on the beach, signing that the ocean is dirty and the beach is closed. The video then cuts to Jones standing in a field: he signs that the trees are cut down, the sky has turned from blue to brown, and trash is piling up. He asks where the animals will make their homes, and where the children will play.

The video then cuts to a large sandy field, with what looks like a landfill in the background. Now Jones is no longer alone in the frame: behind him stand two women, forming a triangle with Jones standing front and center. This visual change signals the start of the chorus, which begins with the repeated refrain "ONE WORLD TWO HANDS." Another cut takes us back to the beach with Jones standing alone, signing the post-chorus, which urges all people to come together with the lyrics: "Roll-up-sleeves DO-DO ALONE-q NO / CAN tap-on-shoulders ALL PEOPLE COME-ON." The chorus and post-chorus then repeat, with the post-chorus varied slightly, followed by another iteration of the chorus.

The song's second verse focuses on the changes that are possible when people work together: people can plant seeds to grow trees and clean up trash from the beaches, and as a result, birds and animals will have a home. After another statement of the chorus, the third verse continues to describe what we can do together: recycle bottles, cups, and paper and stop wasting precious water, and finally children will be able to play freely. The third verse is followed by another chorus/post-chorus pair, and the song concludes with a final chorus.

In "One World, Two Hands," Jones tells a story of contrast between two states: the world in a state of decay and damage, as opposed to the world in a state of cleanliness and joy, created by people working together. This contrast between two states is supported by a conceptual blend between musical parameters and the text. The musical parameters employed by Jones are very similar to those used by Timm in "River Song," with the important addition of creative camerawork. In Jones's ASL song, as in many pieces of sign language music, the camera is an important musical element in its own right.[6]

At the song's opening, the camera pans down from a cloudy sky to focus on Jones, who is walking on the beach (Example 6.16, ⊙ Video Example 6.14). The camera then zooms in on Jones's upper body from his right side as he begins to sign, looking to his right and directly into the camera: SEE WORLD (here). The camera then zooms out, facing Jones, as he signs YELL + HELP HELP HELP. Jones's facial expression is concerned: his brow is furrowed and as he signs HELP, his lips draw back, his open mouth imitating a cry for help. His signing establishes a meter that alternates between simple triple and simple duple through sign onset and sign emphasis. The constant metrical changes create a distinct sense of instability and unpredictability in the verse. As Jones begins to sign about the topic of the verse, the downtrodden state of the planet, the camera faces Jones directly, zooming in on his face again. The camera repeatedly zooms in and out, panning from Jones's right to his left, in large circular motions. Many of the signs used by Jones mimic this circular motion: for example, signs like RIVER, WATER, and WAVE show water moving back and forth across the signing space as well as away from Jones's body.

Both the camera and Jones continue to use circular movements as the location shifts to a field for the second half of the first verse. The camera pans from right to left and zooms in and out, circling in front of Jones as he signs. Signs like TREE + are signed across the signing space, first from left to right and then from right to left, and signs like BARE move away from his body, continuing to mimic the circular motions of the camera. Jones's facial expression remains concerned and disgusted: his brow is generally furrowed, and his tongue often sticks out, showing his disgust for the dirty trash piling

---

[6] In many pieces of sign language music, captions are an equally important musical element as well.

Example 6.16 Notation of "One World, Two Hands," verse 1.

SEE WORLD   (here) YELL   HELP HELP RIVER   OCEAN–fs (here)

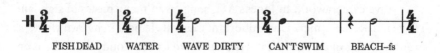

FISH DEAD   WATER   WAVE DIRTY   CAN'T SWIM   BEACH–fs

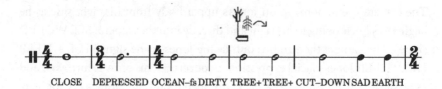

CLOSE   DEPRESSED OCEAN–fs DIRTY TREE+ TREE+ CUT–DOWN SAD EARTH

BARE   ANIMAL+ HOME WHERE   SKY–fs BLUE   WHERE HAZY

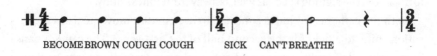

BECOME BROWN COUGH COUGH   SICK   CAN'T BREATHE

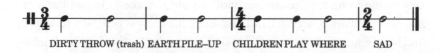

DIRTY THROW (trash) EARTH PILE–UP   CHILDREN PLAY WHERE   SAD

up. As in the first part of the verse, he largely faces the camera directly, except when he indicates the sky by looking upward and to the right.

The formal shift to the song's chorus is made evident to the viewer through another change in location, the addition of two backup singers, and a change in camera work (Example 6.17, ▶ Video Example 6.15). The signers are now shown from a great distance and from above, rather than facing the camera head on and from a close distance as in the verse. The camera also stays steady for the first iteration of the refrain (ONE WORLD TWO HANDS), which contrasts starkly with the constant motion in the first verse. For the second iteration of the chorus, the camera angle lowers and slowly pans from right to left, zooming in slightly. Overall, however, the camera is much more stable and stationary in the chorus than in the verse. The meter is now a stable simple triple as well, in contrast to the constant alternation between simple triple and duple in the first verse.

The arrival of the post-chorus is marked by several important changes: the backup singers disappear, centering Jones once more; the meter changes to simple quadruple; and the camera becomes mobile again. However, instead of making circular motions around Jones, the camera now largely zooms in and out, while Jones remains constantly facing the camera. Jones's

Example 6.17 Notation of "One World, Two Hands," chorus.

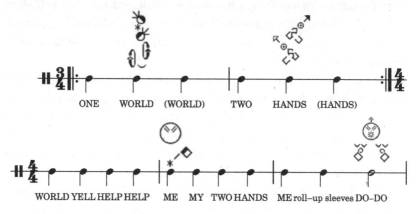

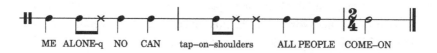

movements are also much stronger, sharper, and more marked: signs like MY, TWO, NO, and CAN, for example, have sharply defined end points in the signing space. The post-chorus also features many repeated signs and movements, such as YELL, HELP, roll-up-sleeves, DO-DO, and tap-on-shoulders. Together, these musical elements create a strong sense of contrast with both the verse and the chorus. The post-chorus directly addresses the viewer, urging the audience to work together with Jones and others to help make the world a better place—this change is marked by a noticeable shift in affect as well. We can understand this change in affect in terms of our musical expectations: we expect, based on expectations established in the verse and chorus, that Jones will continue in a simple triple meter, and that the camera, when it begins to move again, will resume its circular motions. The denial of these expectations contributes to the change in affect that characterizes the post-chorus.

In the final two verses, Jones makes two important musical changes: his facial expressions become more open, relaxed, and happy, and he begins to freely explore and expand the signing space, turning away from the camera when signing about the ocean, for example, and turning his gaze to the sign for TREE + s when he is signing about not cutting down the earth's precious trees (▶ Video Example 6.16). In verse 3, he expands the space even more on the line FINALLY CHILDREN PLAY: he looks away from the camera and around himself with a joyous expression, as if watching imaginary children at play, before lifting his hands up and outside of the normal signing space on the sign PLAY. He looks up into the sky, and the camera follows his gaze by panning upward from below.

There are several central musical parameters in "One World, Two Hands" that establish both the form and the meaning of the song: vocal quality (facial expressions, eye gaze, and body positioning), melody (movement type and directionality), meter, and camerawork. The musical parameters of meter and camerawork establish the work's formal structure. The change from the circling camerawork to a stable angle helps distinguish the verse from the chorus. The post-chorus is distinguishable from both the verse and the chorus by the camerawork, which mostly involves zooming in and out with Jones facing the camera head on, and by the meter, which is simple quadruple in the post-chorus instead of the simple triple of the chorus or the alternating triple and duple of the verse.

The text of "One World, Two Hands" makes use of an overall conceptual blend in which human emotional states are mapped onto the state of the

Example 6.18 CIN for text of verse 1, "One World, Two Hands."

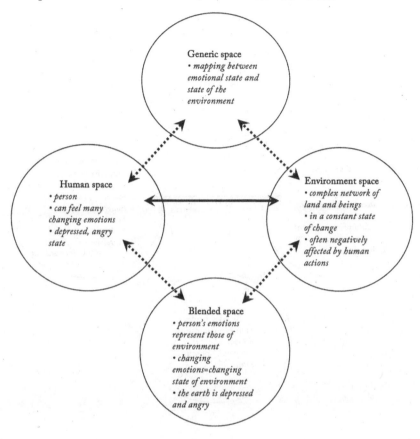

environment. Example 6.18 shows the conceptual blend in verse 1, where Jones's emotional state is depressed and angry, which is mapped onto the state of the environment—we can understand through this conceptual blend that the earth is in a dire state and needs our help.

Jones further creates a blended space in which changes in the state of the environment are reflected in changes in musical parameters such as use of space, movement type, positioning of the body, and facial expressions (Example 6.19). In the first verse, the environment is portrayed as unhappy and depressed; Jones's facial expressions are harsh and negative, his use of the signing space is constricted, and he focuses his gaze intently on the camera. Jones's use of shifting meters in the first verse also helps the audience perceive the constantly changing state of the environment. In the second and

Example 6.19 CIN for "One World, Two Hands."

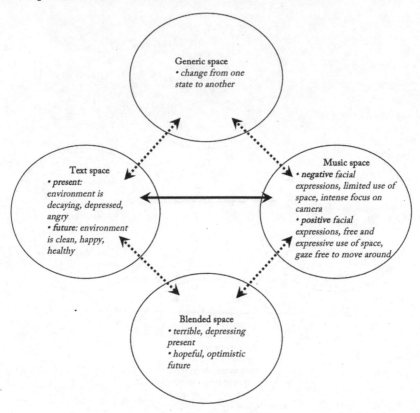

third verses, by contrast, Jones uses positive, smiling facial expressions, he uses the signing space much more freely and expressively, and his gaze moves around freely instead of being locked onto the camera.

6.5 Conclusion

As Cripps et al. observe, not all signed music must include words, and thus not all signed music should be categorized as song. However, signed music that does not include words, or only includes a few words, still conveys musical meaning and affect. When discussing his video "Rain," Jody Cripps describes how both his aunt and his wife felt the video conveyed different affects:

I showed them my video after it was completed, they both watched it and they both understand ASL, but both came to a different conclusion. For example, my aunt said that it had an angry tone and looked serious. My wife felt touched by it and said that it resembled hard work and navigating barriers your whole life. . . . I didn't feel that at all while filming myself, but I used that mouth expression displaying emotions while signing the rain. I expressed emotions and facial expressions in signing the patterns of the rain while being under the rain with it hitting my skin, it was hard work. . . . Really, the perception varies from one person to another. This is why the music itself is very abstract and allows for different interpretations and perspectives. ("Signed Music and the Deaf Musicians" 2020)

As with sounding music, signed music allows for many interpretations depending on the viewpoint and experiences of the perceiver. As Cripps observes, when re-watching a piece of signed music, one's analysis and inter-pretation of the music may also change: "Sometimes when I watch a Signed Music performance, and every time I re-watch it, I tend to see something dif-ferent, to learn something new and my perspective and conclusions changes" (Signed Music and the Deaf Musicians 2020). Cripps's words remind us that, as with any music, meaning in signed music emerges from the interactions of the performer and perceiver and is thus changeable, contingent, and ever-evolving.

The cultural experience and orientation of the perceiver are crucial for their understanding of affect and meaning in any musical style. As Cripps notes, music "has a strong connection with culture. It can sometimes be linked to language but strongly tied to culture. Culture is the under-standing of related experiences and shared understanding" (Signed Music and the Deaf Musicians 2020). Therefore, there may be aspects of sign lan-guage music that are less accessible or understandable to audiences who are steeped in hearing culture and hearing music, and who may not be fa-miliar with a signed language. There are also differences in understanding and interpreting sign language music within the Deaf, hard-of-hearing, and DeafBlind, communities, which are not monolithic and contain a variety of perspectives and orientations on music.

Musical meaning can emerge in a variety of unexpected places, as long as we are willing to understanding music as culturally defined, organized move-ment. For example, in a conversation with John Lee Clark about DeafBlind experiences of music, he describes a haptic musical experience:

We've enjoyed certain experiences that we call "music," such as the gurgling of a hot tub while we're chatting, and when the gurgling stops, one of us will say "more music" and go and hit that button for fifteen minutes of more gurgling. We enjoy things like that, and may call it music, but it has nothing to do with existing auditory music, a concert, lyrics, or anything. (Clark, personal communication, July 22, 2021)

My initial correspondence with Clark provides a small glimpse into the richness of DeafBlind experiences of music. Clark describes a kind of musical experience that has meaning within a specific culture and that involves organized movement, experienced through touch. In considering the musical meaning created and perceived by visual and haptic means, we can better understand music's resiliency across cultures, experiences, and abilities. In other words, analyzing signed music and other visual-kinesthetic forms of music presents a compelling step forward on the path toward understanding human musical perception more broadly.

Epilogue

> I'd like to see more, to see [signed music] flourish, to have more Deaf
> artists express themselves in this medium. For the sake of the chil-
> dren too, because children need exposure. Most people think that
> Deaf children don't need music, but that isn't true. They have music
> within them—we need to foster it and feed it.
> —Pamela Witcher (Canadian Cultural Society of the Deaf 2016)

As I have demonstrated through numerous and varied examples, sign language music has a long, rich history and enormous potential to inform our
theories about music. Sign language music originates from within Deaf culture and finds its natural performers among members of the Deaf community, but members of the hearing community have been drawn to it as well,
as I have noted (Maler 2015). In addition to the controversial phenomenon
of hearing persons creating sign language covers of popular songs (and often
posting these covers on social media websites such as Facebook, YouTube,
and TikTok), the rising popularity of "baby sign language" (which uses signs
from a natural sign language in communicating with hearing babies) has
led to some interest in "music and baby sign" classes geared toward hearing
children.[1]

Despite recent interest in teaching sign language music to hearing children, little attention has been paid toward teaching sign language music to
Deaf children. The authors of the only study of the effects of ASL rhyme and
rhythm on Deaf children's engagement and behavior note that Deaf children have "extremely limited exposure to and experience with ASL rhythm
and rhyme," and that many professionals serving Deaf children in schools
"lacked rhyme awareness themselves" (Holcomb and Wolbers 2020, 23).

---

[1] See, e.g., Happy Baby Signs (2021); Baby Fingers (2022); Klosterman.

Seeing Voices. Anabel Maler, Oxford University Press. © Oxford University Press 2024.
DOI: 10.1093/oso/9780197601976.003.0008

Ironically—and sadly—hearing children may now receive more exposure to ASL rhythm than Deaf children in their early years.

Throughout this book, I have showcased music's resilience. I have argued that throughout the history of Deaf music-making, musicality has been resilient across modalities. I have proposed that vocality, rhythm and meter, melody, and meaning and form are resilient properties of music that emerge in visual-kinesthetic and tactile music as well as aurally produced music. But the resilience of musicality within Deaf communities is only remarkable because of the ways in which the hearing majority have oppressed Deaf music-making and imposed hearing standards upon Deaf ways of knowing and creating music. This oppression continues to the present day, leaving many Deaf children without access to sign language music despite the fact that, as Pamela Witcher puts it, "they have music within them" (Canadian Cultural Society of the Deaf 2016).

What would valuing Deaf musical knowledge and practice look like? It would involve changing the way we think about and teach music at all levels: a fundamental ideological shift away from music as *sound* and toward music as *movement*. It would involve major changes to our music curricula (especially in the realm of aural skills and musicianship) in order to place musical hearing in a more equitable relationship with musical seeing and musical touching. Most crucially, it would involve making space in music scholarship for our Deaf, DeafBlind, and hard-of-hearing colleagues, respecting their musical expertise, and following their lead.

Members of the Deaf, DeafBlind, hard-of-hearing, and signing communities have a great deal to teach us about music. Sign language music in particular teaches us that fundamental elements of music such as vocal technique, entrainment, pulse, rhythm, meter, melody, meaning, and form can thrive in visual and tactile forms of music-making. These concepts are not merely shadows of their sonic cousins. Thus, it will not be fruitful to press and prod sign language music into the mold of aural music, searching for exact equivalents to concepts like timbre or harmony. On that note, basing one's aesthetic judgments of signed music on the parameters of aural music will be equally fruitless: an ASL song like "Boat, Drink, Fun, Enjoy" falls short when compared to the harmonic complexity of a Beethoven piano sonata, but Beethoven too falls short when compared to the spatial complexity of "Boat, Drink, Fun, Enjoy." Instead, signed music deserves to be analyzed and understood on its own terms, as a visual-kinesthetic type of music with its own history, cultural contexts, priorities, challenges, and complexities.

John Lee Clark perfectly encapsulates this concept in his essay "Against Access." He writes:

> The question I am asked most frequently by hearing and sighted people is "How can I make my—Web site, gallery exhibit, film, performance, concert, whatever—accessible to you?" Companies, schools, nonprofits, and state and federal agencies approach me and other DeafBlind people all the time, demanding, "How do we make it more accessible?"
>
> Such a frenzy around access is suffocating. I want to tell them, *Listen, I don't care about your whatever.* But the desperation on their breath holds me dumbfounded. The arrogance is astounding. Why is it always about them? Why is it about their including or not including us? Why is it never about us and whether or not *we* include *them*? (Clark 2021a)

As Clark points out, access is crucially important, but at the same time, it "revolves around the assumption that there's only one world and ignores realms of possibility nestled within those same modes" (Clark 2021a). The same is true, I think, about how we understand music. Too often, we conceptualize music from a hearing perspective and ask how we can make it accessible to those who do not hear, or who hear differently. But perhaps we should instead ask: how can the Deaf, DeafBlind, and hard-of-hearing communities make their knowledge of music accessible to us?

I am reminded of how difficult it is for sighted persons to describe colors—we struggle to describe something that seems so ineffable, so inevitable. By contrast, descriptions of colors by blind persons can be extraordinarily rich, bubbling over with sensory information and meaning. For example, in a video in which she describes various colors from her perspective as a blind person, Molly Burke describes turquoise as follows:

> Turquoise makes me think of vacation. Turquoise makes me think of warm water on my feet after just walking through super soft, silky white sand. It makes me think of piña coladas and daiquiris. It makes me think of being on an island somewhere. It makes me think of going on a cruise and going jewelry shopping. It makes me think of umbrellas on the beach.... It makes me think of a specific turtle necklace that I own that has turquoise in the middle that I always wear when I'm on vacation. (Burke 2021)

One might even go as far as to say that blind persons are *experts* at describing color in a way that those of us with sight can never fully access. Along the same lines, we can think of Deaf, DeafBlind, and hard-of-hearing knowers as experts on understanding and imagining sound and music in ways that the hearing community can never access. Instead of imposing hearing notions of music on Deaf communities, then, we should ask what we can learn from these expert knowers about the world of music and sound.

In an email exchange, Clark bubbled over with possibilities for moving beyond the traditional model of musical access for DeafBlind persons. He suggested finding or creating instruments that DeafBlind persons could easily control, asking: "Would that then inspire us to compose?" He gives an example:

> I can easily imagine us having a lot of fun with a vibrating pad of some kind, where we [p]ut it under the cushions of a sofa, or under a mattress, and you have this box with levers. You can [manipulate] the levers for increasing the vibrations, lowering, patterning, and so on. I can imagine lying on a bed and experimenting, finding out what pleases me, then inviting someone else to experience it, see what they think. Taking turns at the levers, often teasing each other with silly or annoying patterns, but getting serious too. (Clark, personal communication, July 22, 2021)

The kind of DeafBlind music-making Clark proposes is community-oriented, playful, embodied, immersive, joyful, and inviting. It is also a musical experience that I, a hearing and sighted music theorist, cannot typically access. My correspondence with Clark, and with the Deaf signing musicians featured throughout this book, opens a small but powerful window of access into a different kind of musicality, one that is equally as rich and complex as that of the hearing community. As I watch the Deaf, hard-of-hearing, and DeafBlind communities continue to innovate and create, I expect that this window will widen to reveal the multisensory vibrancy and resilience of music in ways that I, as a hearing person, cannot begin to imagine.

Works Cited

Abbate, Carolyn. 1991. *Unsung Voices. Opera and Musical Narrative in the Nineteenth Century*. Princeton, NJ: Princeton University Press.

Abbate, Carolyn. 1999. "Outside Ravel's Tomb." *Journal of the American Musicological Society* 52 (3): 465–530.

Accinno, Michael. 2019. "Extraordinary Voices: Helen Keller, Music and the Limits of Oralism." *Journal of Interdisciplinary Voice Studies* 4 (2): 139–156.

Adams, Kyle. 2008. "Aspects of the Music/Text Relationship in Rap." *Music Theory Online* 14 (2).

Agawu, Victor Kofi. 1992. "Theory and Practice in the Analysis of the Nineteenth-Century Lied." *Music Analysis* 11: 3–36.

Allen, Edward E. 1903. "Proceedings of Department of Special Education." *The Association Review* 5 (4): 343–362.

Alper, Meryl. 2017. *Giving Voice: Mobile Communication, Disability, and Inequality*. The John D. and Catherine T. MacArthur Foundation Series on Digital Media and Learning. Cambridge, MA: MIT Press.

Amman, Johann Conrad. 1692. *The Talking Deaf Man: Or, A Method Proposed, Whereby He Who Is Born Deaf, May Learn to Speak*. Translated by D.F. M.D. Amsterdam: Henry Westein.

Amman, Johann Conrad. 1873. *A Dissertation on Speech*. London: Sampson Low, Marston, Low, and Searle. Originally printed in Latin, 1700.

Anonymous. 1807. "An Account of the Institution in Paris for the Education of the Deaf and Dumb." *The Monthly Anthology and Boston Review* 1807: 525.

Anonymous. October 21, 1820. "The Deaf and Dumb Fond of Music." *The National Recorder (1819–1821)*, October 21, 1820, 266.

Antzakas, Klimis, and Bencie Woll. 2001. "Head Movements and Negation in Greek Sign Language." In *Gesture and Sign Language in Human-Computer Interaction*, edited by Ipke Wachsmuth and Timo Sowa, 193–196. Berlin: Springer.

Arnold, Thomas. 1923. *Arnold on the Education of the Deaf: A Manual for Teachers*. Edited by Abraham Farrar. 2nd ed. London: National College of Teachers of the Deaf.

Arrowsmith, John Pauncefort. 1819. *The Art of Instructing the Infant Deaf and Dumb*. London: Taylor and Hessey.

awti. 2014. "Deaf Parents: Voice with Hearing Children?" https://youtu.be/ZoTRY3u-oAY?si=_0zTqr3WHfATTTLd

Ayres, J. A. 1848. "A Complete Education for the Deaf and Dumb." *American Annals of the Deaf and Dumb* 2 (1): 24–31.

Baby Fingers. 2022. "Baby Fingers: A Musical Journey through Language and Learning." Accessed July 29, 2022. https://mybabyfingers.com.

Bahan, Benjamin. 1996. "Non-Manual Realization of Agreement in American Sign Language." PhD diss., Boston University.

Bahan, Benjamin. 2006. "Face-to-Face Tradition in the American Deaf Community: Dynamics of the Teller, the Tale, and the Audience." In *Signing the Body Poetic: Essays on American Sign Language Literature*, edited by H-Dirksen L. Bauman, Jennifer L. Nelson, and Heidi M. Rose, 21–50. Berkeley: University of California Press.

Bahan, Benjamin, Judy Kegl, Robert G. Lee, Dawn MacLaughlin, and Carol Neidle. 2000. "The Licensing of Null Arguments in American Sign Language." *Linguistic Inquiry* 31 (1): 1–27.

Baker, Nancy K. 1976. "Heinrich Koch and the Theory of Melody." *Journal of Music Theory* 20 (1): 1–48.

Ballin, Albert. 1998. *The Deaf Mute Howls*. Edited by John V. Van Cleve. Gallaudet Classics in Deaf Studies. Washington, DC: Gallaudet University Press.

Bauer, Anastasia. 2014. *The Use of Signing Space in a Shared Sign Language of Australia*. Boston/Berlin: de Gruyter.

Bauman, H-Dirksen L. 2006a. "Getting out of Line: Toward a Visual and Cinematic Poetics of ASL." In *Signing the Body Poetic: Essays on American Sign Language Literature*, edited by H-Dirksen L. Bauman, Jennifer L. Nelson, and Heidi M. Rose, 95–117. Berkeley: University of California Press.

Bauman, H-Dirksen L. 2006b. "Toward a Poetics of Vision, Space and the Body: Sign Language and Literary Theory." In *Disability Studies Reader*, edited by Lennard J. Davis, 355–366. New York: Routledge.

Bauman, H-Dirksen L. 2008. "Listening to Phonocentrism with Deaf Eyes." *Essays in Philosophy* 9 (1): 41–54.

Baynton, Douglas C. 1992. "'A Silent Exile on this Earth': The Metaphorical Construction of Deafness in the Nineteenth Century." *American Quarterly* 44 (2): 216–243.

Baynton, Douglas C. 1996. *Forbidden Signs: American Culture and the Campaign against Sign Language*. Chicago: University of Chicago Press.

Bell, Alexander Graham. 1883. *Memoir upon the Formation of a Deaf Variety of the Human Race*. Washington, DC: National Academy of Sciences.

Bellugi, Ursula, and Susan Fischer. 1972. "A Comparison of Sign Language and Spoken Language." *Cognition* 1 (2–3): 173–200.

Best, Katelyn E. 2015/2016. "'We Still Have a Dream': The Deaf Hip Hop Movement and the Struggle against the Socio-Cultural Marginalization of Deaf People." *Lied und popülare Kulture/Song and Popular Culture* 60/61: 61–86.

Best, Katelyn E. 2018. "Musical Belonging in a Hearing-Centric Society: Adapting and Contesting Dominant Cultural Norms through Deaf Hip Hop." *Journal of American Sign Languages and Literature*: 1–7.

"Bible Class Gives a Funny Show." 1905. *The Deaf-Mutes' Journal* 1905: 3.

Bickford, J. Albert, and Kathy Fraychinaud. 2006. "Mouth Morphemes in ASL: A Closer Look." In *Sign Languages: Spinning and Unraveling the Past, Present and Future*, edited by R. M. de Quadros, 32–47. Theoretical Issues in Sign Language Research 9. Florianopolis, Brazil: Editora Arara Azul.

Birkenshaw, Lois. 1965. "Teaching Music to Deaf Children." *The Volta Review* 67 (5): 352–387.

Boethius, Anicius Manlius Severinus (c. 480–524). 1989. *Fundamentals of Music*. Translated by Calvin Bower. New Haven, CT: Yale University Press.

Bohlman, Philip V. 2002. *World Music: A Very Short Introduction*. Oxford: Oxford University Press.

Boone, R. Thomas, and Joseph G. Cunningham. 2001. "Children's Expression of Emotional Meaning in Mmusic through Expressive Body Movement." *Journal of Nonverbal Behavior* 25 (1): 21–41.

Boutet, Dominique, and Brigitte Garcia. 2006. "Finalités et enjeux linguistiques d'une formalisation graphique de la Langue des Signes Française (LSF)." *Les langues des signes (LS): recherches sociolinguistiques et linguistiques*. Accessed January 7, 2020. http://www. univ-rouen.fr/dyalang/glottopol/numero_7.html.

Boyes-Braem, Penny, and Rachel Sutton-Spence. 2001. *The Hands Are the Head of the Mouth: The Mouth as Articulator in Sign Languages*. Hamburg: Signum.

Brower, Candace. 1997–1998. "Pathway, Blockage, and Containment in 'Density 21.5.'" *Theory and Practice* 22/23: 35–54.

Browner, Tara. 2002. *Heartbeat of the People: Music and Dance of the Northern Pow-Wow*. Urbana: University of Illinois Press.

Browner, Tara. 2009. *Music of the First Nations: Tradition and Innovation in Native North America*. Urbana: University of Illinois Press.

Brownlow, Sheila, Amy R. Dixon, Carrie A. Egbert, and Rebecca D. Radcliffe. 1997. "Perception of Movement and Dancer Characteristics from Point-Light Displays of Dance." *The Psychological Record* 47: 411–421.

Brunell, Natalie. October 2, 2012. "Deaf Filmmaker Truly Hears Music for the First Time." *CNN*, October 2, 2012. Accessed July 7, 2020. https://www.cnn.com/2012/09/29/us/california-deaf-filmmaker/index.html.

Buchanan, Robert. 1993. "The Silent Worker Newspaper and the Building of a Deaf Community: 1890-1929." In *Deaf History Unveiled: Interpretations from the New Scholarship*, edited by John V. Van Cleve, 172–197. Washington, DC: Gallaudet University Press.

Burke, Molly. 2021. "Describing What I Think Colors Look Like! (No Visual Memory)." YouTube video. https://youtu.be/2XFKltB8beg.

Câmara, Guilherme Schmidt, and Anne Danielsen. 2020. "Groove." In *The Oxford Handbook of Critical Concepts in Music Theory*, edited by Alexander Rehding and Steven Rings, 271–294. New York: Oxford University Press.

Cambouropoulos, Emilios. 2009. "How Similar Is Similar?" *Musicae Scientiae* 13 (1_suppl): 7–24. https://doi.org/10.1177/102986490901300102.

Camp, Henry. 1848. "Claims of the Deaf and Dumb upon Public Sympathy and Aid." *American Annals of the Deaf and Dumb* 1 (4): 210–215.

Canadian Cultural Society of the Deaf. 2016. "Signed Music Rhythm of the Heart HD." https://youtu.be/FLazgI_phNQ?si=lG_gKgLJx3WY4AdS

Caswell, Estelle. 2017. "How Sign Language Innovators Are Bringing Music to the Deaf." *Vox*, March 27, 2017. Accessed July 7, 2020. https://www.vox.com/videos/2017/3/27/15072526/asl-music-interpreter.

Cavarero, Adriana. 2005. *For More than One Voice: Toward a Philosophy of Vocal Expression*. Translated by Paul A. Kottman. Stanford, CA: Stanford University Press.

Chakraborty, Mukta, and Erich D. Jarvis. 2015. "Brain Evolution by Brain Pathway." *Philosophical Transactions B* 370 (1684): 1–12.

Chapple, Bennett. 1903. "Curing the Deaf by Electricity." *The National Magazine* 18 (1): 129–131.

Cheng, Qi, Austin Roth, Eric Halgren, and Rachel I. Mayberry. 2019. "Effects of Early Language Deprivation on Brain Connectivity: Language Pathways in Deaf Native and Late First-Language Learners of American Sign Language." *Frontiers in Human Neuroscience* 13: 320.

Chew, Geoffrey, Thomas J. Mathiesen, Thomas B. Payne, and David Fallows. 2001. *Song*. Oxford: Oxford University Press.

Christie, Karen, and Dorothy M. Wilkins. 2007. "Themes and Symbols in ASL Poetry: Resistance, Affirmation, and Liberation." *DeafWorlds* 22 (3): 1–49.

Chung, Andrew J. 2019. "What Is Musical Meaning? Theorizing Music as Performative Utterance." *Music Theory Online* 25 (1).

Clague, Mark. 2014. "Poets & Patriots: A Tuneful History of 'The Star-Spangled Banner.'" Liner notes for *Poets & Patriots: A Tuneful History of 'The Star-Spangled Banner*. Mark Clague, executive producer, Jerry Blackstone, conductor. Star Spangled Music Foundation.

Clark, Adrean, and John Lee Clark. 2016. "A Brief Introduction to the Signing Community Concept." https://youtu.be/CAiqTuJnBrI?si=fdH50YVTm594X4hA

Clark, John Lee. 2021. "Against Access." *McSweeney's*.

Clarke, Eric F. 2001. "Meaning and Specification of Motion in Music." *Musicae Scientiae* 5 (2): 213–234.

Clayton, Martin. 2012. "What is Entrainment? Definition and Applications in Musical Research." *Empirical Musicology Review* 7 (1–2): 49–56.

Clayton, Martin, Byron Dueck, and Laura Leante, eds. 2013. *Experience and Meaning in Music Performance*. New York: Oxford University Press.

Cohn, Richard. 1992. "Metric and Hypermetric Dissonance in the Menuetto of Mozart's Symphony in G minor, K.550." *Intégral* 6: 1–33.

Condit-Schultz, Nathaniel. 2016. "MCFlow: A Digital Corpus of Rap Transcriptions." *Empirical Musicology Review* 11 (2): 124–147.

Convention of Articulation Teachers of the Deaf—1884: Official Report. 1884. Albany: E.S. Werner, The Voice Press.

Cooper, Grosvenor W., and Leonard B. Meyer. 1963. *Rhythmic Structure of Music.* Chicago: Chicago University Press.

Cripps, Jody H., and Ely Lyonblum. 2017. "Understanding Signed Music." *Society for American Sign Language Journal* 1 (1): 78–96.

Cripps, Jody H., Ely Rosenblum, Anita Small, and Samuel J. Supalla. 2017. "A Case Study on Signed Music: The Emergence of an Inter-performance Art." *Liminalities: A Journal of Performance Studies* 13 (2): 1–24.

Cripps, Jody H., Anita Small, Ely Rosenblum, Samuel J. Supalla, Aimee K. Whyte, and Joanne S. Cripps. Forthcoming. "Signed Music and the Deaf Community." In *Culture, Deafness & Music: Disability Studies and a Path to Social Justice* edited by A. Cruz. Rotterdam, NL: Brill-Sense Publishers.

Cuddy, Lola L., and Carole A. Lunney. 1995. "Expectancies Generated by Melodic Intervals: Perceptual Judgments of Melodic Continuity." *Perception & Psychophysics* 57 (4): 451–462. https://doi.org/10.3758/BF03213071.

Dachkovsky, Svetlana, and Wendy Sandler. 2009. "Visual Intonation in the Prosody of a Sign Language." *Language and Speech* 52 (2–3): 287–314.

Dahl, Sofia, and Anders Friberg. 2007. "Visual Perception of Expressiveness in Musicians' Body Movements." *Music Perception* 24 (5): 433–454.

Davidson, Michael. 2006. "Hearing Things: The Scandal of Speech in Deaf Performance." In *Signing the Body Poetic: Essays on American Sign Language Literature*, edited by H-Dirksen L. Bauman, Jennifer L. Nelson, and Heidi M. Rose, 216–234. Berkeley: University of California Press.

Davis, Lennard J. 1995. *Enforcing Normalcy: Disability, Deafness, and the Body.* London: Verso.

"Deaf Girl Is Expert Pianist." 1918. *The Silent Worker*, 1918.

DeChaine, D. Robert. 2002. "Affect and Embodied Understanding in Musical Experience." *Text and Performance Quarterly* 22 (2): 79–98.

Deliège, Irène. 2007. "Similarity Relations in Listening to Music: How Do They Come into Play?" *Musicae Scientiae* 11 (1_suppl): 9–37. https://doi.org/10.1177/102986490701 1001021.

Deutsch, Diana, Trevor Henthorn, and Rachael Lapidis. 2011. "Illusary Transformation from Speech to Song." *Journal of the Acoustical Society of America* 129 (4): 2245–2252.

Di Renzo, Alessio, Luca Lamano, Tommaso Lucioli, Barbara Pennacchi, and Luca Ponzo. 2006. "Italian Sign Language: Can We Write It and Transcribe It with Sign Writing?" LREC 2006—Workshop Proceedings (W-15): Second Workship on the Representation and Processing of Sign Languages.

Dissanayake, Ellen. 2000. "Antecedents of the Temporal Arts in Early Mother-Infant Interaction." In *The Origins of Music*, edited by Steven Brown, Björn Merker, and Nils L. Wallin. Cambridge, MA: MIT Press.

Dittrich, Winand H., Tom Troscianko, Stephen E. G. Lea, and Dawn Morgan. 1996. "Perception of Emotion from Dynamic Point-Light Displays Represented in Dance." *Perception* 25: 727–738.

Dolar, Mladen. 2006. *A Voice and Nothing More.* Cambridge, MA: MIT Press.

Downing, Thomas A. 1995. *Music and the Origins of Language: Theories from the French Enlightenment.* Cambridge: Cambridge University Press.

Dunn, Lindsay. 2008. "The Burden of Racism and Audism." In *Open Your Eyes: Deaf Studies Talking*, edited by H-Dirksen L. Bauman, 235–250. Minneapolis: University of Minnesota Press.

Dunning, Jennifer. 1983. "Dance: Musign Group." *New York Times*, August 28, 60, 1.

Edwards, R. A. R. 2012. *Words Made Flesh: Nineteenth-century Deaf Education and the Growth of Deaf Culture*. New York: New York University Press.

Edwards, Terra. 2018. "Re-Channeling Language: The Mutual Restructuring of Language and Infrastructure among DeafBlind People at Gallaudet University." *Journal of Linguistic Anthropology* 28 (3): 273–292.

Eidsheim, Nina Sun. 2015. *Sensing Sound: Singing and Listening as Vibrational Practice*. Durham, NC: Duke University Press.

Eidsheim, Nina Sun, and Annette Schlichter. 2014. "Introduction: Voice Matters." *Postmodern Culture* 24 (3). http://www.pomoculture.org/2017/09/09/introduction-voice-matters/.

Eitan, Zohar, and Inbar Rothschild. 2010. "How Music Touches: Musical Parameters and Listeners' Audio-Tactile Metaphorical Mappings." *Psychology of Music* 39 (4): 449–467.

Eitan, Zohar, and Renee Timmers. 2010. "Beethoven's Last Piano Sonata and Those Who Follow Crocodiles: Cross-Domain Mappings of Auditory Pitch in a Musical Context." *Cognition* 114 (3): 405–422.

Fauconnier, Gilles, and Mark Turner. 2002. *The Way We Think: Conceptual Blending and the Mind's Hidden Complexities*. New York: Basic Books.

Fernald, Anne. 1992. "Human Maternal Vocalizations to Infants as Biologically Relevant Signals: An Evolutionary Perspective." In *The Adapted Mind: Evolutionary Psychology and the Generation of Culture*, edited by Jerome H. Barkow, Leda Cosmides, and John Tooby, 391–428. New York: Oxford University Press.

Ferreri, G. 1906. "The American Institutions for the Education of the Deaf." *The Association Review* 8 (5): 397–405.

Freeman, Walter J. 2000. "A Neurobiological Role of Music in Social Bonding." In *The Origins of Music*, edited by Steven Brown, Björn Merker, and Nils L. Wallin, 411–424. Cambridge, MA: MIT Press.

Friedner, Michele. 2022. *Sensory Futures: Deafness and Cochlear Implant Infrastructures in India*. Minneapolis: University of Minnesota Press.

Friedner, Michele, and Stefan Helmreich. 2012. "Sound Studies Meets Deaf Studies." *The Senses and Society* 7 (1): 72–86.

Fulka, Josef. 2020. *Deafness, Gesture and Sign Language in the 18th Century French Philosophy*. Amsterdam: John Benjamins.

Gallaudet, Edward Miner. 1875. "Deaf-Mutism." *American Annals of the Deaf and Dumb* 20 (4): 230–248.

Garcia, Brigitte. 2006. "The Methodological, Linguistic and Semiological Bases for the Elaboration of a Written Form of LSF (French Sign Language)." LREC 2006—Workshop Proceedings (W-15), Second Workshop on the Representation and Processing of Sign Languages.

Garcia, Brigitte. 2010. "Sourds, surdité, langue(s) des signes et épistémologie des sciences du langage. Problématiques de la scripturisation et modélisation des bas niveaux en Langue des Signes Française (LSF)." Mémoire d'Habilitation à Diriger les Recherches, Université Paris.

Garland-Thomson, Rosemarie. 2012. "The Case for Conserving Disability." *Bioethical Inquiry* 9: 339–355.

Gertz, Genie. 2008. "Dysconscious Audism: A Theoretical Proposition." In *Open Your Eyes: Deaf Studies Talking*, edited by H-Dirksen L. Bauman, 219–234. Minneapolis: University of Minnesota Press.

GlassMenagerie (@DaddyGlassBaby). 2021. "Ok I think this will be the last one for a while BUT: Do. Not. Learn. ASL. From. Hearing. People." Twitter.

Glickman, Neil. 2007. "Do You Hear Voices? Problems in Assessment of Mental Status in Deaf Persons with Severe Language Deprivation." *Journal of Deaf Studies and Deaf Education* 12 (2): 127–147.

Godøy, Rolf Inge. 2003. "Motor-Mimetic Music Cognition." *Leonardo* 36 (4): 317–319.

Godøy, Rolf Inge. 2010. "Gestural Affordances of Musical Sound." In *Musical Gestures: Sound, Movement, and Meaning*, edited by Rolf Inge Godøy and Marc Leman, 103–125. New York: Routledge.

Godøy, Rolf Inge, Egil Haga, and Alexander Refsum Jensenius. 2005. "Playing 'Air Instruments': Mimicry of Sound-Producing Gestures by Novices and Experts." In *Gesture in Human-Computer Interaction and Simulation*, edited by Silvie Gibet, Nicolas Courty, and Jean-François Kamp, 256–267. Berlin: Springer.

Goel, Divya, and Jason Eli Schwartz. 2019. "I Think You're Wonderful—Protactile American Sign Language Version." https://youtu.be/Ay7RmGP0z3Q.

Goff, M. L. Roy, and Frank W. Finger. 1966. "Activity Rhythms and Adiurnal Light-Dark Control." *Science* 154 (3754): 1346–1349.

Goldin-Meadow, Susan. 2003. *The Resilience of Language: What Gesture Creation in Deaf Children Can Tell Us about How All Children Learn Language*. New York: Psychology Press.

Granda, AJ, and Jelica Nuccio. "Protactile Principles." Accessed July 21, 2020. https://wasli.org/wp-content/uploads/2018/05/PT-Principles-Movies-Final.pdf.

Greenwald, Brian H., and John Vickrey Van Cleve. 2014. "'A DEAF VARIETY OF THE HUMAN RACE': HISTORICAL MEMORY, ALEXANDER GRAHAM BELL, AND EUGENICS." *Journal of the Gilded Age and Progressive Era* 14 (1): 28–48. https://doi.org/10.1017/S1537781414000528.

Griffith, A. L. 1903. "The Acousticon." *World Today* 5 (1): 855–858.

Gulati, Sanjay. 2019. "Language Deprivation Syndrome." In *Language Deprivation and Deaf Mental Health*, edited by Neil Glickman and Wyatte C. Hall, 24–46. New York: Routledge.

Gur, Golan. 2008. "Body, Forces, and Paths: Metaphor and Embodiment in Jean-Philippe Rameau's Conceptualization of Tonal Space." *Music Theory Online* 14 (1).

Haigh, Josh. 2014. "Formerly Deaf Woman Hears Music for the First Time in 40 Years—Watch." *New Musical Express*, 2014. Accessed July 7, 2020. https://www.nme.com/news/music/various-artists-2230-1239610.

Hall, Matthew L., Inge-Marie Eigsti, Heather Bortfeld, and Diane Lillo-Martin. 2017. "Auditory Deprivation Does Not Impair Executive Function, but Language Deprivation Might: Evidence from a Parent-Report Measure in Deaf Native Signing Children." *Journal of Deaf Studies and Deaf Education* 22 (1): 9–21.

Hall, Wyatte C. 2017. "What You Don't Know Can Hurt You: The Risk of Language Deprivation by Impairing Sign Language Development in Deaf Children." *Maternal and Child Health Journal* 21: 961–965.

Hall, Wyatte C., Leonard L. Levin, and Melissa L. Anderson. 2017. "Language Deprivation Syndrome: A Possible Neurodevelopmental Disorder with Sociocultural Origins." *Social Psychiatry and Psychiatric Epidemiology* 52: 761–776.

Happy Baby Signs. 2021. "Happy Baby Signs." Accessed July 29, 2022. https://www.happybabysigns.com/online-classes.html.

Hartmann, Arthur. 1881. *Deafmutism and the Education of Deaf-Mutes by Lipreading and Articulation*. London: Ballière, Tindall and Cox.

Hasty, Christopher. 1997. *Meter as Rhythm*. New York: Oxford University Press.

Herschleifer, Lena. 1917. "Musical Vibrations as an Aid in Developing the Voices of the Deaf." *The Silent Worker* 29 (7): 106.

Holcomb, Leala, and Kimberly Wolbers. 2020. "Effects of ASL Rhyme and Rhythm on Deaf Children's Engagement Behavior and Accuracy in Recitation: Evidence from a Single Case Design." *Children* 7 (256): 1–31.

Holmes, Jessica A. 2016. "Singing beyond Hearing." *Journal of the American Musicological Society* 69 (2): 542–548.

Holmes, Jessica A. 2017. "Expert Listening beyond the Limits of Hearing: Music and Deafness." *Journal of the American Musicological Society* 70 (1): 171–220.

Humphries, Tom. 1975. *Audism: The Making Of A Word*. Unpublished essay.

Huron, David. 2006. *Sweet Anticipation: Music and the Psychology of Expectation*. Cambridge, MA: MIT Press.

Hyde, Merv, and Des Power. 2005. "Some Ethical Dimensions of Cochlear Implantation for Deaf Children and Their Families." *Journal of Deaf Studies and Deaf Education* 11 (1): 102–111. https://doi.org/10.1093/deafed/enj009.

"An Impressive Incident." 1898. *The Silent Worker* 1898: 37.

Jacques-Dalcroze, Émile. 1973. *Rhythm, Music and Education*. Translated by Harold F. Rubenstein. London: Dalcroze Society.

Jaffe, Joseph, Beatrice Beebe, Stanley Feldstein, Cynthia L. Crown, Michael D. Jasnow, Philippe Rochat, and Daniel N. Stern. 2001. "Rhythms of Dialogue in Infancy: Coordinated Timing in Development." *Monographs of the Society for Research in Child Development* 66 (2): i–149. www.jstor.org/stable/3181589.

Jones, Jeannette DiBernardo. 2015. "Imagined Hearing: Music-Making in Deaf Culture." In *The Oxford Handbook of Music and Disability Studies*, edited by Blake Howe, Stephanie Jensen-Moulton, Neil Lerner, and Joseph N. Straus, 54–72. New York: Oxford University Press.

Jones, Mari Riess, and Marilyn Boltz. 1989. "Dynamic Attending and Responses to Time." *Psychological Review* 96 (3): 459–491.

Jusczyk, Peter W., Kathy Hirsh-Pasek, Deborah G. Kemler Nelson, Lori J. Kennedy, Amanda Woodward, and Julie Piwoz. 1992. "Perception of Acoustic Correlates of Major Phrasal Units by Young Infants." *Cognitive Psychology* 24 (2): 252–293. https://doi.org/10.1016/0010-0285(92)90009-q.

Kane, Brian. 2014. *Sound Unseen: Acousmatic Sound in Theory and Practice*. New York: Oxford University Press.

Kane, Brian. 2015. "The Model Voice." *Journal of the American Musicological Society* 68 (3): 671–677.

Kaneko, Michiko. 2020. "Onomatopoeic Mouth Gestures in Creative Sign Language." *Sign Language Studies* 20 (3): 467–490.

Kemler Nelson, Deborah G., Kathy Hirsh-Pasek, Peter W. Jusczyk, and Kimberly W. Cassidy. 1989. "How the Prosodic Cues in Motherese Might Assist Language Learning." *Journal of Child Language* 16 (1): 55–68. https://doi.org/10.1017/s030500090001343x.

Kim, Christine Sun. 2015. "The Enchanting Music of Sign Language." TED. https://www.ted.com/talks/christine_sun_kim_the_enchanting_music_of_sign_language

Klima, Edward S., and Ursula Bellugi. 1979. *The Signs of Language*. Cambridge, MA: Harvard University Press.

Klosterman, Lisa. "Music on the Move: Classes for Kids!" Accessed July 29, 2022. https://mymusiconthemove.com.

Komaniecki, Robert. 2017. "Analyzing Collaborative Flow in Rap Music." *Music Theory Online* 23 (4).

Komaniecki, Robert. 2019. "Analyzing the Parameters of Flow in Rap Music." PhD diss., Indiana University.

Kramer, Jonathan. 1988. *The Time of Music: New Meanings, New Temporalities, New Listening Strategies*. New York: Schirmer Books.

Krebs, Harald. 1999. *Fantasy Pieces: Metrical Dissonances in the Music of Robert Schumann*. New York: Oxford University Press.

Krumhansl, Carol L. 1995. "Effects of Musical Context on Similarity and Expectancy." *Systematische Musikwissenschaft* 3 (2): 211–250.

Krumhansl, Carol L., and Diana L. Schenck. 1997. "Can Dance Reflect the Structural and Expressive Qualities of Music? A Perceptual Experiment on Balanchine's Choreography of Mozart's Divertimento No. 15." *Musicae Scientiae* 1: 63–85.

Ladd, Paddy. 2003. *Understanding Deaf Culture: In Search of Deafhood*. Clevedon: Multilingual Matters.

Lamont, Alexandra, and Nicola Dibben. 2001. "Motivic Structure and the Perception of Similarity." *Music Perception: An Interdisciplinary Journal* 18 (3): 245–274. https://doi.org/10.1525/mp.2001.18.3.245.

Lane, Harlan. 1992. *The Mask of Benevolence: Disabling the Deaf Community*. New York: Alfred A. Knopf.

Lane, Harlan. 2008. "Do Deaf People Have a Disability?" In *Open Your Eyes: Deaf Studies Talking*, edited by H-Dirksen L. Bauman, 277–292. Minneapolis: University of Minnesota Press.

Lane, Harlan, and Benjamin Bahan. 1998. "Article Commentary: Ethics of Cochlear Implantation in Young Children: A Review and Reply from a Deaf-World Perspective." *Otolaryngology—Head and Neck Surgery* 119 (4): 297–313. https://doi.org/10.1016/s0194-5998(98)70070-1.

Lane, Harlan, Robert Hoffmeister, and Ben Bahan. 1996. *A Journey into the Deaf-World*. San Diego: DawnSign Press.

Larson, Steve. 1997–1998. "Musical Forces and Melodic Patterns." *Theory and Practice* 22/23: 55–71.

Leman, Marc. 2007. *Embodied Music Cognition and Mediation Technology*. Cambridge, MA: MIT Press.

Lerdahl, Fred, and Ray Jackendoff. 1983. *A Generative Theory of Tonal Music*. Cambridge, MA: MIT Press.

Leslie, Grace, Alejandro Ojeda, and Scott Makeig. 2014. "Measuring and Classifying Musical Engagement Using EEG and Motion Capture." *Psychomusicology: Music, Mind, and Brain* 24: 75–91.

Lester, Joel. 1986. *The Rhythms of Tonal Music*. Carbondale: Southern Illinois University Press.

Li, Edwin K. C. 2021. "Cantopop and Speech-Melody Complex." *Music Theory Online* 27 (1).

Liddell, Scott K. 1990. "Four Functions of a Locus: Reexamining the Structure of Space in ASL." In *Sign Language Research: Theoretical Issues*, edited by Ceil Lucas, 176–198. Washington, DC: Gallaudet University Press.

Liddell, Scott K. 1995. "Real, Surrogate, and Token Space: Grammatical Consequences in ASL." In *Language, Gesture, and Space*, edited by Karen Emmorey and Judy S. Reilly, 19–41. Hillsdale, NJ: Lawrence Erlbaum.

Lincoln, Harvey. 1897. "Music for the Deaf and Dumb: Providence Journal." *Current Literature (1888–1912)*, 1897: 66. Accessed March 11, 2013.

Linton, Simi. 1998. *Claiming Disability: Knowledge and Identity*. New York: New York University Press.

Listman, Jason, Summer C. Loeffler, and Rosa L. Timm. 2018. "Deaf Musicality and Unearthing the Translation Process." *Journal of American Sign Languages and Literature* 1–9.

Liu, Huei-Mei, Patricia K. Kuhl, and Feng-Ming Tsao. 2003. "An Association between Mothers' Speech Clarity and Infants' Speech Discrimination Skills." *Developmental Science* 6 (3): 1–10.

Liversidge, Anne. 2021. Personal correspondence.

Lloyd, Abby Lynn. 2017. "Music's Role in the American Oralist Movement, 1900–1960." MA thesis, Arizona State University.

Loeffler, Summer C. 2014. "Deaf Music: Embodying Language and Rhythm." In *Deaf Gain: Raising the Stakes for Human Diversity*, edited by H-Dirksen L. Bauman and Joseph J. Murray, 436–456. Minneapolis: University of Minnesota Press.

London, Justin. 2004. *Hearing in Time: Psychological Aspects of Musical Meter*. New York: Oxford University Press.

Longhi, Elena. 2009. "'Songese': Maternal Structuring of Musical Interaction with Infants." *Psychology of Music* 37 (2): 195–213. https://doi.org/10.1177/0305735608097042.

Lupton, Linda. 1998. "Fluency in American Sign Language." *Journal of Deaf Studies and Deaf Education* 3 (4): 320–328.

Lye, Colleen. 2004. *America's Asia: Racial Form and American Literature, 1893–1945*. Princeton, NJ: Princeton University Press.

MacIntyre, Alexis Deighton. 2018. "The Signification of the Signed Voice." *Journal of Interdisciplinary Voice Studies* 3 (2): 167–183.

Mackin, Molly. 2011. "Sean Forbes—Not Hard to Hear." *Ability Magazine* 2011, 10–11.

Malawey, Victoria. 2020. *A Blaze of Light in Every Word: Analyzing the Popular Singing Voice*. Oxford Studies in Music Theory. New York: Oxford University Press.

Maler, Anabel. 2013. "Songs for Hands: Analyzing Interactions of Sign Language and Music." *Music Theory Online* 19 (1).

Maler, Anabel. 2015. "Musical Expression among Deaf and Hearing Song Signers." In *The Oxford Handbook of Music and Disability Studies*, edited by Blake Howe, Stephanie Jensen-Moulton, Neil Lerner, and Joseph N. Straus, 73–91. New York: Oxford University Press.

Maler, Anabel. 2018. "Hearing Form in Post-Tonal Music." PhD diss., University of Chicago.

Maler, Anabel. 2022. "Listening to Phrase Structure and Formal Function in Post-Tonal Music." *Intégral* 35: 45–68.

Maler, Anabel, and Robert Komaniecki. 2021. "Rhythmic Techniques in Deaf Hip Hop." *Music Theory Online* 27 (1).

Mangelsdorf, Heather Harden, Jason Listman, and Anabel Maler. 2021. "Perception of Musicality and Emotion in Signed Songs." *Music Perception* 39 (2): 160–180.

Mansfield, Jeffrey. 2015. "Christine Sun Kim with Jeffrey Mansfield." *Coronagraph*. https://cargocollective.com/coronagraph/Christine-Sun-Kim-with-Jeffrey-Mansfield

Margulis, Elizabeth Hellmuth. 2012. "Musical Repetition Detection across Multiple Exposures." *Music Perception: An Interdisciplinary Journal* 29 (4): 377–385. https://doi.org/10.1525/mp.2012.29.4.377.

Margulis, Elizabeth Hellmuth. 2014. *On Repeat: How Music Plays the Mind*. New York: Oxford University Press.

Margulis, Elizabeth Hellmuth. 2020. "Repetition." In *The Oxford Handbook of Critical Concepts in Music Theory*, edited by Alexander Rehding and Steven Rings, 187–206. New York: Oxford University Press.

Mark, Michael L., and Charles L. Gary. 2007. *A History of American Music Education*. 3rd ed. Lanham, Maryland: Rowman & Littlefield Education.

Masataka, Nobuo. 1996. "Perception of Motherese in a Signed Language by 6-Month-Old Deaf Infants." *Developmental Psychology* 32 (5): 874–879.

Mathiesen, Thomas J. 2002. "Greek Music Theory." In *The Cambridge History of Western Music Theory*, edited by Thomas Christensen, 109–135. Cambridge: Cambridge University Press.

McAlister, Elizabeth A. 2002. *Rara!: Vodou, Power, and Performance in Haiti and Its Diaspora*. Berkeley: University of California Press.

McCaskill, Carolyn, Ceil Lucas, Robert Bayley, and Joseph Hill. 2011. *The Hidden Treasure of Black ASL: Its History and Structure*. Washington, DC: Gallaudet University Press.

McLaren, Angus. 2012. *Reproduction by Design: Sex, Robots, Trees, and Test-Tube Babies in Interwar Britain*. Chicago: University of Chicago Press.

McNeill, William H. 1995. *Keeping Together in Time: Dance and Drill in Human History*. Cambridge, MA: Harvard University Press.

Meintjes, Louise. 2017. *Dust of the Zulu: Ngoma Aesthetics after Apartheid*. Durham, NC: Duke University Press.

Meyer, Leonard B. 1956. *Emotion and Meaning in Music*. Chicago: University of Chicago Press.

Meyer, Leonard B. 1957. "Meaning in Music and Information Theory." *Journal of Aesthetics and Art Criticism* 15 (4): 412–424.

Meyer, Leonard B. 1973. *Explaining Music: Essays and Explorations*. Berkeley: University of California Press.

Miller, John. 2010. "The Difference between ASL and English Signs." Accessed May 28, 2022. https://www.signingsavvy.com/blog/45/The+difference+between+ASL+and+English+signs.

Mills, Mara. 2011a. "Do Signals Have Politics? Inscribing Abilities in Cochlear Implants." In *The Oxford Handbook of Sound Studies*, edited by Trevor Pinch and Karin Bijsterveld, 320–346. Oxford: Oxford University Press.

Mills, Mara. 2011b. "On Disability and Cybernetics: Helen Keller, Norbert Wiener, and the Hearing Glove." *differences: A Journal of Feminist Cultural Studies* 22 (2–3): 74–111.

Mills, Mara. 2014. "Cochlear Implants after 50 Years: A History and an Interview with Charles Graser." In *The Oxford Handbook of Mobile Music Studies*, edited by Jason Stanyek and Sumanth Gopinath, 261–297. Oxford: Oxford University Press.

Mills, Mara. 2015. "Deafness." In *Keywords in Sound*, edited by David Novak and Matt Sakakeeny, 45–54. Durham, NC: Duke University Press.

Mirzoeff, Nicholas. 1995. *Silent Poetry: Deafness, Sign, and Visual Culture in Modern France*. Princeton, NJ: Princeton University Press.

Montague, Eugene. 2019. "Entrainment and Embodiment in Musical Performance." In *The Oxford Handbook of Music and the Body*, edited by Youn Kim and Sander L. Gilman, 177–192. Oxford: Oxford University Press.

Narmour, Eugene. 1990. *The Analysis and Cognition of Basic Melodic Structures: The Implication-Realization Model*. Chicago: University of Chicago Press.

National Theatre of the Deaf. 1971. "My Third Eye" WTTW-TV. Video Cassette/59:00.

Neidle, Carol, Judy Kegl, Dawn MacLaughlin, Benjamin Bahan, and Robert G. Lee. 2000. *The Syntax of American Sign Language: Functional Categories and Hierarchical Structure*. Cambridge, MA: MIT Press.

Nespor, Marina, and Wendy Sandler. 1999. "Prosody in Israeli Sign Language." *Language and Speech* 42 (2–3): 143–176.

Nimjee, Ameera. 2018. "Playing Dance and Dancing Music: The Work of Intimacy in *Kathak*." In *Dance Matters Too: Memories, Markets, Identities*, edited by Pallabi Chakravorty and Nilanjana Gupta, 176–189. New Delhi: Routledge.

Nimjee, Ameera. 2019. "Moving Bodies: The Politics of Mobility in Indian Contemporary Dance." Doctoral diss., University of Chicago.

Norman, Donald A. 1988. *The Psychology of Everyday Things*. New York: Basic Books.

Norman, Donald A. 2013. *The Design of Everyday Things*. Rev. ed. New York: Basic Books.

Nutting, Diane. 2019. "Breaking through the Sound Barrier: Deaf Perspectives from the Music Industry." *Smithsonian Folklife Festival Blog* (blog), *Center for Folklife and Cultural Heritage*. https://festival.si.edu/blog/breaking-sound-barrier-wawa-dj-supalee.

Ohriner, Mitchell. 2016. "Metric Ambiguity and Flow in Rap Music: A Corpus-Assisted Study of Outkast's 'Mainstream' (1996)." *Empirical Musicology Review* 11 (2): 153–179.

Olson, Ben, and Andy Olson. 2007. "CODA BROTHERS: CODA VOICE." https://youtu.be/puQ-D89Nc7g?si=w9RdolSFBAjgn0lI

Ormsby, Alec. 1995. "Poetic Cohesion in American Sign Language: Valli's 'Snowflake' & Coleridge's 'Frost at Midnight'." *Sign Language Studies* 88: 227–244.

Padden, Carol. 1990. "The Relation between Space and Grammar in ASL Verb Morphology." In *Sign Language Research: Theoretical Issues*, edited by Ceil Lucas, 118–132. Washington, DC: Gallaudet University Press.

Padden, Carol, and Tom Humphries. 1988. *Deaf in America: Voices from a Culture*. Cambridge, MA: Harvard University Press.

Patel, Aniruddh D., Edward Gibson, Jennifer Ratner, Mireille Besson, and Phillip J. Holcomb. 2008. "Processing Syntactic Relations in Language and Music: An Event-Related Potential Study." *Journal of Cognitive Neuroscience* 10 (6): 717–733.

Peisner, David. 2013. "Deaf Jams: The Surprising, Conflicted, Thriving World of Hearing-Impaired Rappers." *Spin Magazine*, 2013.

Peritz, Jessica Gabriel. 2022. *The Lyric Myth of Voice: Civilizing Song in Enlightenment Italy*. Oakland: University of California Press.

Perkins School for the Blind. 2018. "Jaimi Lard Learns the Cupid Shuffle." https://youtu.be/XsyYLPrywOQ.

Peters, Cynthia. 2000. *Deaf American Literature: From Carnival to the Canon*. Washington, DC: Gallaudet University Press.

Pettingill, Benjamin D. 1873. "The Sign Language." *Annals* 18: 1.

Pfau, Roland, and Josep Quer. 2010. "Nonmanuals: Their Grammatical and Prosodic Roles." In *Sign Languages*, edited by Diane Brentari, 381–402. Cambridge: Cambridge University Press.

Phillips-Silver, Jessica, and Laurel J. Trainor. 2005. "Feeling the Beat: Movement Influences Infant Rhythm Perception." *Science* 308 (5727): 1430.

Pizzuto, Elena, Paolo Rossini, and Tommaso Russo. 2006. "Representing Signed Languages in Written Form: Questions That Need to Be Posed." LREC 2006—Workshop Proceedings (W-15): Second Workship on the Representation and Processing of Sign Languages.

Porter, Sarah Harvey. 1917. "Musical Vibrations for the Deaf." *The Silent Worker*, 1917, 106.

Powers, Harold S. 2015 [1986]. "Melody." In *The Harvard Dictionary of Music*, edited by Don Randel, 499–502. Boston: Credo Reference.

Rahaim, Matthew. 2012. *Musicking Bodies: Gesture and Voice in Hindustani Music.* Middletown, CT: Wesleyan University Press.

Rameau, Jean-Philippe. 1971. *Treatise on Harmony.* Translated by Philip Gossett. New York: Dover.

Reilly, Judy S., Marina McIntire, and Ursula Bellugi. 1990a. "The Acquisition of Conditionals in American Sign Language: Grammaticized Facial Expressions." *Applied Psycholinguistics* 11 (4): 369–392.

Reilly, Judy S., Marina McIntire, and Ursula Bellugi. 1990b. "Faces: The Relationship between Language and Affect." In *From Gesture to Language in Hearing and Deaf Children*, edited by Virginia Volterra and Carol Erting, 128–141. Berlin: Springer-Verlag.

Rensberger, Boyce. 1979. "For the Deaf, the Language Gap Is Unbridgeable." *New York Times*, 1979, 12.

"Rhythm Work in the New Jersey School for Deaf." 1917. *The Silent Worker*, 1917, 105–106.

Ringer, Alexander L. 2015 [1980]. "Melody." In *Grove Music Online*. Oxford: Oxford University Press.

Roberts, Herbert. 1905. "Silent Songsters of Toronto, Canada." *The Silent Worker* 17 (9): 137–138.

Roberts, Shepherd K. 1965. "Photoreception and Entrainment of Cockroach Activity Rhythms." *Science* 146: 958–959.

Roeder, John. 2001. "Pulse Streams and Problems of Grouping and Metrical Dissonance in Bartók's 'With Drums and Pipes." *Music Theory Online* 7 (1).

Rosen, Rebecca J. August 29, 2012. "What It's Like for a Deaf Person to Hear Music for the First Time." *The Atlantic*, August 29, 2012. Accessed July 7, 2020. https://www.theatlantic.com/technology/archive/2012/08/what-its-like-for-a-deaf-person-to-hear-music-for-the-first-time/260890/.

Rothfarb, Lee A. 1988. *Ernst Kurth as Theorist and Analyst.* Philadelphia: University of Pennsylvania Press.

Rothstein, William. 1990. *Phrase Rhythm in Tonal Music.* New York: Schirmer.

Rousseau, Jean-Jacques. 2010. *Émile or On Education.* Translated by Allan Bloom. In *The Collected Writings of Rousseau*, Vol. 13. Lebanon, NH: University Press of New England.

Samarotto, Frank. 2009. "'Plays of Opposing Motion': Contra-Structural Melodic Impulses in Voice-leading Analysis." *Music Theory Online* 15 (2).

Sandler, Wendy. 1999a. "The Medium and the Message: Prosodic Interpretation of Linguistic Content in Israeli Sign Language." *Sign Language and Linguistics* 2: 187–216.

Sandler, Wendy. 1999b. "Prosody in Two Natural Language Modalities." *Language and Speech* 42: 127–142.

Sandler, Wendy. 2010. "Prosody and Syntax in Sign Languages." *Transactions of the Philological Society* 108 (3): 298–328.

Saslaw, Janna. 1996. "Forces, Containers, and Paths: The Role of Body-Derived Image Schemas in the Conceptualization of Music." *Journal of Music Theory* 40 (2): 217–243.

Sawada, Misako, Kazuhiro Suda, and Motonobu Ishii. 2003. "Expression of Emotions in Dance: Relation between Arm Movement Characteristics and Emotion." *Perceptual and Motor Skills* 97: 697–708. https://journals.sagepub.com/doi/10.2466/pms.2003.97.3.697.

Schachter, Carl. 1999. *Unfoldings: Essays in Schenkerian Theory and Analysis.* Edited by Joseph N. Straus. New York: Oxford University Press.

Schellenberg, E. Glenn. 1996. "Expectancy in Melody: Tests of the Implication-Realisation Model." *Cognition* 58 (1): 75–125.

Schmuckler, Mark A. 1989. "Expectation in Music: Investigation of Melodic and Harmonic Processes." *Music Perception* 7 (2): 109–149. https://doi.org/10.2307/40285454.

Schwaiger, Seth Orion. 2015. "Sound and Silence." *Arts and Culture Texas.* Accessed July 17, 2024. http://artsandculturetx.com/20173/

Seigworth, Gregory J., and Melissa Gregg. 2010. "An Inventory of Shimmers." In *The Affect Theory Reader,* edited by Gregory J. Seigworth and Melissa Gregg, 1–25. Durham, NC: Duke University Press.

Selisker, Scott. 2011. "'Simply by Reacting?': The Sociology of Race and Invisible Man's Automata." *American Literature* 83 (3): 571–596. https://doi.org/10.1215/00029831-1339872.

Selisker, Scott. 2016. *Human Programming: Brainwashing, Automatons, and American Unfreedom.* Minneapolis: University of Minnesota Press.

Shannon, Rogan. 2016. "Simultaneous Communication | Deaf Awareness Month." https://youtu.be/PEBwwe0PLZ8?si=Gj1CDJmvUMBgDzGD

Sheldon, Deborah A. 1997. "The Illinois School for the Deaf Band: A Historical Perspective." *Journal of Research in Music Education* 45 (4): 580.

Shove, Patrick, and Bruno Repp. 1995. "Musical Motion and Performance: Theoretical and Empirical Perspectives." In *The Practice of Performance,* edited by John Rink, 55–83. Cambridge: Cambrige University Press.

"Signed Music and the Deaf Musicians." 2020. Canadian Association for Theatre Research Conference: Partition/Ensemble 2020, Montréal, Quebec.

Skotara, Nils, Uta Salden, Monique Kügow, Barbara Hänel-Faulhaber, and Brigitte Röder. 2012. "The Influence of Language Deprivation in Early Childhood on L2 Processing: An ERP Comparison of Deaf Native Signers and Deaf Signers with a Delayed Language Acquisition." *BMC Neuroscience* 13 (44).

Stefani, Gino. 1987. "Melody: A Popular Perspective." *Popular Music* 6 (1): 21–35.

Stokoe, William. 1960. "Sign Language Structure: An Outline of the Visual Communication Systems of the American Deaf." *Studies in Linguistics: Occasional Papers* 8.

Straus, Joseph N. 2011. *Extraordinary Measures: Disability in Music.* New York: Oxford University Press.

Supalla, Ted, and Joe Dannis. 1994. *Charles Krauel: A Profile of a Deaf Filmmaker.* Dawn-Sign Pictures.

Sutton, Valerie. 1990. *Lesson in SignWriting.* La Jolla, CA: The SignWriting Press.

Sutton-Spence, Rachel. 2005. *Analysing Sign Language Poetry.* Basingstoke: Palgrave Macmillan.

Taub, Sarah F. 2001. *Language from the Body: Iconicity and Metaphor in American Sign Language.* New York: Cambridge University Press.

Thompson, Robin L. 2006. "Eye Gaze in American Sign Language: Linguistic Functions for Verbs and Pronoun." PhD diss., UC San Diego.

Todd, Neil P. M. 1999. "Motion in Music: A Neurobiological Perspective." *Music Perception* 17: 115–126.

Todd, Neil P. M., and Christopher S. Lee. 2015. "The Sensory-Motor Theory of Rhythm and Beat Induction 20 Uears On: A New Synthesis and Future Perspectives." *Frontiers* 9 (444).

Trainor, Laurel J. 1996. "Infant Preferences for Infant-Directed versus Noninfant-Directed Playsongs and Lullabies." *Infant Behavior and Development* 19 (1): 83–92. https://doi.org/https://doi.org/10.1016/S0163-6383(96)90046-6.

Trainor, Laurel J., Elissa D. Clark, Anita Huntley, and Beth A. Adams. 1997. "The Acoustic Basis of Preferences for Infant-Directed Singing." *Infant Behavior and Development* 20 (3): 383–396. https://doi.org/10.1016/S0163-6383(97)90009-6.

Trippett, David. 2019. "Melody." In *The Oxford Handbook of Critical Concepts in Music Theory*, edited by Alexander Rehding and Steven Rings, 397–436. Oxford: Oxford University Press.

Turner, William W., and David E. Bartlett. 1848. "Music among the Deaf and Dumb." *American Annals of the Deaf and Dumb* 2 (1): 1–6.

Tyler, William E. 1856. "Qualifications Demanded in an Instructor of the Deaf and Dumb." *American Annals of the Deaf and Dumb* 8 (4): 202–207.

Valli, Clayton. 1990. *Poetry in Motion*. Burtonsville: Sign Media.

Valli, Clayton. 1993. "Poetics of American Sign Language Poetry." PhD diss., Union Institute Graduate School.

Valli, Clayton, Ceil Lucas, Kristin J. Mulrooney, and Miako Villanueva. 2011. *Linguistics of American Sign Language: An Introduction*. 5th ed. Washington, DC: Gallaudet University Press.

Veinberg, Silvana C. 1993. "Nonmanual Negation & Assertion in Argentine Sign Language." *Sign Language Studies* 79: 95–112.

Vines, Bradley W., Marcelo M. Wanderley, Carol L. Krumhansl, Regina L. Nuzzo, and Daniel J. Levitin. 2003. "Performance Gestures of Musicians: What Structural and Emotional Information Do They Convey?" International gesture workshop, Genova, Italy.

Walk, Richard D., and Carolyn P. Homan. 1984. "Emotion and Dance in Dynamic Light Displays." *Bulletin of the Psychonomic Society* 22: 437–440.

Wecker, Karl. 1939. "Music for Totally Deaf Children." *Music Educators Journal* 25 (6): 45, 47.

Weidman, Amanda. 2014. "Anthropology and Voice." *Annual Review of Anthropology* 42: 37–51.

Wilbur, Ronnie. 2000. "Phonological and Prosodic Layering of Non-Manuals in American Sign Language." In *The Signs of Language Revisited*, edited by Karen Emmorey and Harlan Lane, 215–247. Mahwah, NJ: Lawrence Erlbaum.

Wilbur, Ronnie B., and Cyntha G. Patschke. 1998. "Body Leans and the Marking of Contrast in American Sign Language." *Journal of Pragmatics* 30: 275–303.

Wilkinson, Dan. January 9, 2014. "We Spoke to a Man Who's Been Deaf His Whole Life about Hearing Music for the First Time." *Vice*, January 9, 2014. Accessed July 7, 2020. https://www.vice.com/en_us/article/645ggr/we-spoke-to-a-man-who-has-been-deaf-his-whole-life-about-hearing-music-for-the-first-time.

Winefield, Richard. 1987. *Never the Twain Shall Meet: Bell, Gallaudet, and the Communications Debate*. Washington, DC: Gallaudet University Press.

Winston, Elizabeth. 2000. "It Just Doesn't Look like ASL! Defining, Recognizing and Teaching Prosody in ASL." Conference of Interpreter Trainers: Celebrating Excellence, Celebrating Partnership, Portland, OR.

Winzer, Margret. 2006. "The Ladies Take Charge: Women Teachers in the Education of Deaf Students." In *Women and Deafness: Double Visions*, edited by Brenda Jo Brueggemann and Susan Burch, 110–129. Washington, DC: Gallaudet University Press.

Yeston, Maury. 1976. *The Stratification of Musical Rhythm*. New Haven, CT: Yale University Press.

Zak, Albin. 2001. *The Poetics of Rock: Cutting Tracks, Making Records*. Berkeley: University of California Press.

Zbikowski, Lawrence. 1993. "*The Analysis and Cognition of Basic Melodic Structures: The Implication-Realization Model* by Eugene Narmour." Book review. *Journal of Music Theory* 37 (1): 177–206. https://doi.org/10.2307/843949.

Zbikowski, Lawrence. 1997–1998. "Des Herzraums Abschied: Mark Johnson's Theory of Embodied Knowledge and Music Theory." *Theory and Practice* 22–23: 1–16.

Zbikowski, Lawrence. 2002. *Conceptualizing Music: Cognitive Structure, Theory, and Analysis*. AMS Studies in Music. New York: Oxford University Press.

Zbikowski, Lawrence. 2010. "Music, Emotion, Analysis." *Music Analysis* 29 (1–3): 37–60. https://doi.org/10.1111/j.1468-2249.2011.00330.x.

Zbikowski, Lawrence. 2012. "Music, Language, and What Falls in Between." *Ethnomusicology* 56 (1): 125–131.

Zbikowski, Lawrence. 2017. *Foundations of Musical Grammar*. Oxford Studies in Music Theory. New York: Oxford University Press.

Index